THEY CALLED ME

SYRUP SOPPER

To my Good Friends

Ray & Nettie Jensen

Best Wishes

[signature]

THEY CALLED ME

SYRUP SOPPER

By
Clyde W. Price

ISBN 1-58500-900-8

1st books – rev. 3/23/00

ABOUT THE BOOK

This is the true story of a boy, born and raised on a poor farm in rural North Alabama. In it he reminisces about his hard working family and their struggles to barely survive during and after the great depression of the thirties. It is about his determination to acquire an education, his career in broadcasting as a country music disc jockey and radio station owner and manager in Tuscaloosa, Alabama. This is about how he at nineteen years of age and his young wife, also nineteen, began from nothing, then retired after forty years as multi-millionaires.

The author intended to write a series of comical stories, things that had actually happened to him and his friends, but in doing so he gets into a serious discussion of some of the not so funny things that happened to him as he pursued his career. His discussion touches on his relationships with friends, family, employees, government, famous broadcasters, politicians, sports figures, including Coach Paul "Bear" Bryant.

He writes about his serving on the Board of Directors of the National Association of Broadcasters and his eight years on the Board of the Associated Press.

The ending chapters describe his almost unbelievable number of health problems from cataracts in his eyes to a leg amputation. The reader should find this work to be easy reading. It was meant to be a funny story, but in case you find something in it that is serious, so be it. We think you will enjoy THEY CALLED ME SYRUP SOPPER.

DEDICATION

To my wife Carol Dean Bailey Price, my two sons Walter Bailey and Ronald Blaine Price, my five grandchildren, Bailey, Brad, Leah, Blaine and Caroline, my sisters Lela Johnson, Aria Decker and my brother Louis Price. In memory of my parents, Walter Marvin and Lou Gertie Victoria DeFoor Price and my sister, Opal Thomas.

INTRODUCTION

These past two years, due to circumstances the reader will understand later, I have had a lot of time on my hands. Thus, in order to keep from going completely "nuts" I began this project about six months ago, simply as something to keep my mind and two forefingers occupied. I cannot guarantee that all of the dates, times and places are absolutely correct. I am a poor researcher, and after all, even though every story you will read here is true, no amount of research would prove them, because none have been recorded before. The early information about my family background comes from a two hour interview I taped with my father, shortly before he died in 1975.

Other information came from Carol, my wife for almost 48 years, friends, sister Lela, and my brother Louis but primarily from my own memory. That is why I say that all dates and times may not be exact, but anything that is pertinent to the story is true. Even the names have not been changed to protect the innocent, they are all, every one guilty.

I could never begin to thank all of those who have influenced my life, in business, education, health, spiritually and financially. I thank my parents for my up-bringing, my in-laws, for giving me Carol, my two sons Wally and Ron for giving me five grandchildren, the late Carroll Eddins, and Tom Todd, for my career in broadcasting, some great teachers, employees, highly skilled doctors and nurses, the hundreds of sponsors of the Syrup Sopper Show, on the radio for almost forty years, and certainly the many thousands of daily listeners to my programs. Without you there would never have been a "Syrup Sopper."

I owe a very special debt of gratitude to Dr. Joab Thomas and his lovely wife Marly. Joab is an educator of the first order. An excellent writer, a University Professor and he has served as President of both The University of Alabama and Penn State University. Marly is an English Major, and together they have spent countless hours in editing my amateurish sentence structure, spelling, capitalization and punctuation. Joab and

Marly, I appreciate every , : ; " " ' ? / - ( ) % # $ & ! you have corrected.

As you read, I hope you may occasionally shed a tear or two, but most of all I hope you enjoy many more chuckles than tears. Please have as much fun reading this as I have writing, MY STORY---THEY CALLED ME "SYRUP SOPPER".

MY STORY
THEY CALLED ME
SYRUP SOPPER
BY

CLYDE WALTER PRICE

Chapter 1
MAMA AND PAPA

He was born on July 20th, 1886 in a small farming community called Fruithurst. Walter Marvin the fourth child and third son of Frank and Malinda Price, he had two older brothers named Oscar and Samuel and a sister named Minnie. Fruithurst was located in the extreme eastern part of Alabama near the Georgia Line in Cleburne county.

Very little is known about the first seven years of his life, however my story will begin in the year 1893. That was the year my grandfather decided to take is family, all of his farming tools, and household goods, load them in his two horse wagon which by the way was pulled by a team of mules, and move to Cullman County. He loaded everything he could on the wagon, tied his cow behind and with the family dog following, set out for Cullman County a distance of about 150 miles. The journey was a hard one, taking about two weeks. Some nights they would arrive at a farm house, where they would be invited to feed the animals, enjoy a hot supper and share whatever bedding was available. When no overnight hosts could be located the Family would set up camp preferably near a stream of fresh water.

When Frank Malinda, Minnie, Oscar, Sam and Walter along with the mules, cow and family dog, Jack, arrived in Cullman County they rented a small farm in the Southwest Corner known as the Trimble Community. They lived there for about two years when Frank decided to take the family to another more suitable location. He purchased 160 acres of land about 7 miles north west of the town of Cullman, the County seat. He and the

1

older boys set to clearing land and preparing it for their first crop to be planted in the spring, at the same time they were busy building a house, barn, corn crib, chicken house and of course a two holer outhouse.

Papa, Walter, my father was seven years old at the time. He lived in that house until he married my mother on December 10, 1910. When he was nine years old his mother died leaving his father, Frank alone with the four children to raise and a newly settled farm and home to establish. Later my grandpaw Price married a widow, Sarah Ann Pullen. She had one son Arthur. I don't remember Papa talking very much about his mother, but I did hear a lot about Sarah Ann, his Stepmother. I don't think he liked her very much. I say all of the above just to illustrate how in my fathers lifetime so many drastic changes in the lives of Alabama people have occurred. In the 89 years of his life from 1886 to 1975 we went from the horse or train as the only mode of transportation to the moon.

Speaking of the land, Papa told me that my Grandfather paid $500 and a mule for the 160 acres. When I was growing up the old, original very small house was still standing. We called it the renter house because Papa would usually have a share cropper family or some laborers living there, especially during fall cotton picking time.

I'll have much more to say about papa later, but now I want you to meet the lady that to me was so very special. I still have a lot of fond memories of her, my mama.

She was a person that we country folks would call a city girl. She was born and grew up in Bessemer, Alabama. The only daughter of Jim and Molly DeFoor, having an older brother named Charlie and a younger brother Elmer. All I know of the early years of her life, is that she was born on August 16, 1893. Her parents named her Lou Gertie Victoria DeFoor. She had very little formal education, much less than high school but I do know that somewhere along the way she learned very well the reading, writing and communicating skills that she diligently taught to her children. She made sure that each one of us were able to read and write even before entering the first grade. I'll always be thankful to her for that.

Her father worked in the steel mills of Fairfield, Al. I'm not sure whether Grandpaw DeFoor retired or just got tired of working and later bought about 35 acres adjoining the Price farm in rural Cullman. My grand parents lived there until they became too old and feeble to take care of themselves, at which time they moved into our house. Mama took care of them until they both died, about six months apart in 1951.

My story really begins when Mama was about 16 years old. She made a trip from Bessemer a suburb of Birmingham, Alabama to visit relatives in Cullman County. Someone introduced her to a young farmer named Walter Price. It seems that they were both smitten by the love bug at about the same time even though there was a seven year difference in their ages. She was barely 16 and he was 23 when they met. There was practically no courtship, because of the distance between their homes and the absence of transportation. They corresponded by mail when possible and as their relationship grew they began thinking about marriage.

In the fall of 1910 Walter Price proposed marriage to Gertie DeFoor. They set the wedding date for December 10, 1910 however there was a real problem. She was under age at only 17, therefore she had to have written permission from her father in order to get a marriage license. The wedding date was fast approaching and still no letter from Mr. DeFoor. Papa was getting very nervous so he rode a mule from his home out in the county to wait for two days at the post office in Cullman for the letter. It arrived just in time for him to take the letter to the Cullman courthouse, buy the marriage license, mount his trusty mule and make it home in time for the wedding.

They were married at Pinehill, a small Methodist church located about one mile from the Price farm. There was no honeymoon, the young couple went by buggy to the home of friends where they spent the first night and then the next day they went back to the home of his parents.

Papa told me many years later they did have a honeymoon

about three weeks after the wedding. They went to Vinemont, a small station on the L&N railroad where they boarded a train for Birmingham. Remember Walter is now 24 years old and has never been out of Cullman County since he was seven years old. He said "When I got off that train at the big Union Station I was scared to death but I was even more scared when we'd boarded a street car and headed down the middle of the street for Bessemer about 10 miles away from the train station. I had seen a train before even though I had never ridden on one, but I had never seen a street car." The couple spent Christmas of 1910 with the Defoor family giving them a chance to meet their new son--in--law.

It seems that all through the lives of the family there are close ties to the city of Anderson, Indiana. You will understand what I mean as my story unfolds. Mama and papa were members of the Methodist church in the early days, but then a new religious movement came out of Anderson, The Church of God. They left the Methodists along with a few people from other denominations and formed a Church Of God congregation. These people were called "come outers", I suppose because they came out of other churches. I remember attending services at the little frame church building they built about two miles north of the highway, near Cottonseed Johnson's place. I've never known why, but the church was called "Old 13" maybe it was because they had 13 original members. When the congregation outgrew the building, Dolphus Yates donated enough land next to his home place on highway U.S. 31 to build a new building at the foot of Longview hill. They named the church Longview Church of God. Every Sunday, Sunday night and Wednesday night the Prices were at church unless there was critical illness or the roads were to muddy to get there, even then, we would sometimes go in the farm wagon.

Mama was an ordained minister. I remember hearing her preach and feeling so proud of her. She never "pastored" a church, but was available when she was needed. For several months during one period she preached at a small church in Kelso, Tennessee. She would go by Greyhound on Saturday and return on Sunday evening. They would give her just a few dollars, most of the time barely enough to cover the bus fare. She didn't mind; she was not in it for the money; she loved teaching, preaching and sharing her love of God with any group at any time.

I never saw my mother read any book except the Bible. She read and studied it every day of her life. Very few times did the children go to bed without mama gathering us all around her and insisting that we listen as she read some scripture and prayed.

Speaking of prayer she prayed every day and regardless of the work she had to do in the house or in the field she would go down to the edge of the creek where a large rock jutted out from the ground, kneel there and pray. That was her special alter. She prayed about everything like the soldiers in the war, for rain, for rain to end, the neighbors, the sick, the poor, even the hungry children in China, but most of all for her family that we would grow up to be good, honest, faithful, Christian citizens and never depart from our "raising". She would always give thanks to God as she knelt there by that rock for all of our many material blessings, which by today's standards were mighty slim. I wish I had that rock now.

Mama was the only person I've ever known who completely wore out a Bible, not just one but I know there were five or six. I still have one and I believe my brother Louis and sisters Aria and Lela each have one. She literally studied, made notes in the margins and wrote wherever there was space until the old book would almost fall apart, then somehow manage to acquire another one. I used to tease and tell her that she wrote more in the Bible than the Apostle Paul. That old worn, faded, scribbled, pages loose, King James Version of the Holy Bible is one of my most prized possessions.

My parents beliefs and the teachings of the church were very strict. They certainly believed in obeying all ten of the commandments but they added a lot more like thou shalt not go to movies, play cards, play marbles for keeps, dance, gossip and for sure don't call someone a "fool" and by all means don't take the name of the Lord in vain. They taught us that it was a sin for

5

a woman to cut her hair, use makeup or wear short dresses, low tops or long pants. Back then mama never cut her hair. She would take those long strands that fell down her back, plat or braid them, then wind that plat into a ball and fasten it to the back of her head with hair pins.

In later years she had her hair cut, and would go regularly to the beauty shop. She even got a permanent wave and started wearing makeup, powder and rouge. She never wore lipstick. Of course they hated gambling, drinking, and smoking. but most of all smoking. I can still almost hear her say after she had given me whatever few cents she had as I left the house, "Honey spend it on something to eat but please don't buy cigarettes."

I know now they were completely right. Long before the Surgeon General's warning, mama was warning about the dangers of smoking because she believed cigarettes would send a person's soul straight to Hell and eternal damnation. At that time no one even thought about cigarettes causing cancer, heart disease and so many terrible health problems. I now wish I had listened to her and followed her advice. If I had, maybe I would not have some of the many health problems that I have now. I smoked my first cigarette when I was a freshman at Auburn University, David Bates my roommate smoked and as I studied at night I would sometimes light one up. I wish I, like President Clinton could say that "I didn't inhale", but I did and before long I was buying a pack about once a month if I had 15 cents. When I was in the army they were provided free. I smoked my last cigarette on the way to the hospital with a heart attack on August 11,1984. I'm sure mama knew that I smoked but having so much respect for her and her strong feelings against it, I never smoked in her presence.

Talking about her teaching, we children got much advice from our parents like, "don't wade in mud puddles barefooted or you will get the toe itch," " a bee can't sting you if you stay in front of it," "if you scratch it, it won't heal," and "a morning rain never lasts all day, at noon it becomes an afternoon rain."

Back to the subject of her Bibles, the last time I saw her alive was at Christmas time in 1969. Carol, the boys and I visited mama and papa at their home in Scottsboro. While there, I noticed she had a brand new Bible on the table. When I picked it up it fell open to the book of Psalms, chapter 73. She had circled verses 22 through 29 and in the margin written "my favorite, use at my funeral." I said "Mama what are you doing writing this, we won't need these instructions for a long time." She replied "Yes son, it won't be long now, look at the front." I turned back to the fly leaf and saw the only words written on it were Psalms 73 verses 22-29 my favorite, use at my funeral.

It was Saturday night barely two months later, the following February 7th Louis called and said mama had died in her sleep from a heart attack. One of my first thoughts was about those verses and our last conversation. The minister, Dr. James Pepper, a Presbyterian, did a great job preaching her funeral including that passage from Psalms in his message. He said later it was one of the easiest funerals he had ever preached, "That great lady preached her own funeral." She was buried on Tuesday at Mt. Zion Methodist church just north of Cullman. It snowed that day.

The first year of marriage papa, with the help of his brothers was busy building a house for the newlyweds just about 500 yards down the road from his parents.

Two little babies were born in the spring of 1912. The twins Opal and Olgia arrived on March 31. On August 6th, just over two years later, another girl they named Lela was born. A son, Homer, followed by another girl named Aria (pronounced "ARA") was next on the scene. Her Yankee husband Paul and the folks up north pronounce her name "area" like what area are you from. Oh well, I guess everybody can't be from the South and talk good English like we'uns do. Paul Decker is a good man and a great brother-in-law. Paul was the only one in our immediate family to serve in the military during the World War II. Louis and I were much too young and the other males were past draft age. When Paul was drafted, in spite of his flat feet, they sent him to Camp Shelby Mississippi for eight weeks of basic training and then on his way to Europe to take care of the Germans. I can't say for sure, but I think he liked The Battle of the Bulge more that the snakes, flies, mosquitoes and heat of Camp Shelby. While he was away, Aria moved back home with us and their first child, Paula, was born at Cullman Hospital while Paul was overseas.

The prolific Prices produced another son, Louis Edgar, born on October 8, 1927, the only brother I ever knew. My older brother, Homer, had died at the age of 22 months from a simple childhood disease, colitis, which is curable now. There was another sibling death. One of the twins, Olgia died after only five months of life on August 6th. Coincidentally, my sister Lela was born on the same date two years later.

Comes time now for me to make my grand entrance, which I did on March 26, 1932, on the Saturday before Easter Sunday during one of the worst tornado seasons ever to hit the state. Many people were killed and hundreds wounded in the storm of 1932. I came into the world just as the great depression was beginning and President Franklin Delano Roosevelt had just been elected. From everything I've been told by the family, there had always been a depression at our place, but in the 1930s it only worsened.

So there it is, the Walter and Gertie Price family is complete, with my being the last of seven children spread over twenty years from 1912 to 1932. I give thanks during these days of family planning that my folks had never heard of such a thing. If they had, I most likely would not be writing this; you see he was 47 and she was 40 when I was born. To me my parents always seemed old because they were much older than the folks of children my own age in school.

They might have been older, but they were tougher. Mama had seven babies including twins, without the benefit of a hospital and sometimes without a doctor when the weather or roads were so bad that old Dr. Martin could not make it to our home on time. We were all born in the little house on Rural Route 5 Cullman, Alabama, the house I will describe later.

Chapter 2

THE PRICE PLACE

I will attempt to locate the Price farm geographically for readers who may not be familiar with the area. We lived about six miles northwest of Cullman, half-way between Vinemont and West Point. That is, if one traveled by mule and wagon or buggy on the dirt road called the Dripping Springs road to Pinehill Church, then turned right on to a narrow, one lane road, which was very seldom traveled by automobile. Another way was drive north from Cullman on highway US 31 to the three filling station, grocery store combinations called Longview, turn left onto the Nebo road for two miles and again on to a smaller road for about a quarter of a mile to our house.

The house that Walter and Gertie Price built in 1911, the first year they were married is still standing. It looks better now than it did back then. The present owners have installed aluminum siding and indoor plumbing. Originally the house was a typical farm "shotgun" house, with a wide covered front porch, large enough on which to pile a whole bale of fresh picked "seed" cotton before loading it on the wagon for the trip to the cotton gin in Cullman. That normally would take a whole day, but if the gin were really busy, it would be after dark before papa would return home from town.

There were six rooms in our house. Entering from the right side of the porch one could go directly to what we called the "front" room, the nicest room, having a sofa and chair and even a well worn wool rug on the floor. That was the room where the girls entertained their "fellers". I got many sticks of chewing gum as bribes to stay out of the front room when they had company.

When the girls married and left home mama put a bed in the room for company and for the girls and their husbands to use when they returned for visits. Upon entering the left front door you were in the "heater" room, the only room with heat other than the kitchen, having a long, low wood burning heater which was not very efficient for keeping the family warm on cold winter nights.

Every Saturday night mama would heat a #2 washtub of water, make Louis and me strip off our overalls and "long handle" underwear and take a bath behind the heater. One fateful night while trying to put on his clean underwear, Louis stumbled and fell backwards on to the red hot heater, branding himself across the butt. He probably still has the scar, I can't say for sure, haven't checked lately. I remember grandmaw coming down from her house across the cotton field to "talk and blow" the fire out of his burn. It was funny to me seeing Louis lying on the bed with his naked ass sticking up and grandmaw down over it blowing and chanting some unintelligible words over it. He said the treatment did not work.

In the spring, summer and fall we bathed in the creek down behind the barn. The heater room had a couple of straight chairs, a large rocker, a bed, and in the winter when mama made quilts she hung her quilting frame from the ceiling on ropes, taking up most of the space in the room. Until I outgrew it, my baby bed was in that room. I remember sleeping in that baby bed till I was so big my feet hung out between the slats at the end and my head rubbed the other end. There was just not enough bed space for five children and two adults in our little two bedroom house.

Next to the heater room was the kitchen with it's wood burning cook stove, wood box, a small counter top work space and cabinet. On one side of the kitchen was another bedroom, and on the other a screened porch that we called the back porch. Actually it was a side porch with an unusual feature. Before the porch was built, papa had a well drilled as near the house as possible, then built the porch around and over the well. We could draw water for cooking or drinking without going outside in the bad weather to draw from a conventional well. You might say our place was so modern that we had no running water but drawing water. We dared not draw more than two buckets of water at a time. The well was so shallow that to do so would "muddy" the well and we'd have to wait for several hours for it to clear before drinking or cooking again.

On one side of the porch was a long table we called the wash- stand, with it's wash-pan everybody used to wash hands, feet, or anything else that couldn't wait till Saturday night, its dish of mama's home made lye soap and the cedar water bucket with the chipped enamel dipper that we all used for drinking from the bucket. The unpardonable sin, as far as us young'uns was concerned, was to misplace the dipper just before papa got thirsty. A towel would always be hanging from a nail papa had driven into a wood stud between the sections of screen wire. We piled enough firewood on the porch for several days in case it rained or snowed and wet the wood at the outside woodpile making it almost impossible to burn. Of course, the woodbox next to the cookstove must never run empty of stove wood and plenty of rich, pine knot kindling, mama would use to start fires in the kitchen stove.

On the third side of the kitchen was the dining room, with it's long table, six chairs and a bench, (enough room so the family could eat together) and what we called the "safe." It was actually a two door glass front cabinet, large enough for storing spare dishes, with a drawer at the bottom where mama kept her extra tablecloth, the one she used to cover the food that was left on the table after dinner to keep the flies off till suppertime. There was no reason to remove the leftovers because there was no refrigeration or storage space except the "warming closet" over the top of the cookstove.

The other room was called the "back room." None of the house had insulation, but the back room didn't even have inside walls, just the outside weather boarding, and it was the farthest room from the heater. The room had a dresser, a length of clothesline strung across one corner for hanging clothes, (there being only one closet in the whole house,) and a bed with a mattress stuffed with feathers. Not very original, but it was called a "feather bed."

I can still remember as a teenager sleeping in that room on cold winter nights, the wind whistling through the cracks in the walls and between the pine boards in the floor and wondering if everybody in the would was as cold as I, surely not, vowing that someday I would have a warm place to sleep. To avoid freezing I would snuggle down into the feather bed with my long underwear, socks and "boggin" cap, under every quilt and blanket I could find. I could always depend on mama to come in the room after I'd gone to bed and say "Son are you alright?" I would most likely say "Mama, I feel like I'm swimming in a cold branch." She would heat a flat iron, wrap it in an old sweater and after digging through all that cover at the foot of the bed, place the sweater with the hot iron inside at my cold feet. What a wonderful feeling. In the summer that old feather bed was just as hot as it was cold in the winter.

Several years later papa built another porch on the back of the house. It too was the entire width of the house and was made of concrete. That was where mama put her new electric washing machine when we got electricity and she could afford the Kenmore machine. As you have guessed by now, in addition to no plumbing, running water, heat except the wood heater, we had NO ELECTRICITY. We read, studied, cooked, sewed and just survived by the light of coal oil (kerosene) lamps or lanterns. Naturally we did not miss electricity as we do now when the power is off. You never miss what you've never had.

Without a doubt, one of the greatest days in the history of Nebo community was when we saw the big TVA trucks coming down the road towing power poles and those huge spools of power line. We believed Mr. Roosevelt had personally sent them to us. I was about six or seven years old when we got "lights" and I remember the occasion very well. Papa had someone to wire the house, just a drop cord hanging from the ceiling with a single low power light bulb, in each room and a chain for turning it on and off. There was no need for wall plugs because we had nothing to plug in to them if we'd had them. It was really primitive, just like everything else we did on the farm, but those lights surely did beat kerosene lamps. I remember the minimum light bill was $1.00 a month and papa would go around turning off lights, fearful the bill would exceed that amount.

So much for the house, now about the farm. After the death of my grandpaw Price the 160 acres was split evenly between papa and my uncle Sam Price, our family ending up with just slightly more than 80 acres. Today it would not even be called a farm, more likely, just timberland. It had virtually no level land, being rocky, hilly, uneven and having such poor soil a modern farmer would not even attempt to farm it.

There was a valley right through the place, with a creek flowing in it. The creek was mostly dry in the summer except after a heavy rain and a few holes in which Louis and I would try to swim after running the water moccasins away. Most of that rough valley was fenced for pasture, growing nothing much but bitterweeds and summer cedars (weeds), but it was enough to support a cow, calf and two or three mules.

I think some of the old cows we had would deliberately eat bitterweeds knowing they would completely ruin the milk, and they really did. There is nothing more foul tasting that milk flavored with bitterweed. At most, of the 80 acres only about 30 had been cleared and made suitable for cultivation. The rest of the farm was in woods, hardwood, (oak, hickory, poplar, elm,) and pine trees.

The woods were as necessary for our survival as the fields, providing hardwood for heat in the house, firing the syrup mill, for lumber and for shingles for roofing. The pine we used for lumber, wood for the cookstove, and the pine straw for the strawberry patches and for the cow stalls in the barn.

The only fresh meat we ever had, other than at "hog killing" time was chicken, and whatever we could kill in the woods, squirrels, rabbits, or an occasional 'possum. We had plenty of wild blackberry briars on the place. Picking them was a real chore, not only from the briar scratches, but they were covered with chiggers, a microscopic red mite that could make a large bump on the skin, itching so much that scratching them off made a sore that lasted awhile, and the blackberry patches were a favorite place for snakes to hide. In spite of the work picking blackberries, it was worth it. Mama would make delicious jam and jelly from some, then can some in fruit jars for making blackberry cobbler in the winter.

The woods produced huckleberries, dewberries, wild raspberries, persimmons, walnuts and hickory nuts, always a pleasant treat for a hungry boy when he found them and ate them on the spot.

Our farmland was not all in one big field. We had a series of patches where the land was most level, no more than 10 acres in one field. Even at that the land had to be terraced and plowed on the contour with the hills to prevent erosion. The type of farming we did was Stone Age compared to the farming operations of today. We had no modern machinery, tractors, cotton or corn pickers, hay balers or planting and cultivating equipment. We only had very primitive tools like a turning plow, disc harrow, section harrow, stalk cutter, Georgia stock, scratcher, planter and fertilizer distributor, all pulled by mules, old Pete and Bill sometimes as a team, but if the load were light enough they worked separately. The team was always used to pull the steel tired farm wagon, a necessity for hauling tools, fertilizer, and seed to the fields in the spring and for harvesting in the fall.

Our main cash crop was cotton, but it was very difficult for the family to plant, chop, hoe and pick more than 10 acres of the stuff a year. We would average about 5 or 6 bales of cotton per year, selling for no more than $50 a bale. Being necessary to keep the seed or trade them for cotton seed meal to be used for cow feed, we had no income from the seed.

To supplement our income we raised strawberries and Irish potatoes in the spring. In the summer we sold butter beans, peas, string beans, sweet potatoes, fresh roas'n ears (corn) and an occasional litter of pigs or a calf.

I used to think my papa was the stingiest man alive. When he would let me go to town with him, if I asked for a nickel or dime to buy myself an RC Cola, a hamburger or a moon pie he would most likely say, "You don't need that" or "You are not really hungry, you just want to by something." I know now that the biggest reason he didn't give me the money was that he just did not have it. As I've thought about it, I figure papa's total cash income even in his best years could not have been more than $1000 to $1500 a year. With that he fed, clothed, educated, as best he could, his family, including paying off the bank loan he had made in the spring to buy fertilizer and seed. It's really hard to comprehend now that I pay more income taxes in a year than that hard working man made in his whole lifetime.

When papa would go to town alone we would always tell him to "Bring us something good." Without fail he would bring a nickel, or if he had it, a dime loaf of store bought bread. It was a great treat at the time, but I'd kill right now for a big slice of mama's hot home made yeast bread with butter spread on it, or one of her a delicious cinnamon rolls.

Yes, farming was hard work with little pay but during the 30s and 40s we always had plenty to eat, so much that two of my uncles, Charlie and Elmer DeFoor at one time or the other moved in with us after losing their jobs in Gary, Indiana, and Fairfield, Alabama. We had milk, eggs, butter, fresh vegetables in spring and summer, and mama canned for winter everything that didn't run away. She would can at least a hundred quarts of beans, peas, tomatoes, cucumbers, beets, strawberries, okra, squash, kraut and as already mentioned, blackberries, and make the most delicious pear preserves, jellies and jams a body ever tasted.

We had a smokehouse full of pork from the two hogs we had raised, fattened and butchered in the fall, as soon as the weather was cold enough, usually around Thanksgiving. Having no refrigeration, the only time we could butcher the hogs was in extremely cold weather. Hog killing day was an exciting time, with several of the neighbors pitching in to help, that help being returned by papa when it was time for the neighbor to kill hogs. I say exciting because of the anticipation of what would be on the table that night and next morning. For supper hog killing night mama would fry a big skillet full of fresh tenderloin rolled in flour, make gravy in the same pan, and bake a batch of her best biscuits. Move over Hardee's, no way can you compete with mama's biscuits. After the hog butchering was done and the meat all cut up into hams, shoulders, backbone, ribs, liver, lights, tenderloin and middlings, it was trimmed of lean meat with just enough fat to make sausage.

That night they would let me grind the sausage in the old hand cranked sausage mill attached to the dining room table, that is, until I gave out and quit turning. The next morning's breakfast was fresh sausage seasoned with just enough sausage seasoning and home raised sage to make it just right, gravy, eggs and biscuits. We stuffed ourselves for a few days but before long the fresh tenderloin and backbone and ribs would be eaten but the sausage and head cheese had to be canned in order to preserve them. We had never heard of barbecue, so everything was either fried or boiled.

The fresh pork was loaded with fat, because we wanted it so. We trimmed the fat, cut it up in small pieces and cooked it in the wash-pot with a wood fire under it in the yard. Cooking the fat turned it into lard, the lard being stored in five gallon lard cans and used for cooking. The small pieces left, after we "cooked out" the lard, we called "cracklins". Mama cooked them in her fresh baked cornbread. I never liked cracklin' bread so mama would put them in only one end of the pone of bread, so that everyone could have a choice.

The hams, shoulders, and middlins (bacon) all were hung in the smokehouse, with a smoldering fire of green hickory wood burning day and night for several days, the more smoke the better, sometimes it looked like the smokehouse was on fire from the smoke coming though the cracks and the roof. The meat took on a darkish or even a greenish color. Then after just enough smoking the meat was taken down and placed in a large wooden box, called, what else, a "meat box." It was covered with a generous supply of course meat salt and left to finish curing.

After the curing process was over the meat would last for many months before going stale, I don't know how long because it was always eaten before it had time to spoil. I used to complain about having to eat that old country-cured ham mama had sliced off, soaked in water overnight to take out part of the salt, and then cooked for breakfast the next morning. Wish I had some for supper tonight.

One big problem with having no refrigeration was keeping milk fresh and cool during the hot days of summer. We had two ways, neither one very successful. We could put it in a bucket or jug, take it to the renter house where there was a dug well, and let it down in the well on a rope attached to the windlass. But all kinds of varmints lived in the well, like spiders, bugs, lizards and frogs, not very appetizing conditions for the milk.

Another way, the one most often used was to take the milk down to the creek, find a spot not too deep and not to shallow, scratch out a smooth bottom just so the milk bucket would not be completely submerged, put the bucket in, lay a nice flat rock on top and hope that an unexpected thunder shower didn't come up during the day and wash the whole thing away. In case there were a summer storm, somebody had better run to the creek and rescue the milk bucket. No matter what the Price kids were doing, whether plowing, chopping, picking, shucking or any number of jobs, if it came up a cloud someone had better GET THAT MILK OUT OF THE CREEK, because papa just hated to eat supper without finishing it off with his usual glass of cornbread and milk.

My parents were the hardest working people I've ever known. On the farm there was always something to do, even in the rainiest seasons of the year. Besides cows to be milked, mules, chickens, dogs and cats to be fed, hogs to be slopped, there was corn to be shucked, peas to be shelled, weeds to be cut between the house and the outhouse, peanuts to be picked off, hay to be cut and hauled to the barn and ditch banks to be cleaned off, just in case we ran out of something to do.

I know now that for what he had to do and what he had to do it with, papa was a special individual. It seemed he could do anything, having no more than a fourth grade education, in a one room, one teacher school located five miles from his home to which he had to walk. He could figure in his head almost as quickly as I can with a calculator. He was a farmer, blacksmith, cotton picker, painter, carpenter, woodcutter, shoe cobbler, mechanic, fence mender, meat cutter, a good cook when mama didn't feel well, and the very best sorghum syrup maker in Cullman County.

On the other hand, to this day, I do not understand how mama did everything she did. Every day she rose before daylight, built a fire in the cookstove, (before she got an electric stove,) and cooked a huge breakfast of meat, eggs, grits if available, gravy and biscuits. After breakfast, she washed the dishes by hand, made the beds, washed the clothes, hung them on the clothesline in the back yard, and then would work in the fields chopping cotton, picking cotton, beans, peas, tomatoes or anything else she could do to help out.

About 10 a.m, she would leave the field, go by the garden, pick enough vegetables for dinner and supper, then to the house, cook them and have a big dinner on the table by noon when we half starved men folks came in to eat. After dinner, as I said before she would cover the leftovers on the table and go back to the field and work all afternoon or till the job was done.

I will always remember how she could fry a chicken. Talk about fresh, she would go to the chicken yard, catch a young pullet, place it's head on the wood chopping block, pick up the ax and with one blow chop that chicken's head clean off. When it stopped flopping around (you've heard the expression "chicken with it's head cut off") she would pick it up, skin it, wash it, cut it up, roll it in flour and have it in the frying pan almost as fast as Col. Sanders. She always made plenty of gravy and biscuits to go with the chicken. We usually had chicken for breakfast on Sunday, but if the preacher were coming to dinner, she would serve it then.

Knowing how I enjoyed fried chicken for breakfast, as long as she lived, she would always fry a chicken when I visited her even when she had to buy them at the grocery. As I grew older, I was the appointed official chicken catcher. Our birds ran free all over the place and my being the fastest, I could hem one up in a corner of the barn, smoke house, or corn crib and catch it, then perform the operation on it's neck.

Seems to me as a kid growing up, the youngest of five, that somebody was always "whupping" on me. It was tough trying to survive an older brother bent on my assassination, and three older sisters. It was like having four mamas and a daddy that didn't wait for excuses or explanations before administering the razor strap or plow line at the slightest provocation.

Like the time Louis and I were enjoying a corncob battle at the barn, throwing wet corncobs at each other, seldom landing one where it hurt. The time I loaded my cob with some fresh, black cow manure, and hearing Louis coming around the corner of the barn, I launched it as hard as I could. The trouble was, it was papa in the line of fire and not Louis. That cow dung loaded corn cob hit papa right between the eyes. Needless to say he did not compliment me on my aim, instead he took me in the barn hall and wore my rear end out with leather wagon line.

Or the time, at the dining room supper table, I broke off the corner of a pone of cornbread and threw it the length of the table hitting my sister Opal in the eye. I got two whippings, one from Opal for hitting her and another from mama for throwing the cornbread. I never threw cornbread again.

Or the time papa sent me from the field he was plowing to the house to get him a drink of water. I filled a quart fruit jar and was hurrying back to the field when a big old red wasp flew out of a briar patch and stung me behind my right ear. The sting was so painful and sudden, it knocked me down, breaking the glass jar and spilling the water. Picking myself up and crying all the way, I went back to the house for more water. By the time I got back to the field with a fresh jar, papa, thinking I had taken much more time than I should have and that I had just been playing along the way, before I could explain, he whopped me several times with his plowline. I didn't deserve that one.

When he learned what had really happened, I know he must have felt terrible about the way he had reacted, but he didn't apologize, thinking I suppose, I would need a whipping sooner or later anyway. Or, the many times too numerous to mention, that mama would separate Louis and me in the middle of a fight with a good strong switch. The worst punishment for both of us was when she would say, "Just wait till your daddy gets home and I tell him what y'all have done. He'll take care of you." The bad part then was the dread not the punishment.

I got a bunch of whippings as a young lad, but the mother of all butt whuppings was the day mama told me to catch a full grown rooster she had been saving for Thanksgiving dinner. Knowing that big old dominecker rooster would be hard to catch and that he would surely spur me to death if I did catch him, I devised what I thought was a brilliant plan. I would take papa's old single barrel 12 gauge shotgun and shoot the rooster. I had never fired a shotgun before, but I knew how, I'd seen papa do it lots of times shooting at rabbits. I got the gun and a shell, loaded it when no one was looking, and went searching for the rooster. I found him flirting with several chickens down in the cotton patch behind the corncrib. The old boy was strutting around between the cotton rows like he owned the place.

Thinking, I'll fix you, I lifted the gun to my shoulder, took dead aim and fired, KABAAAAAMMM. That old shotgun kicked me flat of my back and after I recovered slightly, raising myself up, all I could see was the air full of chicken feathers. My intended target, the rooster was nowhere in sight but there were two laying hens on the ground dying. I had shot over the rooster and killed two of mama's best hens. Talk about whipping, it seemed for days after that when mama or papa happened to think about what I had done they would give me another one. Papa whipped me for taking the shotgun, for loading it and for firing it. Mama whipped me for killing two of her laying hens, and for letting the rooster escape her Thanksgiving dinner table. I never saw that old dominecker again, somebody said when that gun went off he headed for Canada.

Mama was a wonderful cook. She could always take the least and make the most of it. She loved to make deserts, apple pie out of scrawny little sour apples, chocolate or cocoanut cakes, fruit cobblers and her specialty was a six layer Lane cake at Christmas time. My all-time favorite of her pies was the butterscotch which she made from scratch. It would take hours to make, but it was worth it. Many Sunday nights while hitch hiking to Auburn, a story I'll tell later, and being stranded somewhere on highway 280 I would open my satchel and find that mama had put a fresh butterscotch pie in there. It would be mashed, but that didn't hurt the taste of it.

There is just no way to describe all that lady did. Of course, when the girls were still at home, they helped her, Louis and I helped too when we were not in the fields. Besides the cooking and cleaning, she scrubbed the wood floors in the house with soap and water, being extra careful not to leave any water standing in the corners. That, according to her was the sign of a bad housekeeper, for instance, like Lilly Alvis.

She washed our clothes by hand on an old rub board in a washtub with water that had to be carried up to the house from the creek or caught in the rain barrel and heated in the cast iron wash pot. Then she would hang the clothes on an outside clothesline to dry in the sun. She made clothes for the girls, sewed quilt tops, carded the cotton and made the quilts, all by hand.

Night time would find her in her big rocking chair, with a child on her lap, usually me, rocking and holding on to the stick attached to the dasher that was in the old crock churn, going up and down as she rocked, turning clabbered milk into delicious buttermilk and butter.

As I mentioned before, we got electricity in 1938. The first electric item in our house was the Silvertone table model radio from Sears and Roebuck. The radio had to have an extensive antenna and ground system. The antenna was a strand of wire from the radio, out the window, up to the top of the house, and along the entire length of the roof. The ground system was a heavy wire connected from the back of the radio to an iron rod driven in the ground outside the window.

What a wonderful new world that radio opened up for the Price family! We could sit right there on Cullman Route 5 and hear the whole world. Having no idea that I would ever actually have an opportunity to talk on the radio, I remember being fascinated by it. I liked to listen to the Grand 'Ole Opry from

Nashville, National Barn Dance from Chicago, WCKY from Cincinnati, and programs like Inner Sanctum, The Lone Ranger, Roy Rogers and Dale Evans, Fibber McGee and Molly, Henry Aldredge, Fred Allen, Red Skelton, and Lum'n Abner. I especially admired the great announcers on the big powerful stations, Louie Buck, Grant Turner, Dave Overton, Hy Averback, and the blow by blow announcing of boxing, we called prize fights.

Being the only house in the Nebo community with a radio, mama and papa invited all the neighbors in to hear the famous fight between Joe Lewis and Max Schmelling. When Lewis knocked out Schmelling, one would have thought the end of the world had come, a black man had beaten a white man. It didn't matter that Schmelling was a German and Joe Lewis was from Alabama, white folks grieved anyway

As president Roosevelt called it "A day that will live in infamy," was December 7, 1941. That early Sunday morning several of us were on our front porch listening to the radio, mama, papa, us kids and I believe a neighbor had stopped by when the program was interrupted by a special news bulletin. The announcer in a very solemn voice was saying the Japanese had bombed Pearl Harbor. Nobody on the porch knew exactly what it meant, and we had never heard of Pearl Harbor, but we figured it must be pretty serious from the announcer's tone of voice. We had no idea where Pearl Harbor was, but it must be awfully close by, maybe down near Blue Hole, the forks of the creek, on Flint creek in Morgan County or surely no further than the Tennessee River. We expected the "Japs" to come marching down the road toward our house at any time.

I can't say for sure, but that old radio may have had more influence on the rest of my life than anything else, I still love broadcasting.

I think it's time to wrap up this chapter of my life. I have already gone too long with it but nobody says you have to read it all. Like drinking an RC Cola, drink just as much as you can hold and leave the rest.

As time went by, mama got a brand new Kenmore washing

machine, but still had to "tote" the water from the creek and hang the wet clothes on the clothesline. She had a Crosley Shelvadoor refrigerator papa bought from a man at Bug Tussle, Alabama For $100. They bought an electric iron, churn, and best of all a Hot Point electric cook stove. Papa did not like the refrigerator, saying it made the milk too cold and the butter too hard.

In 1956 the folks had grown older, in their seventies, the work on the farm was no easier, they were alone, and unable to continue as in the past. Papa tried to rent out the place, even buying the renter a new Farmall tractor, but it just didn't work. He sold the place including the 35 acres mama had inherited from her parents for $9500. He held an auction to dispose of goods they would not need or could not use when they would move into the little house they were buying next to Louis and Maggie, on Wilson street in Scottsboro.

They lived there the rest of their lives. Mama died in her sleep on February 7, 1970 and papa died after a two year bout with colon cancer on June 3, 1975. Quoting directly from the sale notice papa had printed; (I still have a framed copy hanging on my office wall,) will illustrate just how few material goods the hardest working couple I've ever known were able to accumulate during their long lifetime. They didn't have much in material goods but they had each other within a few months of sixty years.

AUCTION SALE ON THURSDAY NOVEMBER 8, 1956
BEGINNING AT 10 O'CLOCK

I Will Sell at Auction To The Highest and
Best Bidder At My Home, All Of My Farming
Tools and Implements, such As:
1 Walking Cultivator
1 Mule Drawn Cotton Duster
1 Two Horse Wagon With Harness
One Farmall A tracter with all Attachments

Turning Plows
2 Milk Cows---1 Springing Heifer
4 Tons of Good Hay, Baled
Wood and Coal Heaters
1 Living Room Suite--One Bedroom Suite
Extra Mattresses etc. Also Items of Interest
In Kitchenware and Furniture Unmentioned

COME AND SEE AND BUY PLEASE
WALTER M. PRICE

Residence On The Nebo Road- 2 Miles South of the Longview
Stores Route 5, Cullman, Alabama
BILL McKENZIE, Auctioneer
IN CASE OF RAIN, SALE WILL BE HELD NEXT DAY

As the reader can plainly see, Walter and Gertie Price came to the end of their working lives with very few possessions, but the things they left behind are a lot more precious than gold. A loving, caring, family with an appreciation for the good things we were taught like love, honesty, integrity, hard work and a strong faith in God.

What happened to the old farm? All but 20 acres, where our house stood was later sold to a group from Cullman. Would you believe that it's now Terri Pines Country Club? It surely is, with a beautiful clubhouse and golf course, surrounded by expensive homes and condominiums. I am told that they are now selling lots for as much as $100,000. Those old poor hillsides where we tried to scratch out a living farming are now covered with grass and Golf carts with people having a good time.

I told Louis the first time we played the course, we should have known it would make a good golf course because all we could ever grow was grass, anyway. He said, "Can't you just see papa sitting on the back porch watching and saying just look at them fools out there chasing that little old ball around? They ought to be working!" If you ever drive northwest of Cullman, Alabama, on the four lane highway, Al. 157, look closely on the right for the little concrete block church, Pine Hill, turn right on the paved road, go down the hill to Terri Pines, then look straight across the golf course. You will see the house with new aluminum siding, a screened porch and indoor plumbing. That's where Walter and Gertie lived and raised Opal, Lela, Aria, Louis and Clyde. By the way, the barn is still there too, still unpainted.

Chapter 3

MORE FAMILY

The George Johnson family was very much like ours, a large family with eight children. They lived on a farm in the Friendship community of western Cullman County. The Prices and Johnsons were very good friends, attending the same church and sharing many Sunday dinners together. Like our family, they had children of all ages. The youngest Johnson was Hilda and you might say that she was my first "Sweetheart" when we were both about 6 years old. In fact I believe my older brother, Louis was sort of sweet on another Johnson girl named Julia Faye.

When I was about five years old, my sister Lela married James Curtis, the third child of George and Nettie Johnson. They moved to Decatur, Alabama where he worked for the state highway department. I don't remember anything about the wedding but I do remember visiting them in Decatur. That's where I saw the first black person I had ever seen. There were no Negroes in Cullman county then and very few until this day.

I remember their first child being born in Decatur. They named him James Clyde for his daddy and me, and called him Jimmy. At six years old I was an uncle.

In 1939 they moved to Anderson, Indiana, his older brother Henry was there in school at Anderson College. Curtis worked in Anderson for a while but soon decided to move back south to a small farm on Highway 31 near the Cullman and Morgan county line. Their other two children Kenny and Linda were both born while they were on the farm.

It was in 1944, during World War II that they moved back to Anderson where they have remained until now. Curtis retired from General Motors Delco Remy division and is still very active with his woodworking, golf and bowling. He is 82 and Lela is 83. Her heath is fair. As my doctor sometimes tells me, "You are in good shape, for you." The same can be said about Lela.

I don't remember when John Webb first started calling on my older sister, Opal. I was much too young to remember anything about their early relationship. It just seemed to me that John was always in the family. My earliest recollection of him was as if he were an older brother or even a daddy. He would come to see Opal, but would spend most of the time with me and Louis. He would sometimes bring a pack or two of firecrackers and it seemed that he always had a pack of Wrigley chewing gum to share with two little country boys who had very few such treats.

After about 8 years of courtship Opal and John were married. They lived in the Eastlake section of Birmingham. What a treat it was for me to get to spend a few days during the summer with them in the city. I saw and tasted wonderful things I had never been privileged to before. For instance, I had never seen store bought sheets. Mama always made sheets from sewing four Royster fertilizer sacks together. She would take the rough cloth sacks left over from planting time in the spring, bleach them in the old cast iron wash-pot out in the yard, the same pot she used to heat water for washing clothes, cooking out lard and dying sack cloth for quilt linings. She used plenty of Red Devil lye trying to remove all of the lettering from the sacks. Most of the time she was successful, but sometimes one could read Royster 6-8-4 or 4-10-7 at bedtime. She would sew the four sacks together to make a sheet. It's true, they were very uncomfortable The sack cloth was rough and the seams were scratchy, but we didn't complain, we just thought that all sheets were supposed to be that way.

After the sacks were emptied, (they were sewn together with tough string,) Louis and I would take those strings, wrap them as tight as we could around a black walnut or a hickory nut to make a pretty good baseball. The balls were OK except when they would start to come apart. After that, when we threw the ball it would most likely have a "tail." We never owned a real baseball.

Looking back now some of the things that charmed me most as a youngster on his first visit to the city seem strange to me. Things like store-bought bacon, movie theaters, ice cream any time, not just on the Fourth of July, electricity, and running water, but most of all, I mean the most fantastic thing was the indoor toilet and soft paper on a roll. I didn't even have to look for a sheet of Sears and Roebuck catalog, a page from Progressive Farmer Magazine, or a fresh corn cob. I just pulled the paper off a roll, like magic.

John Webb was employed by the Conservation Department of the state of Alabama. After working in Jefferson County for a few years he was transferred to Jackson County. They moved to Scottsboro, the County Seat, where he continued to work for the state as a forest ranger responsible for the entire county. One of my fondest memories is when I would be allowed to go home with them, sometimes in the summer for as much as two weeks. John would let me go with him to his office and when he had to go up in the mountains to investigate a forest fire or to try to locate some moonshiner who had started a fire, he would let me go with him in his state owned pickup truck.

He and Opal lived in Scottsboro until their divorce in 1953. I remember the date so well. Carol and I had just moved to Tuscaloosa to go to the University when we got a call saying that they were divorced. To me it was almost like a death in the family because John had always been there. I have never known all of the details, and of course I would not disclose them if I did. I have always believed that part of their trouble was after so many years of marriage John loved and wanted children so much, and because Opal could not bare any, he just couldn't face the future and old age without having some of his own. I say this because soon after the divorce he remarried and right away he and is new wife had four children. John died suddenly with a heart attack at a young age. I loved John Webb.

My sister Opal after living in Scottsboro where she had been for so long, wanted a change of scenery so she went to visit Lela and Curtis in Anderson. There, after a while she met one of the most perfect gentleman one could ever hope to find. Fred Thomas was a classic. He was educated, loved music, played the bass violin in the local concert orchestra and loved my sister very much. He was a good man. His wife had died when she was very young leaving him with two small children Danny and Sharon.

Opal never moved back to Alabama to live. She married Fred, moved into his big two story house with the apple orchard in the back and assumed the role of wife to Fred and stepmother to Danny and Sharon. They had a good life together until she developed cancer and died in 1970. Fred died shortly there after. Danny and Sharon still live in the Anderson area and have families of their own.

My sister Aria left West Point High School in her eleventh year. She, like her two older sisters caught a Greyhound bus headed for Indiana. After a while Mama and Papa started receiving letters from her about her job but mostly about men she had met. One was a dream whose name was Blackwelder. I remember that the folks were trying to figure out how they could afford to go to the wedding so far away. Soon after, they received another letter in which Aria informed them that she had met another man who was even more wonderful. His name was Paul Decker, from Lansing, Michigan, but living in Anderson, and they planned to marry right away. Papa said, "Well, I guess I would rather see her married to a Yankee than to a black welder."

Paul and Aria had two children, Paula and Dennis. Paula now lives in Ohio. Dennis is deceased. He was the victim of an aneurysm while in his early forties, Very tragic.

In the summer of 1950, just after graduating from high school my folks allowed me to go to Anderson to try to find a job. Perhaps I could make enough money to start to college in the fall. I lived with Aria, Paul and the baby Paula for several weeks, sleeping on the couch in the living room at 519 Park Avenue. That sounds like a really fancy, rich folks address, but Park Avenue in Anderson is about as wide as my back porch now It was and still is a very nice neighborhood. In fact the Deckers still live with in a half block of that original house. Paul helped me get a job with a friend of his, Joe Perkey, a painting contractor paying $1.00 an hour. The work was hard, the hours long and the weeks went by before I had been able to save more than a few dollars. I will always be grateful to them for giving me the opportunity to discover that I did not want to make a career of painting houses. It's not as bad as picking cotton, but almost.

When my brother Louis graduated from Cullman high school in 1946 he went to live with Opal and John in Scottsboro. He was working at Copeland's hardware store when he was drafted into the army. The last year of high school Louis drove a school bus on the route from our house to Cullman High by way of Vinemont. The county paid him a whopping $25 a month, which at that time seemed like untold riches to me.

Because of that driving job Louis wound up with something a lot better than money. There was a pretty little girl named Maggie Blair who rode his bus every day. He was so impressed with her, that as soon as she was old enough and her daddy would let her go out, they started dating. Later while on leave from the army he and Maggie made a fast trip over the Georgia line to Rising Faun where they were married.

When he was discharged from the army he joined the National Guard. His unit was one of the first of the Alabama Guard to be mobilized during the Korean War. Louis was stationed at Fort Campbell Kentucky when their first child was born. Nita was born on Christmas Eve. I remember going with my brother in law, Curtis, to Fort Campbell to pick him up and bring him back to Scottsboro on a three day pass so that he could see the new baby before he shipped out to Korea.

When he returned from the war he went to work for the city of Scottsboro in the electric power department and at the same time he attended classes at a junior college nearby. Maggie gave birth to another daughter soon after his return. They named her Lynn. She and her husband John Morgan now live in Chattanooga, Tennessee. They have no children of their own, but John has two from a previous marriage.

Louis and Maggie's third child was a son named David. He and his wife Lynn live in West Palm Beach, Florida. David is the golf superintendent at the famous Breakers Hotel golf course. He is the good golfer in the family.

Nita married an exceptional young man, Larry Derrick. Larry was from a good family, well respected in the town, and was one of the most enjoyable people to be with I have ever known. He loved all of us but especially my wife Carol, Nita's aunt. I don't know who loved each other more Larry or Carol, but it was wonderful to see them together especially after he was stricken by a slowly developing brain tumor. He would tell her his true feeling more that anyone else. His condition gradually worsened. He had surgery at Mayo Clinic in Rochester, Minnesota, but there was nothing they could do. Larry died at the age of 42.

Nita and Larry had two children, Price a recent graduate of Jacksonville State University and Drew, 13 years old, living in Huntsville with Nita, his stepfather Robbie and Charlie his younger half brother. A couple of years after Larry's death Nita married Robbie Farquar from Huntsville, originally from Greensboro, Alabama.

The state of Alabama owns a 4000 acre cattle and catfish prison ranch about ten miles west of Greensboro. You may say "What does that have to do with my story?" Absolutely nothing, except it involves the parents of my new nephew, Robbie. That farm was the scene of one of the most heinous crimes ever committed in Alabama. Mr. Charlie Farquar, Robbie's father and his mother had lived on the farm for a long time in a very nice house with every thing a couple in their 70s could want or need. Charlie was the general manager, responsible for the cattle, catfish production, hatchery, and managing the wild life, deer, turkey and quail. The farm is a favorite place for Alabama politicians to go and take guests for organized deer, dove and quail hunts.

Workers on the ranch were state prisoners. The barracks in which they lived housed about 100 prisoners. Supposedly those prisoners were all well screened determined to be trustworthy, and sent to the prison farm to work where there were no fences, locks or guards. They were not allowed to leave but had free range of the ranch.

Soon after my niece Nita and their son Robbie married,

tragedy struck suddenly and without warning. It was a nice warm Sunday morning. A beautiful day was beginning, the sun was rising over the ranch, all was quiet and peaceful. Mr. Charlie got out of bed, dressed as he usually did and left the house for his morning walk around the farm. The house was about a quarter of a mile from the prisoners' barracks.

While Charlie was walking, a prisoner, (by the way from Tuscaloosa, an attempted murderer who should never been at the farm) left the prison quarters, went to the Farquar house, broke in, raped Mrs. Farquar and deliberately set fire to the house.

Two other prisoners, when they saw the smoke and flames ran to investigate. When they arrived at the house, the convict shot and killed both of them with one of Charlie's shotguns. Shortly after that Mr. Charlie, hearing all the commotion and seeing the fire hurried back to the house to see what was going on. The killer was waiting for him. He shot Charlie in the chest with his own gun. Charlie died instantly. Mrs. Farquar died in the burning house. She was so badly wounded she could not get out. The big house and all its contents were completely destroyed.

That Sunday morning four people died needlessly, Mr. and Mrs. Farquar and two prisoners. The killer then took Charlie's truck, but instead of running as far as the truck would take him and possibly getting away completely, the fool went back to the barracks and crawled back in his bunk. Of course, he was soon arrested, tried and convicted and sentenced to life in prison without parole.

In my opinion he should have been electrocuted for what he did. In fact I don't believe he even deserved a trial. Maybe a good old fashioned lynching would have been more appropriate. As I said, this has nothing to do with the story I set out to tell, but since Robbie is a member of our family now I believe it should be recorded in the family records.

Louis continued to work for the Scottsboro Power Board, being promoted to the manager's position, which he held for more than 30 years. Retiring about 10 years ago, he became bored with golfing, fishing and loafing, he decided to get into politics by running for Mayor of the town. He is now about to end his second four year term saying he will not run again. I think the position of Mayor has been very challenging and rewarding for him. At least it has kept him very busy.

Well there you have the story about the Price family in-laws, all except one. That one was Carol Dean Bailey, my beautiful, loving, wonderful, sweet, and sometimes bullheaded wife for almost 48 years. Before this project is through you will read a lot more about Carol Dean. I will tell you how we met, but first I must give you some background information.

I attended Vinemont elementary and junior high school from grade one through nine. Cullman County High School was located in the city of Cullman, therefore most "country" kids would attend a junior high and then be bussed to town for grades ten through twelve. It always seemed to the country boys, like myself, that the town kids who had gone to school together since the first grade thought that they were superior to us. They thought they were smarter, more handsome and especially more wealthy. No question about it most of their parents were extremely wealthy compared to mine.

The town kids were very clannish, especially the girls. I found it hard to even talk to most of them. There was one in particular, a pretty little freshman that I had never even spoken to, but had seen many times on campus with her stuck up friends looking down their city slicker noses at me because I was country and really showed it, with my blue denim shirt, faded overalls, Vasoline Hair Tonic slicked back hair and looking almost as undernourished as a war orphan. Her name was Carol Dean the only child of W. H. (Henderson) better known as "Cy," and Mildred Bailey. She was a majorette in the marching band, a School Yearbook (The Bearcat) beauty and a former Queen of the Cullman County Strawberry Festival, Miss Strawberry.

From what I had seen and heard of her I had determined that she was a girl that I just did not care to meet. Besides, I still had my good ole country girls, Ima Nell, Quova June, Christine, Polly, Ahhhh Polly, I fell in love with her in the third grade.

Mrs. Thelma Drake our teacher selected Polly and me to do a special May Pole dance, just the two of us, for the entire Vinemont School. Polly was to be a fairy and I a brownie.

I had not intended to tell this at this point in my story, but it's so good I want to hear it again myself. Here's what happened. The May Day celebration was held at the school house at night. It was customary back then to run the regular school bus routes to pick up both parents and children if there were an activity at the school. So, that night my sister Aria and I planned to board the bus for the 10 or 12 mile ride to the school house. Where were my parents? They very seldom, if ever, attended anything at school. Sometimes I thought they just didn't care about things we were doing at school but I know now that they were just too tired from hard work all day, and expecting another hard-working day tomorrow, to go out at night. Besides, the old '28 Chevrolet probably didn't have any gas in it. The day that Mrs. Drake told me she wanted me to be a brownie and dance with Polly Bullard I ran all the way from the school bus stop at our mailbox, which was a quarter of a mile from the house, to tell mama that I was going to be a brownie and Mrs. Drake said for mama to make me a brownie suit. Mama said "Son what is a brownie? I've never seen one. What do they look like?" I said, "Mama I don't know. The teacher didn't tell me." Bless Mama's sweet heart, she could always take nothing and make something of it. She figured a brownie suit would be brown, so she got some of her Royster guano sacks, put them in a wash-pot full of boiling water, and added her secret ingredient, a big batch of green, black walnut hulls from the walnut tree in our front yard. Sure enough those sacks turned the prettiest brown you've ever seen.

She had always made clothes for herself and the girls, so making a suit for me was no problem on the old Singer treadle sewing machine. She made the suit and a little brown cap that looked sorta like a little soldier cap or a dunce cap with the pointed top cut off. Just before time for me to catch the bus to go to the school house we discovered a problem. Not having any buttons, and certainly not having anything as expensive as a zipper to put in it, mama decided the only thing to do was simply sew me up in the suit and send me and Aria on our way.

There was a large crowd at the school. I was so excited. I must have believed that everybody had heard that little third grader nine year old Clyde Price from the Nebo community was making his first public appearance, and they all came to see me in my home-made brownie suit dancing with the prettiest girl anyone had ever seen, Polly. Whooeee!!!, She was lovely all dressed up in that little Shirley Temple dress, sticking out all the way around and those cute little leggins showing her little panties underneath. I can still see her. The fairy suit was all very white with a beautiful set of white wings that stood out and back as if she were flying. On her head, on top of her blonde hair hanging down in long curls was a sparkling crown. I know one thing for sure, her mama did not make that fairy suit. It had to be store bought. No telling how much it cost.

The May Pole dance with the entire third grade, except me and Polly, holding long ribbons attached to the top went fine. The kids danced and sang as they went around the pole winding and unwinding their ribbons. Then it came time for Polly and me to come on stage. Our big moment had arrived. We took center stage and danced to the May Pole music. Oh my, it was beautiful. I was a child star. I was so proud of myself. I was in my brownie suit dancing with the a lovely fairy named Polly. The audience went wild. I had never heard such an ovation. In fact I had never heard ANY ovation before.

After the program was over I strutted out to the front of the school house to wait for the bus to return after having run another route. I knew I would have a long wait but that was OK. More people would have a chance to see me in my brownie suit and brag about how wonderful Polly and I looked dancing together.

While waiting for the bus in front of the school a terrible thing happened. I had a terrific pain in my stomach. If you've ever eaten too many green apples or drunk too much sorghum cane juice you know what I mean. Did you see the movie Dumb and Dumber? If you did, I felt like the old boy that had been given a whole cup full of laxative and barely made it to his girlfriend's house.

The toilets a Vinemont school were outside, some distance behind the building. As I started to run toward the boys outhouse it was so dark back there that I couldn't see where I was going and besides, I was scared to death of the dark. I would not have made it to the toilet anyway, but a chilling thought came over me as I backed up into the shrubbery by the side of the building, I panicked! HOW AM I GOING TO GET THIS BROWNIE SUIT OFF? I'M SEWED IN IT!!!!!.

One thing mama did when she made that blasted suit; she made it good. She even sewed in rubber bands cut from a innertube around the ankles so the legs would not flop as I danced. Needless to say, it seemed that everything I had eaten since Christmas came out of me and stayed in that suit, some of it leaked down into my shoes.

I then started looking for Aria. She was supposed to watch out for me and see that I got on the right bus. I could not find her. I panicked again! Here I was all alone, frightened, and crying with a brownie suit filled to the brim with the foulest smelling mess I has ever experienced, waiting to get on a school bus full of people, Nobody would even come close enough to me to ask what was wrong. Every time I tried to tell someone my trouble they ran away as if I were carrying the plague. All of my fans had deserted me, even the ones who had given such applause for Polly and me just a short while ago, and to make it worse my own sister was hiding from me. I learned later that Aria had met up with her boyfriend Tallmadge Nesmith and he had taken her home. I could never figure how I got home before she did. Strange.

Finally the bus arrived. The school bus route was at least ten miles of mostly dirt roads. We lived at the very end of the route. When I boarded the bus I went all the way back as far as I could go to the back seat. The bus was full but nobody shared a seat with me. When I sat down that mess in my suit went SLOOOSH and I think some of it even came out the collar. The bus made many stops along the way to let people off and at every stop those remaining on there would move to the front like rats abandoning ship. It was a very cold night for the first of May but every window in that old bus was all the way down, some folks even had their heads hanging out like a hound dog in a pickup truck.

After what seemed like hours the bus came to a stop at our mailbox. I left my back seat, walked to the front to get off praying that the driver would not shine his flashlight on the steps of the bus as he had done for all of the other passengers, but no such luck. The fool lit up the steps, the ground and my soiled brownie suit for everyone to see.

As you know our house was about a quarter mile down a one lane dirt road from the big road where I left the bus. As I started walking down that dark road every step was horrible. By now a lot more had drained into my shoes. I can still hear that SLOSH, SLOSH, SLOSH every step I took.

Just before I got to the house, I could see a familiar figure on the front porch. It was mama. I think she had waited up for me, but it could have been that she smelled me coming. About that time I decided it would be a good time to cry again. I did and for the first time in my life my sweet mama did not take me in her arms, love me and rock me in her big old rocking chair. Instead she told me "Don't come in the house! Stay in the yard! I'll be right back!"

She went in the house and came back with the big pair of scissors. Starting at my neck and working down, she cut that brownie suit off of me. She eased my shoes off and left me standing naked in the front yard with only my brownie cap on. We had no running water and the only way to get warm water was to draw it from the well and heat it on the wood stove. She didn't have time for all of that. Her baby was standing in the yard at eleven o'clock on a cold night, freezing and covered with dodo.

We had a big rain barrel by the side of the house placed so that when it rained the rainwater would run off the roof and into the barrel. Mama used that water to wash the family clothes. That night she ruined her wash water. She led me around to the side of the house, picked me up and doused me in that barrel of cold water, I don't mean just one time, I mean I went up and down, up and down until I thought I would either drown or freeze to death. At that time I really didn't care which. I must tell you that to my delight when Aria got home she got a real good ole country whuppin' for leaving me alone at the schoolhouse and for letting me get into that mess. Come to think of it, I don't know what she could have done if she had been there.

Whew! That story took much longer to tell than I had expected, but every word is true. I was madly in love with pretty Polly from the third to the sixth grade, when she ran off with a sailor and married. She was 12 years old. I never saw her again, but Polly, where ever you are, I still love you Honey and I hope you are happy. When she married, I didn't even know there was a difference in our anatomies except that she had long curly hair. Now, let's get back to my story.....

The plot thickens. Carol Dean's best friend was a girl named Dot Clark and my good friend was another country boy, Elmas Howlett. Elmas wanted to date Dot so badly that he was about to lose his mind over her. The trouble was that Dot would not go with him unless he got Carol Dean a date too. Guess what! I was the chosen one to go with them on a double date. Elmas's father let him borrow his 1946 Ford coupe. We went to a 25 cent movie at the Cullman theater, afterwards bought the girls a 5 cent coke at the Globe Drive-in, went for a ride and maybe we stopped for a little while down by the city park, you understand just to save on Mr. Howlett's gas. Anyway, I got to know Carol Dean pretty well that night in 1949. If you have never been in the back seat of a '46 Ford Coupe, I'll tell you that little bitty back seat can get pretty crowded.

As Paul Harvey would say "Now the rest of the story." That was the ONLY DATE Elmas ever had with Dot, and after my first date with Carol Dean, I dated very few other girls. On November 25, 1951 Carol Dean and I were married at 4:00 p.m. by Dr. Gilbert Speake, Pastor at the Seventh Street Baptist Church in Cullman, Alabama.

Before I move on, I need to relate a couple more stories about my youth and my relationship to my older brother, Louis. He is four years older than me and could always whip me in a fist fight, but I could run faster and most times get away from him before there was a killing. We could fight about anything or nothing, but sooner or later Mama would break it up with a switch from a nearby lilac bush.

There was one incident that may have affected my brain to this day, It was a Saturday afternoon. Mama and papa had gone to town, papa leaving instructions for Louis and me to go to the south field and pick dry whippoorwill peas. Near the pea patch was a terrace row of watermelon vines. Being early fall and frost had not killed them, the vines had put on some second growth watermelons about the size of baseballs or a little bigger. As we picked peas from the vines, putting them in our long cotton pick sacks, the fight started. I don't remember what it was about, probably Louis thought I was not picking fast enough. I would certainly lose the fight, so for protection, I dropped the pick sack strap from my shoulder and started running as I usually did in a situation like that.

Louis picked up one of those little old watermelons and threw a strike that would have made Catfish Hunter envious, hitting me in the back of the head. That was on Saturday. I woke up the next Tuesday, lying on a pallet of quilts mama had placed on the floor. I suppose the reason they didn't put me on a bed was because beds were so scarce at our house, they figured since I was unconscious it wouldn't make any difference. Please understand, not for one minute do I believe Louis meant to hit me in the head with that melon to kill me. He simply wanted to cripple me.

According to what I was told later, when he saw I was knocked out he dragged me down to the creek and splashed water in my face, having no luck reviving me he dragged me on up to the house. I'm sure all the while he was praying papa would not murder him for killing his baby boy. I must have had a serious concussion, but we'll never know because they did not think of taking me to a doctor.

Another incident, about that same time, again on Saturday when mama and papa went to town leaving Louis, me and our sister Aria at home involved my cutting my nose almost off. No one was living in our old renter house, so papa had run one strand of barb wire from the pasture to the corner of the porch so the cow could go in the yard to eat the grass. That day, as kids will, Louis and I along with Leo and Billy Huffstutler were playing in and around the old house when one of them chased me around the corner of the house. Forgetting about that wire, I hit it full speed across the bridge of my nose so hard that I hit the ground. I don't think I was knocked out that time, but the sight and smell of the blood spurting from the wound must have caused me to faint.

When I recovered I was lying on the front porch of our house smelling nothing but coal oil. Louis and the Huffstutler boys had somehow managed to drag me to the house where Aria, not knowing what to do, managed to stop the bleeding, poured the kerosene on the cut and taped my nose back together with several pieces of white adhesive tape.

I've worn that scar all my life, just being thankful that Aria got the end of my nose lined up pretty good, else I might be smelling up side down. Again no doctor ever saw it.

When I was in the seventh grade at Vinemont, Louis had turned 16 and had his driver's license. Papa consented for him to drive his 1938 Ford pickup to the school house, but he had to take me along and see that I got back O K. I think the folks still remembered the famous May Pole incident. The happening at school that night was a cake walk and box supper. For the uneducated, that meant the girls would pack a supper in a box, bucket or whatever and the boys would bid on it, the high bidder would get to share the food with the young lady that brought it. Most of the time the prettiest box did not belong to the prettiest girl.

My teacher, Mrs. Copeland had baked the biggest, prettiest coconut cake I'd ever seen, a huge cake with white icing and lots of coconut, with a big red cherry right in the middle of the top. The deal on the cake was, she had baked something inside it and

41

for a dime a person could have one guess as to what that item was. Being so fond of coconut cake and only having one dime, I spent it on a guess. I guessed that she had put a whole pecan in the cake. I WON. What a prize. I was the proud owner of the biggest cake at the cake walk and I bought it for a dime.

When the program was over, I took my cake, went out to the parking lot to ride home with Louis in the pickup truck. The truck was gone! I looked all over the school ground for it but it was nowhere in sight.

The bus route from our house to Vinemont was 10 miles. The pickup truck route via the two-mile dirt road to the highway and then to the school was 6 miles. There was a short-cut through the woods of about 4 miles, but the only time we used it was in the daytime, in case we missed the school bus or had a belly ache during the day and the principle, Mr. L.C. Camp sent us home. Occasionally we went that way just hoping to get a glimpse of the three Roden sisters Irene, O'Dell and Bee-At. The Rodens invented the word ugly, especially Beatrice, or as she was known far and wide by every man in the county, Bee-At.

My dilemma that night was what to do about getting me and my cake safely home. I know now that part of my decision to walk, carrying the cake, was to get Louis in trouble for leaving me. No doubt he would have returned looking for me when he got home after delivering several other kids he had offered a ride and his girlfriend Quova June Quick home. That was not enough. I wanted all kinds of bad things to happen to him for his negligence.

There must have been a relatively bright moon that night or I would never have found my way from the school, across the highway down a dirt road, past Johnson's dairy barn, through the pasture, and into the darkest, deepest woods I had ever seen. There was a small trail, but I had trouble finding it in the dark. I imagined all sorts of "boogers" were chasing me and that surely there must be a wildcat or a "haint" behind every tree.

After what seemed like an eternity, I crawled through the fence of 'Kinley Roden's pasture. I was in the open at last with my cake still intact. I crossed the pasture coming out at Bent Alvis's old house, a big black two story, spooky looking place to a 13 year old boy on a dark night. I crawled through the fence between his garage where he kept his T-model Ford and the big house, hoping the old man was in bed and would not see me.

Having accomplished that much of the walk home I was feeling pretty good except for being tired of walking with that big cake. I had entered Nebo road at the top of Alvis hill, between Bent Alvis' house and that of Frog Martin on the other side. It seemed then that the road down Alvis hill was a mile long, full of curves, and there was no telling who or what would be lurking in the dark for me. Afraid of what might come out of the ditches on either side, I walked down the middle of the road, continuously looking back to see how far I'd come and if anything was following me.

There were three more main obstacles before me. First about half way down the hill I had to pass by an old unused "dipping vat," a hole in the ground lined with concrete with one end slanted enough to put cows in there in order to "dip" them in whatever chemical farmers had to kill parasites. Everybody in the community knew that dipping vat was haunted and would avoid walking by there at night if at all possible. That night I had no choice. I wanted to run, but was afraid I'd drop my cake. I never knew what kind of haint was supposed to be in the vat unless it was the ghost of a bull who drowned while being "dipped".

At the bottom of the hill was Alvis creek with its long wooden bridge that made all sorts of weird squeaky, bumpy noises that night. The old bridge was so noisy as I walked, I would have sworn something was following me for sure. After crossing the bridge and walking up the hill on the other side I had to pass the home of Eb and Bessie Alvis. Hoping they would be asleep, I tip-toed by, afraid I would hear Bessie scream as she often did after Eb drank too much of his moonshine whiskey and was beating her up or threatening her with a butcher knife. When Eb would finally drink enough and was tired of whipping on Bessie, he would fall asleep. Then came

Bessie's revenge; she would take Eb's glass eye out of its socket and hide it for several days. Anytime we saw Eb with a black patch over his right eye socket we knew there had been a big fight at the Alvis house.

Right across from their house was the mailbox and the little road down to our house. I was almost home after that long walk carrying my heavy load. Before I could make it on down to the house, I saw the lights of our old truck coming my way. Sure enough Louis had taken a bunch of kids home from the cake walk, driven on home and discovered I was not in the back of the truck. In near panic he turned around in the yard and headed back to the school house to find me. He was surprised to see me not more that 500 yards from our front door. He opened the truck door and told me to get in. I said "NO." So far, I had not taken time or effort to cry, saving my tears for when I would get home. I thought now might be a good time so I let it all out.

By that time Louis was pleading for me to get in the truck, he and I both knowing Hell would break loose if he parked the truck and I was not in it. Still I refused, kept walking down the road with him following close behind in the truck. I believe he thought if he stayed close enough to me it would appear to mama and papa we had both arrived at the same time in the truck.

As I stumbled up the front porch steps still carrying my cake which by then was looking very ragged, (some of the icing was dripping off from the warm tears falling on it,) there was both mama and papa standing, waiting to hear why I was walking with a cake from the cake walk. I couldn't wait to tell them the whole story, crying awhile in between the details of how Louis had left me and I had to walk all the way home from Vinemont.

Louis got an old fashioned butt "whupping" and lost his driving privileges for months. I got revenge for the watermelon and the pleasure of showing mama what was once a beautiful white coconut cake, it's cherry on top had been long gone, but it still had it's whole pecan in the middle. Come to think of it, I may be eligible for the Guinness book of World Records for the longest cake walk ever.

I don't want to leave an impression that Louis and I don't get along. Now, we are as close as two brothers can be, and I think we were no different than any other brothers growing up, I know I was a pest to him because he was older and did not deserve me hanging around and demanding to go every place he went. Certainly we were no different from the two boys Carol Dean and I would produce later.

I hope you will allow me one more short story about Louis. Just about every spring papa would go to Kenny's mule sales barn in Cullman to buy an old plug mule or, as he did one year an old mare we named Maude. Talk about a "plug," old Maude was not only old, but she looked like she was ready for the soap factory. As we say, "She was as pore as Job's turkey." You could count her ribs from 20 feet away and her swayed backbone stuck up about three inches above her sides. With plenty of corn, hay and oats in her belly, she gained some weight and started looking like she was alive enough to pull a light plow.

We had no saddle, so I would ride her bareback on Sunday afternoons until I made blisters on my butt. It was tough on Monday morning having to walk behind a plow with those half dollar size blisters. Old Maude even became healthy enough to breed, and in about eleven months she gave us a little mule colt, which I promptly claimed as my own. I had better explain some animal husbandry to the really uneducated. A mule is a hybrid, a cross between a mare and a jackass. Male and female mules cannot reproduce. Mules make much better work animals than horses because they never think about sex, come to think of it, maybe we should elect a mule President. They earn their keep by pulling a plow, a loaded wagon, or "snaking" logs in the woods.

From the day the colt was born, I named him Star, because of the white spot on his tan forehead. I was a happy boy, petting, brushing, feeding and taking care of him. The colt would follow me around like a dog. We were good buddies, enjoying each other's company. I think he would have slept with me if mama would have let him in the house. Star was about a year old when one day Hoyt Bridges came by in his pickup truck, with the cattle bed on it, to see if papa had a pig or a calf to sell. Papa said, "No, I don't but I do have a mule colt I will sell you." Hearing that I said, " Please, Papa you can't sell STAR. He's mine, and I love him." Papa said, "Now, son, you know that little old mule won't be able to work for several more years, and we just can't afford to feed him. Any animal that eats has to work around here." He sold my pet for a few dollars, which I'm sure he desperately needed, but for days I cried and I still almost cry when I think about how hurt I was and how much I missed that little old mule. In fact I cried so much that papa threatened to whip me for crying. I never could figure why grown-ups whipped kids for crying. After all that was usually why they were crying in the first place.

Pardon me for the digression from my story about Louis. Having the extra animal to work with our good team of mules, old Pete and Bill, meant that we could get the spring planting done in a shorter time. This story is about the year papa bought old John. It would be hard to describe old John to those who are unfamiliar with mules, but if you can imagine the worst looking, down trodden, flop eared, toothless mule, (by the way, to tell a mule's age you look at his teeth and judge his age by the amount of wear they show.) Since John didn't have any teeth nobody had the slightest idea how old he really was. He was slow as molasses in the wintertime, he was almost deaf and the poorest excuse for a work animal we had ever seen. I think papa paid $5.00 for him. He should have gotten some change.

One late Saturday afternoon, just before sunset, mama told Louis to go over to Susie Crisco's house and bring back her canner that Susie had borrowed. What's a canner? Well, a canner is a metal, enamel covered vessel large enough to hold about twelve quart fruit jars, with a lid on top and a wire rack inside to separate the jars. Mama would pack the jars with peas, beans, cucumbers, or whatever, arrange them on the rack, fill the canner with water and put it on the stove to boil a length of time before sealing them. That was called water bath canning.

Back to my story. Louis, instead of walking the half mile to the Crisco house, decided to ride old John, knowing I'm sure that the trip would be faster walking, but he just wanted to ride. He mounted old John and rode off into the sunset toward his destination.

At the Crisco's he didn't even dismount. Ben Crisco handed the canner up to him and he and John started home, old John poking along with his head down almost between his knees, Louis with both arms wrapped around the canner, not even holding the reins. Everything was going fine until they turned off the big road and headed the quarter mile from our mailbox down to the house.

About that time, John being almost blind, and in the twilight not seeing a rut in the road, stumbled, and when he did the rack in the canner rattled making a noise barely audible to old John but one he had never heard before. The noise startled the old mule so much that he broke into a trot. Of course, that made the canner rattle much more, and the more the thing rattled, the faster old John ran, picking up speed with every gallop. Every time a hoof hit the ground there was more rattling and the mule would go faster. Instead of throwing the canner down, knowing he would get a whipping if it were damaged, Louis held on to it, wrapping his legs as best he could around old John's belly and hanging on to his mane with one hand and the canner with the other.

Opal, our sister, and brother-in-law John Webb had just arrived from Scottsboro for the weekend. We were all out in the front yard greeting them, that is mama, papa, and me when we heard the most terrible racket, strange noises between the house and the mailbox.

Suddenly the air was filled with totally unfamiliar noises for a quiet late spring, Saturday afternoon. We heard clanging, banging, yelling, clopping, snorting, all blended into one great chorus. Old John was doing the cloppity, cloppity, cloppity, snort, snort, snorting, the canner was doing the clangity, clangity, clangity. Louis was doing the yelling WHOA JOHN, WHOA JOHN, WHOA, clang, clang, clang, clop, clop, clop, snort, snort, snort, WHOA JOHN, WHOA, WHOA YOU OLD SON-OF-BITCH!!!

When mama realized what was happening to her boy she started hollering at papa to do something, "Walter, that old mule is gonna kill that young'un". Stop him. Hang on Louis, Jump off Louis, Don't you dare drop the canner, Louis, Walter DO SOMETHING," she screamed. Of course papa was helpless.
Louis couldn't hear any of the yelling from the yard, the yelling being drowned out by the clopping, clanging, banging, and old John's snorting with every clop, and Louis's own yelling "WHOA, WHOA, WHOA JOHN!!!" That evening the question in all our minds was what would happen when old John and his rider reached the house? Would he go on by, only giving Louis a chance to wave, like Paul Revere? Or, would the mule drop dead with a heart attack from fright and exhaustion? Would he be going so fast he couldn't make the turn around the big walnut tree at the front of our house, and if he did, would he stop before he reached the barn?

By the increased volume we could tell that our questions would soon be answered. The mule with Louis and the canner still on board, turned the corner around the walnut tree on two old legs, never breaking stride.

Mama, Papa, John and Opal were standing in the drive between the house and barn, determined to stop the mule, waving their arms and shouting in unison with the banging, clanging, clopping, snorting and yelling all blending perfectly.
Meanwhile, I am on the front porch enjoying every minute of the spectacle, and laughing till my stomach hurt. By-the-way, I'm still laughing as I write this.

They didn't succeed in stopping him. Old John ran right between the grownups, through the barn lot gate, which happened to be open. With his speed, old John could have jumped the fence if the gate hadn't been open. He ran into the barn hall and without slowing down leaped over the threshold and suddenly stopped in his stable.

Louis, still cradling the noisy canner in his arms had to dismount in the stable, miring up to his ankles in mule manure. I don't think old John would have won the Kentucky Derby that day, but I do believe he would have finished no further back than second. He still holds the record for the fastest quarter mile in Nebo Community history. And I'll tell you something else, Willy Shumaker never made a better ride than Louis did that evening. Mama and papa were so happy Louis was not hurt, they didn't even whip him for saying that ugly word. He was not hurt, the canner was not damaged, and old John survived long enough for papa to sell him when the planting season was over.

Chapter 4

FARM AND SCHOOL BOY

After my sisters left the farm, to begin homes and families of their own, only papa, mama, Louis and me were left. The family was smaller, but the work was no lighter or easier. There was always work to be done. Every day chores included feeding and watering the mules, milking the cow, slopping the hogs, feeding the chickens and drawing water out of the well. On mama's wash day, water had to be carried up from the creek unless it had recently rained and left water in the barrel by the side of the house.

In the winter there was wood to be cut, hauled and stacked, enough to last for a whole year . For cutting there was no such thing as a power saw. We chopped with a double bitted ax and sawed with a crosscut saw. Most of the wood we used for heat in the house, but we had to cut, split and dry enough for the sweet potato bed and the syrup mill. Another early spring job I simply hated was cleaning out the cow's stalls and mule's stables. That meant loading the manure on the wagon with pitch forks and shovels, then, what we called "broadcasting" it over the strawberry patches. It was great fertilizer, but I don't recommend throwing it off the wagon into a stiff March wind. Thinking about that makes me wonder why I ever made a career of "broadcasting."

Farm work really got underway in early spring with cutting and burning the previous year's corn stalks, running the stalk cutter over the old cotton stalks, turning the land and preparing it for planting. Then came the planting of the early garden vegetables, Irish potatoes, sweet potatoes, watermelons cantaloupes, corn and okra. Then the cotton, pole beans, butter beans and purple hull peas had to be planted for selling on the farm market in the summer. During late spring and into the early summer everything we grew had to be cultivated, chopped, hoed, thinned, picked or dug, all by hand or with primitive mule drawn plows. Summer meant going into the corn fields and cutting the tops and pulling the fodder (corn leaf blades), bundling and stacking them to dry for a few days, then storing the bundles, along with the fresh mown hay and oats in the barn loft as feed for the animals.

Summer was the time for picking the beans, peas, fresh corn or whatever was in season, loading them on the old '38 Ford pickup truck and hauling them to the big curb market on First Avenue in Birmingham. We had to be there very early in the morning because the buyers would start coming around to buy at three or four a.m. So, we would leave home in the late afternoon, drive the 50 miles to Birmingham. We would arrive there as early in the evening as possible in order to get a good parking place, sleep in, on or under the truck waiting for the action to begin the next morning. The sooner we sold our produce the better. When everything was sold, we hurried back home to gather another load and head back to the market.

These days when I visit a supermarket produce department I get sticker shock just comparing today's prices with some typical prices for which we sold vegetables on the curb market, such as tomatoes 50 cents a basket, butter beans 2-5 cents a pound, pole beans 3-6 cents a pound, fresh corn 25 cents a dozen ears, strawberries for as little as $1 a crate of 24 quarts, sweet potatoes at 1-4 cents lb. Now, it breaks my heart to pay $1.89 a pint for berries and $1.69 lb. or more for tomatoes and 79 cents lb. for potatoes.

Typically, county schools would begin in mid July, be in session for about six weeks then dismiss for six to eight weeks for "cotton pickin," so the children could help with that back-breaking job. I hated picking cotton, and I was always anxious to start back to school. I don't have the space and you don't have the time for me to mention all the work on the farm, like shucking and shelling corn, shelling dry peas, picking peanuts off the dried vines, drying apples, making lye soap and cooking the fat of the hog carcass at butchering time in the old faithful wash-pot to make a year's supply of lard, and making sorghum syrup in the fall from cane we had grown, stripped, cut and hauled to the syrup mill.

I mentioned before that my grandpaw and grandmaw DeFoor lived near us. Actually, by way of the little road it was about a mile, but if we took the path through the cotton field it was only a short distance. You wonder why I bring this up now when the subject is work? I'll tell you. My grandpaw did not believe in it. He was no farmer, but he would stand around in his Sunday suit bossing the sharecroppers or hired hands as they worked. A very tall, thin, good natured, fun loving man with a mustache usually stained by snuff, he was the only person I ever saw sniff snuff up his nose. Guess that's where they got the name snuff. Grandmaw "dipped" snuff. She would have one of us boys cut a small limb, about four or five inches long, off of a hickory bush. She called it her "toothbrush." She would chew on it till it was just right, frazzled on one end and moist enough to dip into her small snuffbox she always carried in her apron pocket. She would get a small amount on the stick and then chew on it till it was gone and then repeat the dipping process. She was very careful not to let the snuff run down her chin like most folks who dipped by placing the snuff between the lower lip and gum. You notice I say grandmaw and grandpaw, that is what we called them, no cute little names like gramma, grampa, paw paw or maw maw. Grandmaw DeFoor was a little bitty woman with her dark hair rolled up neatly in a ball on the back of her head. Granny on the Beverly Hillbillies reminds me so much of my grandmaw DeFoor. The only part of her anatomy I ever saw was her face and hands. She always wore high neck, long sleeve full cut dresses down to her high top shoes. I never saw them, but she wore stiff petticoats under her dress, causing it to stand way out from her body.

For someone who had lived in town most of her life she was very old fashioned. For instance she would never ride in a car. One time when she just had to go to the doctor in Cullman she would not let papa take her in our car so she got a neighbor, McGlon Snow, to take her ON his car. It was a car chassis with no body, just two seats on the running gear much like a dune buggy. Molly said that if something happened she could jump off. I promise I'll leave grandmaw in peace, but I've just got to tell you about the day she rode a hog.

I didn't see this, but papa swore to me that it actually happened before I was born. Seems that one day grandpaw's big old sow got out of the hog pen and he was trying to coax her back in by trying to drive her from behind. Any farmer will tell you that you cannot "drive" a hog. You can lead them with a bucket of slop or an ear of corn. At any rate, as he was trying to get the sow back in the pen, grandmaw thought she would help. She stood in front of the hog, started flopping and waving that long dress and those petticoats at the animal. Suddenly the old hog ran right between grandmaw's legs, with its nose catching on the inside back of her dress, and seating grandmaw squarely on the hog's back like a rodeo bull rider only she was riding backwards.

The blinded hog ran down across the cotton field with grandmaw hanging on for dear life until she fell off. She was not hurt in the fracas, but I remember she would get mad enough to bite when papa or grandpaw would tease her about it. As I remember, for years after that incident every time a hog would root out of the pen, grandpaw would always yell, "SOMEBODY HOLD MOLLY, SHE'LL BE WANTING TO RIDE IT." He would laugh and grandmaw would be fighting mad.

Papa was the very best sorghum, we called "soggum", syrup (pronounced surp. not sirrup or syrup its surp) maker in Cullman County. When sugar for making jams and jellies was rationed and almost impossible to buy during WWII, papa found a used syrup mill over in Georgia. He bought it and set it up down by the creek in our pasture. For you that don't know what a syrup mill is, it is a large grinder with rollers inside to squeeze the juice from the cane. It was powered by a mule hitched to the end of a long pole (about the size of an electric power pole) attached to the top of the mill. The mule walked around and around in a circle and someone, usually Louis or me would stand and "feed" the cane into the mill. It was hazardous duty if the feeder forgot to duck when the pole came around. If he forgot once, it didn't take very many whops on the head to encourage him to remember to "duck."

Two other problems were yellow jackets, drawn like flies to the sweet juice and a young lad's temptation to drink too much of that wonderful tasting stuff. It would make him sick in a hurry. After the grinding, the juice was fed by gravity to the cooking area just down the hill. Papa built a long narrow wood burning furnace and placed the copper "syrup pan" on top. The fire underneath would cook the juice and as it cooked, the syrup maker, papa, had to attend to it constantly. He would not trust anyone else to work the front end of the long pan, where the syrup came off. Somebody else could work the lower end just to dip off the "skimmins."

I don't know where or when he learned the art of making syrup, but he really had mastered it. He made the clearest, brightest, bronze colored, best tasting soggum in the county. People would come from miles around to buy his syrup. I remember selling it for as little as $1.00 a gallon. Just last fall I paid $10.00 at a craft show for a ½ pint of something they called soggum, but it was nothing like papa used to make. Why am I spending so much space writing about syrup, you ask?

Home made soggum syrup was a large part of our diet. The folks always managed to have enough flour, which was bought by the barrel in cotton print sacks that mama would use to make dresses for herself and the girls. We would have a big pan of biscuits made with lard every morning and there was always a pitcher of papa's syrup on the table to "sop" with the biscuits.

There is definitely an art to sopping syrup. First you pour some on your plate, put a good portion of butter on it, and then with a kitchen knife, stir it up real good until the butter and syrup are mixed. Then take either the top or bottom half of A biscuit, drag it toward you through the syrup collecting a generous portion of syrup on the biscuit, and get it to your mouth before any drips off. Or if you prefer, you butter the biscuit first and then take your knife and put a portion of plain soggum on it and then go to your mouth. You spill less that way. Sopping was sometimes difficult in the summertime when the syrup was thin, but in the winter it would be so thick that it had to be helped onto the biscuit with a knife. I personally liked to put butter in the syrup and stir it up real good, turning it a nice golden color while it was still on the plate and then sop it. Glory!!! Wish I had some now. As you will learn later, syrup played a most important role in my later career in broadcasting. So stay tuned.

Sure, our family was poor, but we didn't know it. We had a lot more material goods than the average family in those days but best of all we had, as coach Bear Bryant used to say "a good mama and papa."

Talking about goods, one of the most exciting days of the year was when Mr. Forney Rasco, the mail carrier would deliver that big brown package from Sears and Roebuck . Another good day was when somebody named Mr. Wrigley would send us chewing gum. For advertising, the Wrigley Company way up there in Chicago would attach a block of Doublemint, Spearmint, or Juicy Fruit to a card and mail it to "boxholder," but I thought that some how he knew about me and was sending the gum to me personally.

When the cotton had been picked, the loans paid off, while they had some cash and the weather was turning cool in the fall mama and papa would place that all-important order to Sears and Roebuck for our annual supply of clothes. It consisted of two long sleeve shirts, two pairs of high back Duckhead overalls, two pairs of long handle underwear, two pairs of socks, a pair of high top brogan shoes and a black cap made of some kind of shiny material (plastic had not been invented,) with identical orders for Louis and me. The cap pulled down over my head, had long ear flaps that buttoned at my Adams apple and goggles. As much as Louis and I hated those caps, we got a new one every year. Somehow we would always manage to lose them. We would get a whipping for it, but at least we didn't have to wear those silly looking caps anymore. As a last resort, if mama made us wear them to school, we would hide them in a culvert at the bus stop and pick them up when we returned in the afternoon.

Why did we get two of everything? That's easy. We would wear the same clothes for a week and change for the next week when we took our baths on Saturday night. What we were not wearing mama washed. I realize that all sounds strange and downright nasty, but you must remember washing, drying and ironing was a major job and mama just didn't have time or the strength to do it every day. In wet weather she had no way to dry clothes except behind the heater, hanging them on a quilting frame.

Christmas was special too, but not like the day the "package" came. Our family emphasized the religious aspect of Christmas more than gift giving which they could not afford anyway. We would always have a sack of oranges and apples, some English walnuts and pecans, peppermint stick candy and maybe even some of those chocolate drops with the white cream inside or orange slices. There were very few toys. Between us, Louis and I would usually get one toy which we had to share. I remember one year we got a little battery operated truck with lights on it that really worked and another year a BB gun. The one thing that I always wanted for Christmas but never got was a tricycle. I have never wanted anything so much in my entire life. Papa and Mama would tell me that tricycles were for city boys who could ride them on the concrete sidewalks, that I would never be able to ride one where we lived with nothing but mud in the yard and the road. That didn't keep me from wanting one. The day after our first son, Wally, was born I bought him a tricycle. Louis and I would usually wind up fighting over the one toy between us, and both getting a whipping.

Our proudest possession was the bicycle that all three married sisters and mama and papa went in together to order from Sears & Roebuck. It was a beauty, the one thing we never dreamed we'd own. Louis had learned to ride on Ellis Leverett's bicycle, but I couldn't ride. While I was learning, Louis would run along beside me just to catch the bicycle if I started to fall. It made no difference to him if I fell, he just didn't want the new bicycle to be damaged.

When Carol and I married, I had told her how few toys I had

received as a child and never one for me only. She has given me a toy every Christmas since 1951 the year we married. There have been toy cars, trucks, airplanes, space ships, boats, just about every kind of mechanical toy imaginable. Last year she gave me a Furby. When our boys were small, we explained to them that they were not to play with daddy's toys. They never even asked and now our grandchildren understand the toys in the cabinet are "Pop's." To me the toys are priceless. Some of the older ones are antiques now and worth quite a lot of money. I will get my 48th one this year, that is, if I'm a good boy from now till Christmas. All of the toys are displayed in a glass cabinet in our downstairs den.

The other big day of the year was the Fourth of July. That was the day we did no work in the fields and had homemade ice cream and lemonade. Papa would go to the ice plant in Cullman early in the morning, buy a 200 lb. block of ice, put it in a toe sack tied to the fender of the old Chevrolet and hurry home. Out of the ice when he got home, we would make two freezers of ice cream. We'd take what ice was left, put it in the water bucket with a dozen lemons and some sugar. We drank lemonade all day instead of water.

As the day went on, when the bucket would become almost empty, mama would add more water. Soon there was nothing left but warm water with lemon peelings in it.

One special year the folks invited all the neighbors to our house for the Fourth. Papa built a long table between two trees down by the creek to hold all the food the neighbors would bring. Everybody brought what they could. There were Joe and Irene Bailey, Buren and Fannie Snow, Eb and Bessie Alvis, Ed and Agnes Huffstutler, Elmer and Maudine Leverett, Ben and Suzie Crisco and of course grandmaw and grandpaw DeFoor. They all brought their young'uns too. We had a great time. No one seemed to care, or know, much about the significance of the 4th of July, we just enjoyed the food, lemonade and ice cream with no work on that day.

In the fall of 1938 at age six I started to school at Vinemont Elementary and Jr. High School. I was lucky to have had an

58

older brother and sister, Louis and Aria precede me at the school. Most of the teachers remembered them and were looking out for me, their baby brother. The first woman I ever loved besides my mama was my first grade teacher, Miss Louise Thompson. When she died a few years later, I cried. She was young, beautiful and an excellent first grade teacher.

I don't remember much about the second grade, but as I have already related, it was in the third that my show business career really got underway with my famous May Pole dance and pretty Polly. That was also the first year I, along with my friends Oscar Pace and Franklin Drake were chosen to sing a verse each of "We Three Kings" in the school Christmas Pageant. Nobody in our family owned a bathrobe, so mama had to make me a king's robe out of guano sacks. That time she did not sew me up in it. With my homemade bathrobe, my brogan shoes, and mama's best towel wrapped around my head, I looked just like a king. Well, I thought so anyway. The three of us were so wonderful that we played that role all the way through the ninth grade.

I used to like to spend the night with Oscar Pace. He, his mother and grandmother lived close to the school house and they always had something store bought and good to eat. I ate Kellogg's corn flakes at Oscar's house for the first time. They are still my favorite cereal.

I don't recall anything special about Mrs. Livingston's fourth grade or Mrs. Graham's fifth except that was when I first heard about "fractions." Most kids did not like her. However, I remember her as very strict but an excellent teacher.

As I recall the sixth grade I think most about the war. Battles were raging in Europe and the Pacific. The husband of my sixth grade teacher, Mrs. Maurice Holmes, was in the navy and fighting in the Pacific area. She made us read every account she could find in newspapers, Life Magazine, Saturday Evening Post and even the uncensored sections of letters from him and give reports to the class.

Ah!! Jr. High School, the seventh grade, I was growing up. That was the year they opened the lunch room at school, the first time we could buy a hot meal with milk for a dime, if our folks had a dime. If not we would take our usual biscuit and syrup or a baked sweet potato . Barbara Johnson, whose daddy owned a dairy farm at Vinemont would bring store-bought cookies to school and trade them to me for mama's home-made tea cakes. I wish I had some of those tea cakes now. I wouldn't trade them for anything.

I made good grades in Jr. High without much effort and especially enjoyed acting in the school plays. Mr. L.C. Camp our principle liked to do three things. He always directed the ninth grade play, taught ninth-grade math and walked the long halls of that horseshoe-shaped school building carrying a big paddle about two and a half feet long just in case he happened to see someone running in the hall. Most of us were scared to death of him, but later he and I became good friends. He was a good man.

Throughout Jr. High School I was active in the 4-H Club. In the ninth grade I was elected President of the county association and got to preside at the annual meeting of all the clubs in the county, held at the Cullman High football stadium. One of my projects was raising a steer, feeding, fattening, and grooming it for the big show and auction at Legion Field in Birmingham the next spring. My calf sold for $87.00, the first big money I had ever seen. Papa said he thought I should give him part of it because he furnished the feed for the steer, but he let me keep all of it. I opened my first bank account at the Parker Bank in Cullman. I was RICH.

The 10th, 11th and 12th grades were at Cullman High School. I did not set any scholastic or athletic records in high school. I was too small for football, to short for basketball and too slow and clumsy for baseball. However I was the 1949 Ping Pong champion of Cullman High. I participated in other activities such as glee club, school politics, being elected vice president of the senior class, (losing the presidency to Betty Sue Hudson by one vote,) and Future Farmers of America (FFA). It was the FFA that ultimately sent me on my way to a career in broadcasting.

Here is how it happened. The FFA sponsored such activities as cattle judging, fruit tree pruning, chicken and hog farming and other farm related activities. The ones in which I was most interested, requiring the least amount of physical labor, were the quartet and string band. I entered the FFA oratorical contest, winning the local, but losing at the county level to a student at Holly Pond High named Guy Hunt. He was later elected governor of the state of Alabama twice, being the only Republican governor of this state since the Civil War. I told Guy when he was elected that "If I had won that contest I would be governor and he would be a "syrup sopper" on the radio."

Two of my good buddies, Elmas Howlett and Oscar Pace, along with George Hartwig and I formed the FFA quartet. Charlie Skinner was our pianist. Elmas was a great steel and electric guitar player. George played guitar and sang. With Charlie at the piano and Oscar on the bass fiddle we not only had a quartet but a string band. We later added Tommy Kohlenberg playing banjo. In the statewide contest at Auburn in 1949 we won the quartet division and finished second in band competition. But the next year 1950 we won it all, both the quartet and band .

We advanced to the district finals at Lake Lanier near Atlanta. I think surely the judges must have cheated or we would have won there too. I appreciate Mr. J. D. Hardeman, our agriculture teacher and FFA leader, for giving us the opportunity and encouragement to participate in these activities. I could not play an instrument, so I wasn't very much good to the band other than as soloist. I tried to sing the Red Foley songs just as he did. I took $50 of my calf money and bought a nice nearly new Gibson guitar which I never learned to play. I practiced a few chords that Elmas taught me but the strings made my fingers so sore I gave it up.

I sang bass in our quartet, George the lead, Elmas baritone and Oscar sang tenor. We are all still very good friends. Elmas and Oscar still live in Cullman, I see them often. Right after school George moved to California, making his fortune in the construction business. We usually get together about once a year when he comes back to Alabama for a visit.

I believe I'll divert our story here to tell you about Elmas, another one of my favorite character. He grew up at Crane Hill in southwest Cullman county, further from town than Nebo. By the time I knew him his folks had moved closer to town. The farm he inherited is now in the city limits of Cullman.

Elmas joined the navy right out of high school, serving three and a half years in Japan as a medic during the Korean war. Returning to Cullman after the war, he met and married Betty Meyer, from Hanceville, a beautiful, smart, hard working girl, a great cook, of German decent. When he's upset with her, he calls her a Nazi.

He went to work for Mr. Leonard Lumsden, at Lumsden Oil Company, the Texaco Distributor, as bookkeeper, straw boss and watcher of the business end of the several small, mostly country service stations. When Leonard retired, he sold Elmas and Betty the distributorship. They have worked hand in hand for the past forty years, building and maintaining the business, until just recently they leased the company, including all of their more than a dozen Texaco super foodmart service station combinations, to an employee for multimillions of dollars. I am very proud of their success. They and their grandchildren will never have to work again unless they want to.

I am telling all this just to prove Elmas is smart. If he were poor, one might consider him to be a "nut," but because he's rich he is only eccentric. He does not believe in credit, paying cash for everything he buys whether its a new gasoline tanker truck, a condominium at the beach or a new home. His business associates call him "Cash Howlett."

Another peculiarity is that, up until just a few years ago he had never been to a doctor, believing that if a person never goes to a doctor he will never be sick. Even if he is sick the person won't know it because no doctor told him about it. That all changed about five years ago. Elmas and Betty were at their weekend home on Smith lake. After finishing mowing the grass on a hot summer Saturday afternoon, having no clothes on except his Bermuda shorts, he ran down to the pier and jumped off into the cool water.

In a couple of minutes, he realized something was wrong, something was definitely biting him. It was a school of small bream, the grand kids had been feeding them off the dock. The fish were biting his toes and legs, one even bit his right nipple off and it was spurting blood everywhere. Elmas scrambled up the piling of the dock yelling and kicking at the fish. As he did, he kicked the piling, wounding his second toe, the one next to the big toe, on his right foot. Getting out of the water he saw that toe was not pointing straight like all the others, it was looking back at him and was beginning to swell.

He struggled up the hill to the house, telling Betty he believed his toe was broken. She said, "Come on, get in the car, I'll drive you to the hospital in Cullman." He refused, saying, "I'm not going to the hospital, I don't believe in hospitals." She said, "O.K. just be stubborn and suffer."

By suppertime the toe was hurting so badly and was so black and blue he finally gave in and let Betty drive him the 15 miles to the hospital. Never having been to an emergency room before, and not knowing that patients could drive right up to the hospital door, they parked about a block away, Elmas hobbling the entire distance on one good foot and a badly broken toe on the other foot.

As soon as they entered the emergency room, a nurse asked, "What can I do for you?" as she was putting a thermometer in his mouth and a blood pressure cuff on his arm. He said, "Look at my toe, it's pointing south instead of north and hurts like hell." The nurse, after reading his blood pressure, said, "Mr. Howlett, does your blood pressure usually run high?" "I don't know, I've never had it checked before, but look at my toe, it's pointing back at me." The nurse left the room, returning with an intern. He said, "Mr. Howlett, how long have you had high blood pressure?" Elmas replied, "Son, I told her I don't know that, but look at my toe, it's getting bigger and bluer pointing the wrong way and hurting like hell."

In a few minutes a doctor came in saying, "Mr. Howlett,

your blood pressure is extremely high, we have got to do something about it." To which Elmas yelled, "DAMMIT, IF YOU'D FIX MY TOE MY BLOOD PRESSURE WOULD GO DOWN." They fixed it, and sure enough his blood pressure went down. I love Elmas, even though he is responsible for my being with Carol Dean all these years.

The only radio station in Cullman at that time was an AM 250 watt station, WKUL, owned by Mr. Hudson Miller, a New Jersey Yankee whose uncle had bought it for him from its original owner Judge Horace Kenny. I think his uncle must have bought the station and sent Miller to run it just to get him out of New Jersey. I don't really remember how it happened. I suppose he heard us someplace. He invited our little band to do a 30 minute radio program each Saturday morning. We all were excited and jumped at the chance to be on the radio. My good fortune was to be chosen as the spokesman for the group and to do the commercials. The first commercial I ever did was for our sponsor, McMinn Auto Parts. As it turned out, in my more than 40 years of radio I did literally thousands of them. Hudson Miller either liked my announcing or was desperate for someone to work at the station. He asked if I would like to be a real radio announcer? "Yes SIR!!!! Just let me at it. He said, "Of course I can't pay you anything until you learn how."

I must have said something like "That's fine I will work hard and learn how to be as good as Lon Waters, Jay Aldredge and Bill Strube, (the other announcers.) My job was to sign on the station at 4:00 a.m. and work until 8 o'clock and then go to school. I would sometimes go back to the station in the afternoon. I did that for about three months-December, January and February.

After that I told Mr. Miller I believed I knew how to do the job pretty well. I'll never forget how my bubble burst when he said " If I have to pay you I can't use you anymore." So he fired me. Fortunately for me, Mr. Carroll Eddins, the previous manager at WKUL had recently applied to the FCC for a license to build and operate WFMH and WFMH-FM. The FM license was approved in short order but an objection to the application for the AM was filed by Hudson Miller, not wanting any competition on AM, certainly not caring about the FM because in those days there were hardly any FM radios in existence.

Carroll Eddins was one of the most easy-going peace-loving gentlemen I have ever known. I had never seen him angry until the day he became so fed up with Miller's antics and objections that he went up to WKUL, marched into Miller's office, grabbed him by the collar punched him in the nose and blacked an eye. The funny part of the story was that they both had the same attorney, Julian Bland. After the fight Carroll went straight to the lawyer's office to report what he had done and no sooner had he arrived than there came Miller with indisputable evidence, a black eye, a bloody nose and shirt.

Needless to say the case was dropped, the objection withdrawn and the license was granted for WFMH-AM.

After I was fired from my non-paying job at WKUL, I went to see Lon Waters the program director at the new station. He gave me a part-time job working most weekends and anytime I was needed during the week, paying me a whole $1.00 an hour. At last, through out my senior year in high school I was a real `disc jockey.

I don't remember how or when I got that tremendous urge to go to college. I always knew I did not want to be a farmer looking forward only to working hard for very little reward like my parents had. My ambition was to become a Greyhound Bus driver, to me the best job in the world. We had a cotton field rented from uncle Arthur Pullen next to the highway and just behind the Longview stores. Every time one of those big busses would stop at the store to let people on and off, I would lean on my hoe handle if I were chopping cotton, or raise up from the row of cotton I was picking, with sore hands and an aching back, to see the driver with his blue uniform and cap, hear those air brakes go WHIISSSH as he pulled back onto the highway. I knew he was headed for such far away and exotic places as Nashville or Birmingham, but best of all I knew it was cool in that bus. I wanted his job.

Many years later Carol bought for me a genuine Greyhound

Bus driver's cap which I still sometimes proudly wear. The drivers don't wear them anymore. They are not even manufactured but she contacted an old friend and former driver from Tuscaloosa, Bobby Martin with her unusual request for a Greyhound driver cap. Bobby, now an executive with Greyhound was able to find a new one for me. Thanks, Bobby.

Chapter 5

AUBURN UNIVERSITY

In 1950, the year I graduated from high school, very few young people went on to college. Several of the boys enlisted in the military, the Korean war was just beginning, and some went to trade schools or directly to work. I was determined to go to college if there were any way possible. I faced several problems, not knowing for sure what I wanted to do with my life, not really knowing where I wanted to go, and not the least of which, **I had no money**. Later I joked that when I told papa I wanted to go to college, he said, "Son you know that's going to cost a lot of money which you don't have. I'll help you all I can. I guess I can sell some stock,"..so he sold a calf and two pigs.

No one in the family had ever been past high school. I wanted to be the first to obtain a college degree, even though I could not expect any financial help from my folks. Some of my teachers had encouraged me, especially Mr. Hardeman, the agriculture teacher. As to where I would go, that was easy. The only university with which I was slightly familiar was Alabama Polytechnic Institute at Auburn, Alabama. Through an act of the legislature several years later the name was changed to Auburn University. I had been on the Auburn campus several times, to the state 4-H club convention and twice to the state FFA contests. I knew there was some kind of school at Tuscaloosa, but it never occurred to me to check it out. In North Alabama, when a person was sent to Tuscaloosa it was usually by a probate judge or a doctor, for mental disorders. You see, the only thing we knew about Tuscaloosa was it was the location of the state mental institutions, Bryce Hospital and Partlow State School. I knew Bryce and Partlow should be avoided at all cost. Some family and friends who had been "sent off to Tuscaloosey" were never heard from again.

After mama and papa moved to Scottsboro, when he was not gardening or fishing papa would go downtown to the Courthouse

Square, find some old buddies, join them on a park bench, whittle on a cedar block, trade knives or argue about the Bible.

He said "One day an old man, I didn't know, sat down by me on the bench. We got acquainted and he asked if I had any children." I said, "Yes, I've got three daughters in Indiana, a son here in Scottsboro and another son a Tuscaloosa." The old man patted papa on the shoulder and said, "Well, they're doing wonders fer 'em now."

As time approached for me to begin really thinking about applying for admission to Auburn, I started taking inventory. I had about $30 of the calf money left, a few dollars I'd save from Indiana and from working some that summer for my brother-in-law, Curtis Johnson, at the Snack Bar, a restaurant he owned in Falkville, Al. My only other asset was my beautiful Gibson guitar which I sold for $85. I was working part-time at WFMH, and Mr. Eddins had said I could keep my job there on weekends if I could manage to travel the 180 miles each way from Auburn to Cullman and back.

Knowing that I just had to have a job at Auburn too, I contacted Mr. H. T. Pruitt, our former high school principle. He was at that time teaching at Auburn in the School of Agriculture. As luck would have it, Mr. Pruitt was also in charge of student on campus employment. He encouraged me to come on down to Auburn early to see what we could do about a job. When I arrived at his office, he said the best job on campus was available beginning with the fall quarter. That was in the School of Chemistry working in their supply store each afternoon from 2-5 Monday through Friday and instead of the usual 50 cents an hour for freshmen, the job would pay a flat $50.00 a month. I said "What if they won't hire me?" Mr. Pruitt said "They will have to because I won't send them anyone else to choose from."

He didn't and they did. I went back the next week for two weeks training for the job with a Mr. Quillen, the manager of the store. Having a very limited background in chemistry, only one year in high school, it was a tough job. The supply store was located in the basement of the Chemistry Building. Our responsibility was to furnish all labs on campus, except

68

Veterinary Medicine the chemicals and equipment needed to operate their labs, including bulk alcohol, ether, organic and inorganic chemicals and glassware.

In addition, students who had broken test tubes, beakers or any of the dozen or more items they used in the lab had to buy replacements from me. The manager of the store, Jim Quillen, and I were the only two employees and he would usually "bug out" shortly after I reported for work at 2 P. M.

While I was at Auburn that two weeks, I made arrangements for a place to live and for meals, when I would return to begin the first quarter of school. I rented a room on South Gay Street from Mrs. Gay. She lived next door to a big old two story house which she rented and sublet to about 30 of us male students. Being there early I had my choice of rooms. A large room on the first floor had a full size bed and a double decker bunk bed. Naturally I took the only double bed in the house, but had to share the room with two other boys. My room cost me $10 a month. About three blocks up the street Mrs. Cook had converted her basement into a dining room for about 300 boys eating in shifts three meals a day. The food was plain, served family style at long tables in big bowls, but it was a bargain at $35 a month for three meals a day except Sunday night.

Have you ever heard the expression "Lonely in a Crowd?" That is exactly how I felt the Sunday afternoon my sister Opal, brother-in-law John and Carol Dean Bailey,(yes our high school romance was still going strong,) drove me to Auburn. We left my cardboard suitcase at my room, and then they delivered me to the quadrangle where I joined about 3000 other freshmen for a convocation in the football stadium, and the beginning of a week of orientation. I'm sure most of them were just as scared and alone as I, but it seemed to me that I was the only one who didn't have at least one friend.

After spending part of my savings for some new pants and shirts, I arrived in Auburn that Sunday afternoon to begin my college career with $85 in my pocket, enough to pay my first months rent, and meals, with $45 left over for books, supplies, and tuition. I would not be paid my $50 at the supply store till the end of the month. I was flat broke, but I could eat and had a good place to sleep for a month, doing pretty good.

Army ROTC was required for all male freshmen. The first day I went to class, the captain said that I must have an army uniform by Thursday and I had better show up on the drill field fully dressed in the uniform, which we would rent from the army for $35 each quarter of school. Thursday being only three days away I was at a loss as to where I was going to come up with $35. I didn't know anybody who had the money and besides, if papa had it I couldn't reach him because the folks didn't have a telephone. In desperation, I called my brother-in-law Curtis. At that time he was running a service station, motel and truck stop combination on Highway U.S. 31 at the top of Lacon Mountain. I explained what I needed; he wired me the money and thanks to Curtis, I was still alive and had not been court martialed by the army for not having a uniform.

I found the next day that all was still not well. Another requirement was physical education. At the first P.E. class the coach said I would have to buy a sweat suit and a pair of tennis shoes, and wear them to class the next morning.

I had seen tennis shoes, but had no idea what a "sweat" suit was. We sweated in any kind of suit back home in the summertime. The Tiger Sporting Goods store was located in "downtown" Auburn, on Toomer's corner across from the campus. That afternoon, as I stood looking in the window, at the tennis shoes and what I assumed were sweat suits, I saw a vision, although an ugly one. It was Bud Tucker from Cullman walking toward me.

Bud and I had never really been friends in high school, my being a freshman when he was a senior. About 6 feet 6 inches tall, Bud was a jock, and A star basketball player, so we didn't have a lot in common. However, he recognized me and said, "What are you doing here?" I told him I had enrolled as a freshman, and the P.E. coach had said I MUST have a sweat suit and tennis shoes by the next morning, that I did not have money to buy them and didn't know what to do.

Bud said "Don't worry about it. I'm a senior and don't have

to take P.E. anymore, I'll give you mine." I said, "Bud I appreciate the offer, but there's no way I could wear your sweat suit and tennis shoes." Bud was not only tall, but he weighed about 230 pounds. I was 5 feet 9 and weighed 120 pounds. He said "The clothes are yours, if you want them. Suit yourself, but, if it were me I'd rather go to class tomorrow in a suit and shoes that were too big than face the meanest coach at Auburn University without them." I said "I'll take them".

Bud said, "Come on over to my room with me and pick them up. When we entered his room I knew without doubt that he still had the suit and shoes, from the odor of sweat caused by two years of wearing them without the benefit of washing. Bud dug them from under his bunk and handed them to me. I thanked him for saving my life and left.

Having no time or money to have them washed, I would just have to make the best of a bad situation. The next morning I got myself ready to go to that dreaded P.E. class by first putting on the sweat pants. The legs were about a foot too long. With the help of rubber bands, I was able to "blouse" them just above my ankles. Same for the sleeves, they too were much too long. Thank you Lord for rubber bands. The tennis shoes were a size 14. Only trouble, I wore a size 8 1/2. I stuffed some paper in the toes, tied them as tight as I could, the left over string ends, I wrapped around and around the entire shoes.

I had to walk all the way across campus from South Gay Street to Cliff Hare Stadium for the class. Every step I took, those tennis shoes went "plop, plop, plop, plop," with the stench from the suit attracting several dogs that started following me. When I arrived at the stadium, class had already started and the coach was saying, "Today we're going to find out what kind of condition you boys are in. You're going to run the 880." I had never heard of an 880, but knowing 280 was the highway between Auburn and Birmingham, I figured right away I was not going to like it. Sure enough, the 880 was a half mile, four times around the track. In Bud Tucker's sweat suit and tennis shoes, I couldn't have run a half mile in three days.

Do I have to tell you the big old football coach posing as a

P.E. instructor was not pleased? I did set a school record that still stands, the longest time for the 880 in Auburn University's history.

As I said before, athletics were never my long suit, no pun intended. Another day in the P.E. class we went to what they called the natatorium. Not knowing what that word meant, I was anxiously awaiting that 7 a.m. class. Maybe it was something I would like. Would you believe it meant swimming? It was a building enclosing an Olympic size swimming pool, the widest, longest pool I'd ever seen. In fact, I don't think I had ever seen a real swimming pool before. Now, the only 'swimmin' I'd ever done was in the creek down behind the barn. Louis and I put two empty syrup buckets in a toe sack, tied the ends and, laying our bodies across the sack between the buckets, learned to swim in water just a little more than knee deep, a muddy waterhole about the size of my kitchen floor.

Our assignment that day was to swim two laps, from one end of the pool to the other and back as fast as we could. I had never been in water over my head, and when I jumped in, I went all the way under, not even touching the bottom. I almost had a panic attack, but thought I'd better start swimming or I'd drown. I made the first lap pretty well, but coming back I was so exhausted I just started "dog paddling," trying to stay afloat, thinking for sure that I saw Jesus coming to meet me.

The second quarter, I could choose from a list of activities for physical education. Not really being interested in any of them, I chose something that didn't seem too strenuous and might even be fun. It was called "apparatus." Not having the slightest idea what the word meant, but thinking it must be driving a tractor, operating a hay baler, a milking machine or hog feeder, since Auburn was an agricultural school, I chose apparatus.

My guess as to what it meant could not have been more wrong. When I reported for class at the Joel Eaves field house, I was shocked to see a young man in the tightest britches and B V D undershirt, with the biggest muscles I'd ever seen. The whole end of the building was covered with mats sorta like mama's quilts, only thicker, and some very strange looking contraptions.

The young muscleman introduced the class to each piece of equipment and demonstrated their use. There was one he called the "pummel horse," about five feet tall covered in leather with two handles on top, that fellow jumped up on the thing and swung his legs around, over, under, higher and wider, in perfect rhythm balanced only on his hands holding to the handles.

That was only the beginning. He leaped out on to those quilts and started doing the strangest contortions. Turning head over heels, forwards and backwards, he would plop flat down on his bottom with one leg pointing north and the other south, all over the quilt, from one side to the other. He moved around, flipping and flopping, running and jumping, turning, "summersets" in mid-air looking like a fellow being pestered by a wasp.

Another piece of apparatus was what he called the "rings," a tall rig with four legs, and a bar across the top, with two cables hanging from it. At the end of each cable was a round circle of metal, a ring. That boy jumped up, caught a ring in each hand and pulled himself up to where he was hanging on to the rings, but his hands were by his sides, not over his head. His legs were perfectly straight and not even swinging one little bit. I discovered that was the idea of that game, see how long you could hang there from the rings without having to move or let go.

The one that really got my attention was the uneven bars. That rig had two horizontal bars mounted on a frame. They were the same length but at different heights about four feet apart. The coach jumped up grabbing the highest bar and began to swing himself round and round over and under the bar. Then he let go, I was thinking for sure he would kill himself hitting the floor, but at the last split second on the way down he caught the lower bar and continued to swing and leap from one bar to the other in perfect rhythm.

When he was through with his demonstration, he swung as high and fast as he could, let go of the bar and in midair turned three somersaults before his feet hit the floor. After the display of perfect coordination and dexterity on the apparatus he said, "I need a volunteer," He said, "Price come forward and show us what you can do on the uneven bars". I said "Do what?" I could only "chin" myself three times. I made a "D" in P.E. that quarter, but I learned some new words and decided once and for all, I was not going to enter the Olympic tryouts.

The third quarter of P.E. I chose golf. I know it sounds unbelievable but until that time I had never seen a golf ball much less a golf club. All I knew about golf was that the player would hit a ball lying on the ground, hit it with a stick and then go look for it so he could hit it again. It's always seemed right silly to me. If he hadn't hit the ball the first time he wouldn't have to look for it. I figured I'd be good at it because at home in the summertime, I could hit a flying bumblebee with an ax handle just about every time I swung at one, and could even hit a black walnut with a broom handle when Louis would pitch it to me. Golf would be a snap. The ball was not even moving.

There were only two requirements for the golf class, first go to the driving range and hit balls each class period and sometime during the quarter go to the Opelika Country Club, about ten miles from campus, play 18 holes of golf, have the pro sign the scorecard, and turn it in. It made no difference what the score was, but the round of golf should be played. Again I was in a terrible bind.

As I explained to the smartass coach who thought he was a cross between Arnold Palmer and Jack Nicklaus, I just did not have the time to play golf. With classes all morning, working in the chemistry supply store all afternoon, and hitch hiking back to Cullman to work at the radio station every week end. There was no time left for golf. The coach said "Don't worry about it, I understand. Your schoolwork comes first." So, I didn't worry about it. At the end of the quarter he gave me a "D." Asking him "How come I got a D?", he said, "You did not play the 18 holes of golf."

I made a D for the round of golf I didn't play. I felt then I was being persecuted, but since that time I've played dozens of

74

rounds of golf for which I didn't even deserve a "D." I'm the only Auburn freshman who ever made three "Ds" in physical education. No wonder I'm a 230 pound weakling, always getting sand kicked in my face.

I realize I have said nothing about the class work at Auburn and have taken most of this chapter to tell about my P.E. experiences, but are you really interested in exciting stories about college algebra, biology, botany, chemistry, English Literature, French, or U.S. History? I liked History most, because the old professor would sit on a stool and without referring to a book, teach history and make it so real you'd think he had actually been there as it was happening.

Chapter 6

SCHOOL BOY TAKES A WIFE

Of all my 67 years, I must say that the school year 1950-51 was the most stressful and frustrating I have experienced. Besides having very little money, even working 2-5 p.m. at the chemistry supply store, Monday through Friday and at the radio station in Cullman on Saturdays and Sundays, it seemed I was always broke. My only mode of transportation between Auburn and Cullman each weekend was my right thumb. As soon as I closed the supply store on Friday, I would walk the ten or so blocks to the edge of town hoping to get a ride toward Birmingham. I always did even though some days it took a long time.

Most of the students with cars had already gone by five p.m. on Friday. After arriving in Birmingham many late nights I have stood on a corner in North Birmingham, on old Highway 31 hoping someone would stop and give me a ride to Cullman. Finally there, it would be too late to try to get to my house, so I would walk over to Carol Dean's, flop on the living room couch, and sleep until her mother would wake me for breakfast and Carol would drive me to WFMH by 7 a.m.

Speaking of money, I am grateful to Carol Dean and her family. Her parents let me sleep at their house, fed me and even let me use their car to go out in the country to see my folks when I could find the time. A senior in high school at that time, Carol Dean was working at the Cullman Drive-in Theater selling tickets, making about $35 a week from which she would give me half to help out with my expenses at school.

I always liked to hitchhike with John Hamrick. He had a club foot, causing a very bad limp when he walked. Drivers would see him limping along, feel sorry for him and stop to pick us up.

One Sunday we were stranded between Childersburg and Sylacauga, when a man with his wife and two little children stopped to give us a ride. They were going to Columbus,

Georgia, passing close to Auburn. Soon after we were in the car and started down the highway, a black cat ran across the road in front of us. The man slammed on the brakes, made a U-turn in the middle of the two lane road and headed back the way we had come. John and I thought he was just kidding and would turn around again, but he never did. In just a couple of minutes, he turned off the main road, and headed we knew not where.

We had to stay in the car because we knew if we got out on a side road we'd never get a ride. I never knew how we did it, but somehow we arrived at Talladega. The fellow remembered he had friends there. He called his friend, who invited him to come on by his house, with me and John still huddled in the back seat with the two kids. After being served cake and coffee, we started out again for Auburn, arriving there just before daylight, all because of a nut afraid of a black cat crossing the road in front of him.

Another time John and I were standing for a very long time on a lonely stretch of highway 280, when two beautiful young ladies went by in a red convertible. They waved to us as they passed. Just as their car faded from view, a farmer in an old pickup truck stopped, we hopped in the back, snuggled as close as we could to the back of the cab and started on down the road.

No sooner were we under way, but to our surprise we met the two girls in the convertible coming back to pick us up. They turned around, followed for a little while but went on by, leaving us to ride in the back of the pickup. They waved and smiled again, as they left us.

Another strange hitch hiking story. One night I was at the corner in Mountain Brook, when a man alone in his car stopped. He asked if I could drive. I told him I could. With that he crawled in the back seat, told me to drive and wake him up when we got to Opelika. Can you imagine anyone doing that today? I can't even imagine myself or my sons or grandsons hitch hiking at all these days.

The 185 mile trip back to Auburn on Sunday night was exciting. The idea was to somehow get to Mountain Brook on the south side of Birmingham where there was a very popular corner for Auburn students to catch rides back to school. If I got a ride all the way to Auburn or Opelika I was extremely lucky. The worse thing was to be stranded in Sylacauga, Alexander City, Dadeville or somewhere in between, on a cold, dark sometimes rainy night. On several occasions I would arrive back at Auburn just in time to go to class on Monday morning. Between working at school in the afternoons, in Cullman on weekends, attending classes in the morning and studying, I had very little time for anything else that year.

I don't want to leave the impression that I was the only student that had to work hard. I'm sure there were plenty more. From what I see today, most college kids think they are being persecuted if they have to work to help their parents with school expenses. I am proud to say that both of our sons worked at our radio station or at the funeral home, digging graves in country cemeteries when they were in school at the University of Alabama.

My point is, in 1950 there was no such things as Pell Grants or government guaranteed student loans. I'm sure there must have been some scholarships available, but no one ever told be about them or even suggested that I apply for one. I must have thought scholarships were only for the disabled or the really "pore" folks, it never occurred to me that I just might be eligible for one . So far as I knew, the only ways to go to college were, have a rich family, on the GI bill, which only applied to veterans of military service, or work.

In the spring of 1951 the school year ended, I moved back home, Mr. Eddins gave me a full time job at WFMH making $55 a week. Carol Dean graduated from high school and went to Birmingham to work at Alabama Gas Company, now called Alagasco, while attending Draughn Business College at night. Living in a small apartment at the home of her uncle Wiley and aunt Bell Hatley in the West-end section of the city. She commuted to work by street car. We only saw each other on weekends when she would come to Cullman by bus and I would usually take her back on Sunday night.

That summer went by really fast. We were both working at

pretty good jobs, and happy, except that we were only together on weekends.

I don't remember when we first started talking about marriage. I'm sure it must have been her that mentioned it first. However the subject did come up. We were both 19 years old. If we were to marry that fall I had some unpleasant things to do. First tell my folks, then ask hers. We had to tell them not only that she was quitting her job, but that I was not going back to school. I dreaded most telling Carroll Eddins, my boss, that I had decided not to go back to school, but I would keep working for him and that Carol Dean and I were making plans to be married in the fall.

Carroll didn't object to the marriage, but he really was upset when I said I was not going back to school. He was so upset that he said "No, you must go back to school. If you don't I will fire you. If I let this little job at WFMH keep you from getting a college education, some day you will hate me." Believe me, I was extremely distraught. Without the job, marriage was impossible, and I was convinced he meant what he said about firing me.

After a day or two I devised a brilliant plan. I told Mr. Eddins "If you will let me keep my job, I will enroll in St. Bernard College." The two year Catholic school was located in Cullman. He said "Fine just as long as you're in school you can keep your job".

My next move was to go to Ward's Jewelry, pay $10 down and promise to pay an additional $2.50 each week on a $135.00 diamond engagement ring. That September I enrolled at St. Bernard, Carol Dean moved back to Cullman, went to work at Leeth National Bank and started making plans for a November wedding, which as I have already said was on November 25, 1951.

I was paid my $55 on the Saturday before the wedding plus Mr. Eddins gave me a $5 raise to $60. After the wedding, with the $60 we left on our "honeymoon". Not knowing exactly where we were going, we just started driving toward

Birmingham in my 1947 Ford that I had managed to buy from a distant cousin, Hoyt Bridges, a used car salesman.

We checked into the Thomas Jefferson Hotel. I was so nervous I dropped my keys in the gutter, the chain broke scattering them in all directions, so I'm crawling around the gutter in my Sunday suit trying to find my keys with my bride saying "Hurry let's go'. I think she was afraid some one would see us checking into a hotel, but I said, "Don't worry about it, we're married".

In the hotel restaurant that evening, I don't remember what she ate but I distinctly remember I had fried oysters. Somebody had told me that oysters were good for a man on such an occasion. They were the first oysters I had ever eaten. I hated them, and besides they didn't work until the second night, which we spent at Opelika.. On Wednesday we went back home with 50 cents left out of the $60. We took that to the Globe Drive-in, bought two hamburgers and two cokes, then went to our little two room apartment which we had rented from P.C. and Julie Simms in the attic of their house. The rest of that week, we ate with our parents because we didn't have money to buy groceries until payday on Friday.

Life in our small apartment settled down to my working at the radio station as an announcer and going to school while Carol Dean was working at the bank.

I think it was about that time I decided to make a career of broadcasting if I could. I really liked being "on the air" and it surely did beat pickin' cotton. I discovered right away that I was never cut out to be a sports play-by-play announcer. Mr. Eddins always did the Cullman high football, and basketball, St. Bernard College basketball and American Legion baseball, his only announcing except in an emergency. I would usually work with him as his "spotter" while he did the play-by-play.

The afternoon before the first high school football game that fall, he and I went up to the stadium to "set up" the equipment in the little press box on top of the bleachers. Remember back then remote equipment was very bulky, and heavy. Setting it up for a broadcast was a major operation. We had to have the phone company install a telephone line back to the station into which we connected our equipment. With no two-way communication between the remote location and the studios, we would proceed to broadcast and hope we were on the air. Cullman high was playing Bessemer the night Carroll Eddins and I went to set up for the broadcast. When we climbed to the top of the bleachers, opened the press box door and went in, too late we saw a big wasp's nest in the corner. They started stinging us, and as we both ran out of that cramped little old press box on to the very top bleacher, Mr. Eddins foot slipped and he fell all the way to the ground below. As he lay there he was moaning, "I believe I've broken my leg, help me to the car and take me to the hospital." On the way there I said "Mr. Eddins Who is going to do the ballgame tonight?" He said "You are." I said "You know I have never done play-by-play before, I don't know how." He said "Now is a good time to learn."

I'll never forget that night. I went to the stadium, contacted both coaches for their lineups, went to the booth, placed the names of the starters on Eddins spotting board, he had invented, and while keeping one eye on the football field and one on the big wasp's nest, at the appropriate time started my first play-by-play of a sporting event.

While I was giving the starting line-ups Cullman kicked off to Bessemer. They had a little 'ole running back named Jimmy Thompson, who later played for Georgia Tech. He took that opening kickoff in his own end zone and ran it 100 yards back for a touchdown, after kicking the extra point, Bessemer was ahead 7 to nothing and I was still announcing the starting line-ups. I would give a lot of money today if I had a tape of that ballgame. After the opening I don't remember much about what happened, but I'm sure it wasn't good. Come to think of it, I could not have had a tape of the broadcast, because tape was not widely in use, especially at small local radio stations.

It seems that every time I tried to do sports, something bad would happen. The boss sent me to Moulton, Alabama that same season on the coldest night of the year for a football game. It was really cold with a mixture of rain, sleet and snow falling.

Moulton had no press box at all. I stood on the top bleacher with my microphone in one hand, the two school's rosters in the other describing, as very best I could, the action on the field, which by-the-way had no visible yard numbers or lines. I thought for sure, while standing in the open all the way through the first half, the halftime and the second half with no one to help me, I would certainly freeze to death. The sad part of the story was, when I got back to the station I learned I had not been on the air at all because of phone line trouble. The good part, I did not catch pneumonia and die, but best of all it was show business.

One other little story about play-by-play and why I decided I was supposed to be a disc jockey and not a sports man, I would leave that job to Keith Jackson, Chris Schenkle or Curt Gowdy. The first college basketball game I ever saw, I did the play-by-play. In a similar situation as the football incident, Carroll Eddins and I went out to the basketball game between St. Bernard and Jacksonville State. Before the game was to start he sensed that something was wrong and we might not be on the air. Being the only engineer, he said "I'll go back to the station and check it out. If the game starts before I get back you go on with it and I'll join you later."

Not only was that the first college basketball game I had ever seen, but to this day it was the highest scoring game I have seen. St. Bernard won the game over Jacksonville by a score of 122-111. One thing I did not have to worry about was "color" comments or filling time. It was more than I could do just to keep up with the score. By the time I announced the score, one of the teams would have scored again.

Needless to say my buddy, my boss, the man I admired most and my friend, and benefactor never came back to the gym that night, and unlike the Moulton football game, when I returned to the station after the game, I learned that I had indeed been on the air the whole time.

By-the-way, his leg was not broken in the fall from the bleachers, but after that night I felt like breaking both of them.

I will always be thankful to Carroll Eddins and his brother

John for giving me the opportunity to begin my broadcasting career at their station, and for giving me a chance to decide what I really wanted to do in the business and what I did not want to do. I learned a lot from some great announcers at WFMH, our country music and early morning man Slim Lay, and my idle, Bill Hoffman, the best voice I had ever heard. I always wanted to sound like him but never could. And, who could ever forget the personality, the courage and the warm friendly voice of Lon Waters. He was a paraplegic, paralyzed from the waist due to an automobile accident while in military service. Although in a wheel chair and in tremendous pain most of the time I never heard him raise his voice in anger or even seem to be upset with any of the staff, as I'm sure he had a right to be as our program director.

My work hours were from 7-9 a.m., 12-1 p.m. and 3-6 p.m. and going to school in between. There being so few radio stations in the 50's and 60's each station tried to please everyone. No station specialized it's programming as they do today, with country, rock, news and talk, and any number of different formats. In those days, at WFMH, Slim played country music in the early morning, I would play "pop" beginning at 7 a.m. My noontime was gospel quartet music and the afternoon was pop music again. At one time, I even played a half hour of classical music from the old RCA Red Seal records.

I didn't have to be a genius to see that the most popular person on the station was Slim Lay, the listeners liked him and the country music he played. Myself, I liked country music, that's how I got into radio in the first place with the FFA band, but I didn't have a chance to program it until much later. I gained a lot of experience in news and other programming, like our "man on the street" program on Saturday mornings, in addition to working when I had time in advertising sales.

Selling our station was pretty tough. We had good people, a good sound, but very few listeners because there were no FM radios in the 1950's FM was brand new . In fact, WFMH-FM was the third FM to go on the air in the state of Alabama. Another big difference in broadcasting then and now, we did everything "live". All news, program intros, and commercials had to be read live from a master book which was prepared the night before. One of my first jobs was to "make up the book" from the program log, being sure that everything was in the proper order for the announcers the next day.

Now days, just about everything you hear on the radio is computerized, or picked up from satellites. Automation is good in some respects, but I believe it has taken too much of the "personality" away and left a cold music playing machine. Why listen to the radio? You can get the same thing from your stereo set, or computer without the commercials. But, that's the way it is whether I like it or not. Maybe that's one reason I'm not doing it anymore.

I managed to squeeze two semesters into three at St. Bernard. As the end of my third semester approached in January of 1953 I realized I had taken every course they offered except those I had not already taken at Auburn my freshman year. That is, unless I wanted to enter the monastery and become a priest. I decided, and with good advice from father Patrick O'Neal, the Dean, that I had at least two strikes against me. First I was not a catholic, second I was married, I was obviously not a candidate for the priesthood.

When I told my boss, Mr. Eddins, my predicament and that my school days were over after only two years, he again gave me that dirty look I still remembered from 18 months before when I told him I was not going back to Auburn. I think he just said, "We'll see about that."

Chapter 7

TUSCALOOSA

After completing that first year at Auburn University and three semesters at St. Bernard College, I decided that I had had it with college, and I was not going back.

Thinking I was secure in my job at WFMH and there would be no more classes and studying, ready to get on with my life, I was shocked one morning in early January 1953 when Carroll Eddins came in the control room and told me that he and I were going to Tuscaloosa that very day, leaving as soon as my shift was over at 9 a.m. My first reaction was surprise, saying "What for?" He said, "We are going to get you a job, and you are going on to school at The University of Alabama." I said "Whoa! Wait a minute. I can't go to the university. That place is for them high falutin' rich folks. They all have money, cars, fancy clothes, and besides, the only folks I had ever known that went to Tuscaloosa never came back."

I thought of many more excuses such as, Carol Dean would have to quit her good job at the bank. I didn't even know where Tuscaloosa was. It must be way too big for us. We didn't have a place to live. I probably could not get a job, and I might just join the army and go fight with General MacArthur in Korea. All to no avail, he said "We are going to Tuscaloosa today. I know all of the radio station managers and owners there and we will get you a job so you can get started in school this winter semester, which would begin in just a few days.

At 9:00 a.m. I called Carol Dean at work and told her that Mr. Eddins was taking me to Tuscaloosa. She said "What have you done?' I said "Nothing, he wants to take me there, find me a job in radio, and then he wants us to move there right now." I don't remember her exact words, but I believe it was "He's out of his mind. We can't just pick up and leave here." Then she thought of some more excuses for not doing such a crazy thing. He would not listen to any of them, so he practically dragged me kicking and screaming to his car and we headed out down highway 69 toward Tuscaloosa passing through Jasper, Oakman, Northport and across the old river drawbridge to Tuscaloosa to look for a job.

The first stop was at WTBC located on the second floor of city hall on Greensboro Avenue. The owner, manager was Bert Bank. He knew Carroll. He invited us to have a seat in his office, inquiring about what he could do for us. Carroll said "Bert, I've got a young fellow with me that wants to come to the University. (That was a lie) He needs a job. He has been working for me for about three years and is a good, dependable employee. He and his wife Carol Dean will be moving here in the next week or so, how about it, do you have anything available?" As ugly as my later very good friend and competitor Bert Bank was, when he leaned back in his big chair, propped his feet up on the desk, resumed reading his comic book or whatever and said, "Carroll, times are hard, I'm losing money, I've got too many employees and I'm planning to let some go next week, I could have kissed him right on the mouth.

We left his office and I'm thinking so far so good, only two more stations to go. The next stop was down on Broad Street at WJRD, Tuscaloosa's oldest station owned by Mrs. Wilamena Echols who's late husband W.R. Doss had put on the air in the 1930s. The manager, John Cooper gave us about the same reaction as Mr. Bank, no job available, sorry. By this time I'm grinning, couldn't wait to get back across the river and out in the field where there was a brand new radio station WNPT. Managed by Mr. Tom Todd, and owned by Todd, Mac Jordan. Ham Gilliard, Wag Thielans and Ruth and Bill Harris, the station had been on the air for less than a year.

The first time I ever saw the man who later, along with his family became some of our dearest friends, Tom Todd, was on a tractor with a blade attached behind leveling a dirt parking lot in front of the new building. He stopped his work long enough to tell us politely that he had no job for me . He did say to me, "If you move to Tuscaloosa, please stay in touch. You never know when a job might be open." I thanked him, thinking all the time

"Yeah, sure, you know I will. I will not be coming back any time soon."

As Carroll and I were on the way home I could tell he had something on his mind but I assumed it was because we didn't find a job for me. He finally spoke, saying, "You are going anyway, I know with your ability, you will get a job sooner or later, so I'm going to keep paying your salary from WFMH until you can go to work at a station in Tuscaloosa." Of course I protested, arguing that I just could not accept charity and that it would not be right for him to pay me for no work. He called it an investment, not only for my future, but I know he fully expected that I would come back to Cullman and work with him after I graduated from the University in two years.

That never happened, as I will explain later. Carroll Eddins had a very long and worthwhile life as a broadcaster, civic and church leader a good citizen and one of the best friends I ever had. He died two years ago at the age of 81. His wife, Elsa, still lives in Cullman. His daughter, Mary Evelyn Jones, and her husband, Clark, are operating WFMH, and have recently purchased two other stations in Cullman.

Moving to Tuscaloosa was not a problem for us because we had very little to move. We had no furniture or appliances. Having lived in furnished apartments since we married, there was no need to buy them, and besides we couldn't afford such things. Neither one of us really wanted to go, but Mr. Eddins had been so persuasive and so positive we could not disappoint him. Being absolutely certain that we would only be in Tuscaloosa for two years, we decided we could do anything for that long and then come back to Cullman when I had finished school.

We loaded everything we owned, our clothes, a few wedding gifts such as pots, pans, silverware, towels, and sheets in the trunk and back seat of our 1951 De Soto and headed for the city which, as it turned out, would be our home for the rest of our lives. We had not arranged for a place to live in Tuscaloosa. Carroll told us the first thing we should do when we arrived was see Mrs. Weatherford on University Boulevard.

Carroll and Elsa had lived with her when he was in school many years before. The first person we met in Tuscaloosa was Mrs. Weatherford. People familiar with this area will remember her as attorney M. T. Ormand's mother. She did not have an apartment available so she sent us to a neighbor, Mrs. Bert Ward, who had two efficiency apartments upstairs in her house.

She said one would be available in two weeks, in the meantime we could sleep in her guest room downstairs, share the dining room, kitchen and bath with her and her husband Bert. So, for two weeks we lived out of the trunk of the car and slept in her bedroom. When we at last saw the apartment, we couldn't believe how small it was. It was basically one room with a bed, chest, and one chair. In a corner the kitchen had a small stove, refrigerator and a small table with two tiny chairs. The bathroom entrance was out in the hallway.

The apartment next door was occupied by three college girls so I was sharing the bathroom with four women. I was allowed very little time in there. The place was small, but cheap. We paid $40 a month rent.

In just a few days we settled down to my going to school at the University, and Carol went to work immediately at Alagasco. Because she had worked for the company in Birmingham before we married, they were glad to have her experience at the Tuscaloosa office. I still didn't have a job, but we did have the $60 each week Mr. Eddins was sending to us. I was miserable, just going to school and not working. I called on the three radio stations asking about work so often I'm sure they must have dreaded to see me coming.

After about six weeks Mr. Todd at WNPT asked if I had ever done any advertising selling. "Yes sir, I'm the very best, but I would rather have an announcing job." He said "If you want to sell, I'll pay you $35 a week draw against commissions." I took the offer gladly, at least I had my foot in the door of a radio station and was making enough money to pay our car payment. Taking home $29 a week with car payments of $100 a month, we had $16 of my pay left each month for groceries.

At that time, selling at WNPT was tough. First, it was a new station, second it was in Northport, third it was daytime only and because of the friction between Northport and the much larger Tuscaloosa there was just not much commerce between the two. Later the owners were so tired of being called "The little Northport station" they applied for and received permission from the FCC to designate their city of license as Tuscaloosa, and for night time programming, even though it never changed locations.

Not only was selling the station not easy, I was scared to death calling on business men and women, total strangers trying to sell them advertising. I knew nothing about the city except how to get from home to the station. All business was in what is now known as downtown or on the "strip" near the University. There were no shopping centers or malls. It seems funny to me now, but at that time I was so nervous about selling I would drive around the block where a business was located hoping I could not find a parking place and wouldn't have to go in. I did manage somehow to sell a little, but I don't think I ever earned my draw. I was so desperate for a sale I even called on the manager of the Paper Mill Cafe. He thought I was crazy. The cafe was at the Gulf States Paper Mill and only catered to the mill employees.

Before long, Mr. Todd must have realized he was not getting his $35 worth from my selling, and when Jack Norman left, he offered me the 5-8 a.m. announcing slot. I don't even remember the pay, probably didn't ask. I was so happy to be "on the air" again. The other two announcers were Keith Barze and Joe Langston. Keith was an engineer and had a great announcing voice. When he left WNPT he was hired as an engineer at WBRC-TV (channel 6) in Birmingham, then was promoted to program director and later was named Associate dean of the Communication School at the University. He and Nancy still live in Tuscaloosa, and we have remained good friends throughout the years.

Joe Langston was the most meticulous radio announcer I've ever known. I mean by that, he had a voice, delivery, enunciation and perfection achieved only by a few. If he made a

mistake reading or mispronounced a word it just tore him apart.
In broadcasting, we call mistakes "Bloopers." The best one I have ever heard, one that should go into the radio blooper hall of fame, was said on the air by Joe. It couldn't have happened to a nicer guy.

It was in the springtime. The station copy writer, Betty Bailey had written a commercial for Morgenthau dry cleaners advertising their cold storage for the ladies' winter furs. The first line of the commercial was, "Tuck your precious furs in Morgenthau's cold storage vaults, etc." Well, my buddy Joe, in that precision delivery of his and after clearing his throat flipped the mike on and proclaimed for all in radioland to hear,

"F--- your precious turs in Morgenthau's cold storage vaults." When he realized what he had said he nearly died. It took us several minutes to revive him.

Some years later Joe would come to work for a while with me at WACT before being hired by Keith as news anchor on Channel 6 in Birmingham. Upon his retirement from television he would become head of the broadcast department at Jacksonville State University where he and Margaret still reside.
At the time I was assigned to do the morning slot at WNPT. The music had been selected at random with no rhyme or reason that I could tell.

Recordings were played in rotation as they happened to be stacked in the shelves. I had never played any Country Music, but was very familiar with it and the performers. I decided that was what I would do with my three hours, one of the best decisions I ever made, not even realizing it at the time.

There was no country music being played in Tuscaloosa at all, another reason for my decision. You may notice I'm using the phrase "Country music". Please remember that to the uninformed any music played on a guitar, fiddle, mandolin, banjo or dobro was "hillbilly" music. The music was not called "country" until several years later when it was being recognized by Hollywood, New York, National TV networks and the public in general as their favorite music. As Barbara Mandrel said in her song, " I was country when country wasn't COOL."

Country music disk jockeys in the 1950s were a different breed. Not only must one know all about the recording artists like Red Foley, Hank Snow, Eddy Arnold, Carl Smith, Roy Acuff, Kitty Wells, Johnnie and Jack, Little Jimmy Dickens, Bill Monroe, Lester Flatt and Earl Scruggs, Hank Williams and many others, he had to know all about their backgrounds, where they could be seen in concert, how many wives or husbands they had had and all sorts of personal information about them.

Country music deejays were expected to talk "country" and the more country the better. Most took on names like Slim, Tex, Happy, Uncle Josh, Smilin' Jim, or Country Boy. I had no trouble with the country talk, being able to do that with the best of them. On my three hour program every morning I did a whole lot of country talkin' and became so familiar with the artists you would think I knew every one personally.

It was just natural at breakfast time for me to talk about mama's cat head biscuits and papa's home made "soggum" soppin' syrup," I would talk about our old farm as if I had just left there on a mule that morning. I always referred to Carol, my wife as Mama with sayings such as, "Mama put the biscuits on. I'm coming home." as my regular sign off at the end of each program. What the listeners did not know was Carol had already gone to work and I was rushing out the door to an 8:10 a.m. class at the University. At first the program did not go over very well. Most Tuscaloosa listeners had never been exposed to "country" on the radio, thinking they were too sophisticated in the University city for that kind of stuff.

Sure, great numbers of folks listened to Joe Rumore on WVOK in Birmingham. He played country music but he was not country. One thing he was though, he was very successful, making a lot of money. However, I persisted in what I was doing and gradually the phone started ringing more for requests and favors, like my helping find lost dogs, cats or kids that had stayed out too late. The best was when the boss and sales manager Ruth Harris started getting calls from business people wanting to buy advertising on the show.

As time went by that first year Carol and I were really

struggling to pay rent, living expenses, tuition, books, etc. One really good thing happened. Through Mrs. Ward we met her sister Mrs. J.D. Caples, a widow living in a two story house on Reed Street about two blocks nearer the University. Mrs. Caples was so particular about tenants, the large furnished apartment upstairs had not been rented for several years. Fortunately she liked us and invited us to move there after about six months at the Wards on Caplewood Drive.

The apartment had a large living room, bedroom, dining room, kitchen and, best of all, we had our own private bathroom, all for $45 a month. We were much happier there. We each had a chair and even a couch in the living room and with our purchase of a Bendix washing machine and an RCA television set were really living at last.

We entertained one very important guest in that apartment. Former Governor of Louisiana Jimmie Davis came to town for a concert. The promoter asked me to pick the Governor up at the airport that afternoon. When I met him I asked if there was anything, maybe the University, he would like to see. He said, "No, I'm worn out. I would just like to go somewhere and rest." Not having any money to take him to a hotel, I took him home with me.

Carol almost passed out from shock when I climbed the stairs with my distinguished guest and introduced him to her. He relaxed, took a nap and just before time to leave for the concert we fed him the only food we had, a peanut butter and jelly sandwich. A few days ago I read in the paper that he had celebrated his one hundredth birthday. The writer of the famous song "You Are My Sunshine," two time Governor of Louisiana and recording artist ate supper with us on Reed Street.

The first loan I ever asked for was at The First National Bank Of Tuskaloosa. Not knowing how to go about acquiring a loan or that banks had installment loan departments, I went in to see the president, Mr. Frank Moody. I introduced myself and told him I wanted a loan to buy a TV and a washing machine. He said "Son, tell me why I should let you have that much money." I said, " Because I'm honest. I'll pay it back. I'm in school and I work for Mr. Tom Todd at WNPT." He said, "Well, if you are good enough for my friend Tom you're good enough for me." At the time I had no idea that little loan was the beginning of a fine relationship between me and First National Bank.

As I got going in sales, calling on retail stores, meeting the merchants and selling spots on the morning program on WNPT most of the people I called on did not connect me with the country nut that had somehow found his way to Tuscaloosa and got a job at a radio station, and I didn't bother to tell them I met some resistance from those who said the fellow is too country, and I'm not interested in associating my business with that silly, "country bumpkin." My favorite come back for that was ,"You must have heard him, or you would not know so much about him." Usually I would get a reply such as, "Yeah, I listen every morning just to see how big a fool he's going to make of himself." I'd come back with, "If you listen, don't you think everybody else does too?"

During that first semester, in addition to my work at WNPT, I took a night job at the educational station on campus, WUOA making $50 a month working 6-10 p.m. I would sign off WUOA at 10 o'clock, go home to sleep a while and then get up early enough to sign on WNPT at 5 a.m. In order to help more with our expenses I got a job selling Kirby vacuum cleaners in my spare time. Mr. G. B. Mitchell was the Kirby distributor for the area. I tried to sell him advertising. I didn't sell him, but he sold me on the idea of working as my time would permit. He really got my attention when he said, "The commission on the $184 machine is $60."

I was not a very good door-to-door salesman, but that experience made me have a greater appreciation for people who make their living doing so. I did sell a few machines, but I found out that if I took an old vacuum cleaner on trade, whatever amount I allowed for it came out of the $60. I didn't make any money, but we did wind up with several old worn out vacuum cleaners, one of which Carol used for years.

I will never forget my first sales call I made alone. I still believe it was a practical joke that the other salesmen played on the young, new salesman. Someone had made an appointment to demonstrate a Kirby machine at a small house on Bridge Avenue in Northport, occupied by a black family, in an all black neighborhood. When I arrived, there were people in the yard, in the driveway, and on the porch, and as I took the big box full of equipment, including the cleaner with all attachments, a grinder, floor polisher, knife sharpener and buffer into the small living room for the demonstration, I saw that the room was already just about full of people, and those outside were crowding in. Obviously neighbors had been invited to see the show.

We salesman always carried what they called a "dust meter," a small six inch in diameter attachment with a glass top and a round piece of filter paper inside which we connected to the machine where the bag would normally be attached. The purpose of it was to show the customer how much dust was being removed from their rug or mattress by the most powerful vacuum cleaner ever invented.

The floor was covered by an old well-worn rug that reminded me of the one we had back hone at Nebo. I plugged the machine cord in a socket, set it in the middle of the crowded room, asking a few people just to back up a little so everyone could see, attached my dust meter and pressed the "on" button. There was so much dirt in that old rug, that instantly the dust meter blew completely off. The machine was sucking dust, and spraying it in all directions, and to make matters worse, it was going around in circles. No Oklahoma dust storm ever stirred up so much dust in such a small space. It was so bad that I could not even see how to catch it and turn it off. The folks in the room scattered as fast as they could out every door, and I think some even went out the windows, all of us gasping for breath. When I finally got the machine stopped, I piled it back in the box, carried it out to the car and left. I didn't even wait to ask for the order.

I need to explain about her name. Before we moved to Tuscaloosa, she was called Carol Dean. Our friends in Tuscaloosa simply called her Carol, so that's what I'll do from now on. I still call her Carol Dean when I'm peeved at her. Now, her legal name is Carol Bailey Price. That, no doubt, is where Hillary Rodham Clinton got the idea of using her maiden name in the middle.

All right, now I'm working at WNPT mornings, going to school, studying when I can, working at WUOA at night and selling vacuum cleaners on the side. Carol was still working at the gas company. We had a nice apartment, and Mrs. Caples supplied us with all the cornbread and collard greens we could eat. She was a very sweet lady, the mother of J. D. Caples Jr. He and his beautiful wife, Lanie, and son Bruce, are very dear friends now.

I will tell you a secret that to this day has never been told to anyone. Mrs. Caples has passed on and I doubt very much if her son and daughter-in law will ever read this, so I'll tell you for the record. Carol and I both hated the smell and the taste of collard greens, but for some reason Mrs. Caples thought we liked them. She cooked enough every day for herself and for our supper. The secret is, we flushed so many collards down the commode that the bowl turned green.

Speaking of secrets, I had at least two others. One was that I went to school at Auburn my freshman year and the other was that at the present I was a student at the University of Alabama. The reason? Simple, no self respecting Alabama man would admit he ever went to the "cow college," and no country music deejay would admit he ever went to any college. Speaking of college, by the time I began my last two years at the University, I had decided I wanted to be involved in some form of broadcasting as a career.

At that time the University had no school of communication, as it does now. The broadcasting department, which primarily radio, (television was just a toy at that time,) was in the school of Arts and Sciences. I enrolled and declared my major in broadcasting with a minor in the School of Commerce. Most of my courses were required for a BA degree, with very few electives after my year at Auburn and a year and a half at St. Bernard. I found the broadcasting courses were fairly easy because I already had been working for four or five years. Class lectures and instructions by some good teachers like Don Smith, Ted Nelson, and Knox Hagood consisted, it seemed to me, of too much theory and not enough practicality. Very few of the students and none of the teachers had ever actually worked in a small radio station.

I did have some excellent and talented classmates. I've already mentioned Joe Langston. There was Stan Siegal, Dick Hartsock, Wendell Harris, Harry Mabry Jim Stewart and others who went on to distinguished careers in the industry. I had better mention a really famous broadcasting alumnus, "Gomer Pyle" whose name is Jim Nabors, had graduated the semester before I started.

No doubt Stan Siegal and I must hold the record for the smallest class ever at the University of Alabama, only we two in the class. Believe it or not it was a class in sports announcing, my worst nightmare. Our only assignment was to broadcast live from Denny Stadium the annual spring "A" Day game, Stan calling the first half and me the second. As I remember, he did a good job. He had done play-by-play of Tuscaloosa High School football for Bert Bank at WTBC. I have always thought that it might have been my announcing of the second half of the spring game that caused the football team to go winless that fall, either that or a lousy quarterback named Bart Starr.

I found the economics and advertising classes in the Commerce School interesting. Though after all these years I still remember how I was sorely disappointed in the advertising class. We had a professor, who, I will not name, that taught and we studied by the text book. During the semester we laid out newspaper and magazine ads by cutting out pictures, pasting them and writing copy. We studied every conceivable form of advertising including direct mail, billboards, calendars, Burma Shave signs, match book covers and even taxicab and bus signs. But near the end of the book there was a one-page chapter headed by the word RADIO. I had been looking forward all semester to something about radio, my favorite subject, but to my surprise that morning the good professor said "I don't know anything about radio, so we will skip this chapter."

The next day when he asked me why I had walked out of his class the day before, I just had to tell him how upset I was about his attitude in regards to my chosen field. I know I probably went too far but I said "Doctor, if you don't know anything about radio and television, and you call yourself an advertising professor, you had better learn something about them because, whether you like it or not, they are here to stay. Furthermore, these other students in the class will most likely be advertising buyers for large retail outlets and ad agencies. One day I will be calling on them for their business and I'm afraid their attitude may be the same as yours, I don't know anything about radio. We skipped that chapter."

I seriously considered not even going back to class after that, being certain I had blown any chance of passing the course, but to my amazement, I made an "A" in the course. Must have had a good instructor.

All in all my university experience was enjoyable except for not having very much time to study or participate in campus activities. My toughest subjects were trigonometry and a whole year of French language.

I had taken the first year at Auburn and three years later had to take the second year. Naturally I had forgotten all I had ever learned, making it really tough. The only way I ever passed that last semester of French was by promising Mr. Menardier, the tennis coach and French teacher, I would never again take a French course. He spoke English about like I spoke French but I understood him when he said " If I let you pass this course, then you take more, they gonna wonder why I gave you a passing grade, but if you promise not to take more French, I give you a "C." I gave him a big loud "Oui" a big kiss on his bald head, not a French kiss mind you, and went away happy, thinking I had made a good deal considering I had come to the end of the semester with a 41 average.

By the end of our first year in Tuscaloosa, things were going quite well, making more money too. I was becoming more popular on the morning program. I was selling most of the advertising on a 15% commission. I still did not have a country handle, but because of the homespun nature of my early morning program and all the talk about home in the country and sopping syrup with mamas biscuits, I noticed that occasionally when I met someone for the first time they would say "Are you that ole' boy who is always sopping syrup on the radio?" or "Are you that syrup sopper?" So gradually I started calling myself 'The Syrup Sopper." The name caught on and to this day people will see me at a restaurant or any public place, introduce themselves and still call me "Syrup Sopper."

Believe me, I love them for it. The only difference between then and now, then the girls and young ladies would smile and say they listen all the time, but now the young ladies say, "My grandmother used to listen to you all the time". If it's a grandmother I'm talking to she will say "I used to listen to you all the time, and I still miss you on the radio every morning." I am pleased that they still remember.

Most people, including our government, would have you believe that radio and TV are strictly for the information and entertainment of the audience, which is absolutely true, except someone has to pay the bills. In other words, it is a business too. The only way we have to pay the expenses is by selling advertising on the local level and being effective in moving merchandise off the shelves of our customers. The better job we do with our commercials, whether delivered formally or as I used to do ad-lib style, the more merchandise we sell, and the more advertising dollars come our way.

I found right away that a store I was advertising would know exactly and without doubt they were getting results from my efforts because I would say something like "When you go to the Piggly Wiggly, be sure to tell them old Syrup Sopper sent you in."

It was amazing how many listeners would do that. I really didn't care what they called me as long as the advertiser knew I sent them to buy his merchandise. People who would never say I heard Clyde Price talking about your store on the radio, would go in and laughingly say "I heard the old Syrup Sopper talking about a refrigerator, or whatever, and I'd like to see it." Great, another sale for them and another point for me.

The morning show was going so well that we added an hour from 3-4 in the afternoon. It, too, was very successful. As time was approaching for me to graduate in January of 1955, it became necessary that Carol and I start making some plans for the future. I talked it over with my boss Mr. Todd. He said he would really like me to stay on with the station after I graduated and would do his best to work out an arrangement whereby we could both benefit.

We developed a plan. I would sell exclusively the three hours in the morning and one in the afternoon, being responsible for all copy, servicing the accounts and doing the programs live for one half, 50 % of what I put on the air and collected. The station would only do the billing. A great deal for me. By that time I knew I could sell advertising and was certain I could sell the goods on the radio.

I developed a style, a very low-key conversational style, more like a friend or neighbor telling the listener, "Now looky here if you've got a hog, cow, chicken, goat, rabbit or a hound dog, you need to be feeding them Bama feeds 'cause Bama feeds are better feeds, made right here in Tuscaloosa at Alabama Feed Mills by Mr. R. E. Winstead, his sons Earl, and R. E. Jr. and all the good folks that have been making quality feeds for 42 years. You would not eat anything but the best yourself, so why feed less than the very best to your animals? And by-the-way, be sure to tell the man at the Alabama Feed Mills feed and farm center the old Syrup Sopper on WNPT sent you to buy your feeds from him."

I actually read very few commercials because it was impossible for a copy writer to write in my style. Therefore, I ad-libbed everything except those the ad agency demanded be read word for word. Syrup Sopper was very successful in selling just about anything, because the audience was faithful to listen, and they believed if Syrup Sopper said it was; it had to be good.

I have always believed that the primary reason for my success as a country deejay in Tuscaloosa was because this is still basically a country town. I know very few people who have city roots, past a single generation. A very large percentage of the population was born and raised in the country, if not, their parents or grandparents were.

I want to go back to November of 1953 to tell you of a very significant happening in my pursuit of knowledge of country music. The radio station received an open invitation from WSM in Nashville, Tennessee to send a country disc jockey, if it had one, to a convention of country music deejays, in conjunction with the 25th anniversary of the Grand Ole' Opry. I talked Mr. Todd into letting me go, and he even gave me some money for expenses. Carol took two days off from work, I skipped school and we were off to Nashville, where neither of us had been before.

The convention was held at the Andrew Jackson Hotel. There were only 50 or 60 deejays attending, including some very famous ones from the larger cities. As an aspiring young radio personality I was in awe of the real pros in the business like Pee Wee King, Dal Stallard, Bob Jennings, Hard Rock Gunter, Eddy Hill, Charlie Lamb, Bob Dunnavant and a real odd-ball Ramblin' Lou Schriver from Niagra Falls, New York. In 1953 it was almost impossible to find a station or anyone who would admit to playing "hillbilly" music from above the Mason/Dixon line and especially from the state of New York. Ramblin' Lou, Carol and I became good friends, continuing to enjoy each other's company throughout the years at conventions . He, like me, later became a radio station owner.

The wonderful part of that anniversary celebration was meeting the famous and not so famous country music artists. They were all there to attend special breakfasts, luncheons, cocktail parties, dinners, and dances, all paid for by the individual record companies, Decca, RCA, Columbia, Capitol and publishing companies Acuff Rose and Tree.

I was impressed at a luncheon when everybody was served a steak and Gene Autry picked up the tab. To name a few of the artists we met who, even though I had been a country deejay for just a few months, I idolized because I had heard their records and listened to them on the Grand Ole' Opry all my life.

There were, Roy Acuff, Minnie Pearl, Stringbean, Bill Carlisle, Rod Brasfield, George Morgan, Little Jimmie Dickens, Bill Monroe, Hank Snow, Mac Wiseman, Lonzo and Oscar, Kitty Wells, Red Foley, Eddy Arnold, Chet Atkins, Lester Flatt and Earl Scruggs, Johnny and Jack, Faron Young, Ferlin Husky, Bill Anderson, The Davis Sisters, Jim Ed, Maxine and Bonnie the Browns, the Carter Family, Mother Maybelle, Helen June and Anita, Marty Robbins, Tex Ritter, and Hank Thompson. You may wonder about the most famous of them all, Hank Williams. Remember Hank had died suddenly on January 1, that same year 1953.

Another pleasure to me was seeing and talking to those great WSM announcers, Eddy Hill, Louie Buck, Grant Turner and Dave Overton who was from Tuscaloosa and Bob Jennings from WLAC. Perhaps the most famous WSM announcer Ralph Emery, at that time was working in Shreveport and did not go to Nashville until the untimely death of their all-night deejay, Eddie Hill. In later years Ralph and I became good friends. Of course the highlight of the weekend was the 25th anniversary performance of the Grand Ole' Opry at the famous old church in downtown Nashville known as the Ryman Auditorium.

That was the first time I had ever seen the Opry and what a thrill it was. They even let us go back-stage to visit with the performers during the show. Even though I've been many times since, to the Ryman and to the beautiful new building on the outskirts of town at Opryland, no visit there has been quite the same as the first.

The most significant outcome of that meeting was the formation of the CMDJ (Country Music Disc Jockey's) association. In private conversation, some of us decided to get as many of the attendees together as we could to see if there was any interest in forming an association. We met. Everyone agreed it would be a good idea, not only for each individual but for the organization through which we could promote Country

Music in general. Someone designed a Charter Member plaque with all of our names on it which I hung proudly on my office wall for many years until I gave it to the Country Music Museum in Nashville.

The way that happened, Ralph Emery was visiting me, saw the plaque and said, "I have never seen one of these before. I'll bet they don't even have one at the museum." The next time I went to Nashville, I showed it to the curator. He likewise had never seen one but he said the museum would certainly like to have it if I would donate it, which I did gladly. I don't know if it has ever been put on public display or not. He showed me literally hundreds of items stored in the basement of the museum which had never been displayed because of the lack of display space. The significance of all this is, our little group of deejays grew to become the largest association of country performers, publishers, promoters and composers in the world, the CMA, the Country Music Association. Carol and I continued to attend the annual convention for many years until it became so large we didn't really enjoy it anymore. It became so large that it lost the intimacy and personal contact with individuals it had in the beginning.

The first ten months of 1955 were very good. I graduated from the University in January. We stayed on in our $45 apartment at Mrs. Caples, Carol was still working at the gas company. The Syrup Sopper show was doing great. I was bringing home between $2000 and $2500 a month in commissions. We had managed to get me through school without going into debt except for the $35 I borrowed from Curtis and the bank loan for the washing machine and television set, which were already paid off. During all those years of not seeing each other very often, because of school and work, we discovered we really did sorta like to be together. In January she became pregnant. All was going real well for us. We had traded the DeSoto for a 1953 Oldsmobile Ninety-eight.

But, there was a dark cloud on the horizon. Soon after graduating in January, I lost my military deferment and was reclassified to 1-A, the highest priority. We worried about my being drafted at first but since I was not called right away we just sort of forgot about it.

Not knowing any doctors personally in Tuscaloosa, Carol wanted to go back to her family physician, Dr. Frank Stitt and to the Cullman Hospital to have the baby, which she did. I was concerned the whole nine months that when the time would come for her to deliver, I would not be able to drive her the one hundred miles to Cullman fast enough and that our child might be born at Bug Tussle or someplace else by the side of the road. Believe it or not, on the afternoon of October first, I started having terrible back pains and feeling just plain awful. I told Carol I thought she must be getting ready to have the baby, but she said she felt fine and not to worry, she was OK.

I did manage to convince her that we should go on to Cullman because the baby was due at anytime. We drove to her parents house late in the afternoon and that night she woke me saying "I think we had better go to the hospital." After a long labor of more than 18 hours, one of the nurses introduced me to my first son, 8 pound 2 ounce Walter Bailey Price, to be known forevermore as "Wally." I not only was the proud daddy of a baby boy but his birth cured my backache. Thank you Wally.

Chapter 8

UNCLE SAM CALLS

Wally was born on October 2, 1955, in Cullman. Then, mothers and babies stayed in the hospital for at least a week. During that week I had to return to work in Tuscaloosa and would go to see them when I could. I remember, like it was this morning, they were still in the Cullman hospital and as I was leaving our apartment on Reed Street for my afternoon program, I met the postman coming up the walk. With tears in his eyes, he handed me a letter that in effect said, "The President of The United States of America is in trouble and he needs you more than your wife and new baby need you, so, they will just have to get along without you for awhile. If you don't mind, how about reporting to the induction center in Montgomery, Alabama on November 1, 1955."

I admit it was a shock, but since January I had known that my number would more than likely come up. I don't mean to complain, except the government's timing could not have been worse. True, there was no shooting war in 1955. The Korean War had just ended and no one I knew had ever heard of a place called Vietnam.

I have always believed that some compulsory military training for every able bodied male graduating from high school would be good for the individual and the country, but at the time I was drafted I had graduated from college, had a good job making lots of money, with a wife and child and ready at last to begin the rest of my life.

As soon as Carol could leave the hospital, she, the baby and I came back to Tuscaloosa and started preparing for my departure in less than three weeks. It's hard to say which of us cried the most during that time, Wally, Carol or me, but it seemed that Wally cried twenty-four hours a day, so much sometimes that Mrs. Caples would climb the steps to our apartment to help with the rocking. Our time for the most part was spent "showing off" the new baby to our friends, my telling my advertisers personally that I was leaving and answering the phone. Calls came from radio listeners, most of whom I had never met, wishing us well and saying please hurry back.

Unlike when we moved to Tuscaloosa in 1953, we had to rent a trailer to move our belongings back to Cullman. We loaded everything and, with the U-Haul behind the car, we went back to Carol's parents' home, where she stayed until I finished basic training and had a permanent assignment. The first ten months of 1955 I had made more than $25,000. That doesn't sound like much now, but then it would have been more like $200,000 today. We had plenty of money to spend. We had saved enough to buy a house, but had not, putting it off until the baby came and the just-right house was available.

With Carol and Wally settled at the Bailey's, on November 1, 1955 I, along with a dozen or so other fellows, most in their teens, left the Cullman bus station headed for Montgomery. After a brief physical examination, consisting of "Open you mouth," a peek inside, then "Bend over and spread your cheeks apart," another quick glance. I've often wondered what they were looking for, what ever, I wished I had one. The doctor said "Move on", to anyone able to walk.

Reminds me of the story about the old boy who, on his way to the induction center, had to stop by the roadside, run into the woods to relieve himself and not having any paper, used a handful of dry leaves. Then at the examination, when the Doctor told old boy to "Spread 'em" he raised up and declared, "I've seen all kinds. I've seen big ones, small ones, fat ones, white ones, black ones and a few yellow ones, but this is the first one I've ever seen with a bird's nest in it."

By the middle of the afternoon, we, along with enough other recruits from over the state to fill a bus, had been sworn to defend our country and its Constitution, and were on our way to Fort Jackson at Columbia, South Carolina, arriving there after mid-night on November 2.

The first real soldier I saw was a little short sawed-off, smart aleck corporal at the supply building, handing out our bedding, consisting of a mattress, a blanket, two sheets, a pillow and pillow case. That was the meanest, foulest mouthed little guy I'd ever seen. I thought he must be either plumb crazy or just mad at the world.

It gets cold in South Carolina in November. After picking up our bedding, we started walking, not to a nice warm building, but to a cold squad tent. Each tent had enough room for about twelve cots with a single small coal heater in the middle, which obviously had not had a fire in it since the previous winter. By the time we built a fire in the heater and were trying to get warm it was about 4 a.m.

Soon another madman, this time a sergeant, came busting into the tent without knocking, kicked over a couple of cots, yelled something about "You morons are not supposed to build a fire in that heater." and said, "I need five volunteers, you, you, you, you", then pointing his finger at me said "You, for KP duty at the consolidated mess." Wow! How about that, I thought . I've been in the army less than twenty four hours and I've already got a good job. Having no idea what a consolidated mess was, I reckoned that it must be a big one and would take a long time to clean it up, so the work would be steady.

On that cold, predawn morning the sergeant marched the five of us about a mile to what must have been the biggest building in the army. We didn't go in the front door, instead we went to the back and into the largest kitchen I had ever seen. The kitchen served a very big dining room for about 1000 soldiers three meals a day.

I'm not very smart, but I soon discovered that consolidated meant a whole lot of folks and mess meant where they all came to eat and KP meant that I was supposed to help wash, peel, grate, chop, blend, brew, slice, cook, and serve three time that day, enough food for that hungry mob, and then wash 3000 metal trays, tons of heavy, stainless steel pots, pans and silverware. In our sparetime, they even allowed us to sweep, mop, scrub and wax the floors throughout the building.

When it came to meanness, that little old corporal and the early morning sergeant were pikers compared to that tyrannical mess sergeant at the consolidated mess. You would have thought that he owned the whole army and the rest of us were slaves, from the way he treated us. After meeting my third soldier, I decided that they all must be mad about everything. I worked on KP from 5 a.m. till 10 p.m. before being allowed to go back to the tent.

I had never seen the place in daylight, all the tents looked alike, but after awhile I stumbled into my assigned tent completely exhausted, falling on my cot and passing out, thinking at that time a day of picking cotton would be a luxury.

So went my first twenty-four hours in the service of my country. As it turned out that day was not too bad after all. Some were even worse.

The first week at the center they kept us busy with orientation speeches about matters like the uniform code of military justice. I had a hard time grasping the meaning of that since so far I had seen very little justice. It seemed to me they were always in a hurry to do nothing, running, or as the sergeants called it, double timing to get to some place so we could wait again. One day was spent getting physical examinations and taking shots in both arms at the same time.

Another day was at the quartermaster being issued our uniforms, including two fatigue, two khaki and one wool dress uniform, two pairs of long-handle underwear, they called long johns. The only difference in those and what we wore at Nebo was they were two piece, rather than one with a "trap door" in the back. We were also issued two pairs of shorts, caps, tee shirts, a pair of black dress shoes, two pairs of brown combat boots and a tie, never being allowed to try them on to see if the clothes actually fit.

Two days of testing our aptitude in math, science, history, geography, and general knowledge, along with IQ tests, just about took all of that week, which seemed more like a month to me.

We finally were allowed to ask questions. I asked the captain in charge, "How much is the army going to pay me?" I remember exactly what he said, "Soldier, you ain't worth a damn, but Uncle Sam is going to feed, clothe, shelter and pay you $78 a month. You get to keep $38 cash, and we will send your wife the other $40 for her to live on. And if you are good enough to deserve it, when you make Private First Class we'll give you a $10 a month raise."

I was almost overwhelmed by the generosity of my government. Before I was drafted, I had been sending Uncle Sam a whole year's pay every month. I was so homesick for my pretty wife and little baby back in Cullman, but one of the lectures I had heard pertained to all the bad things that could happen if I decided to leave Fort Jackson and go home. They called it AWOL. When they explained what it meant, I decided I'd better stay with them.

The second week in the army was what they called zero week, meaning we didn't even start basic training until our third week. That week was spent moving into our permanent wooden barracks, learning how to make up beds, clean the latrine (toilet), wash windows, buff floors, how to hang our clothes in a locker and how to place everything we owned in the right place in a footlocker according to army SOP (standard order of procedure,) and being chewed out like a pack of dogs by the drill sergeant, the "baddest" soldier I had met yet.

There's always one thing that has haunted me about that second week. I had just been drafted, sent all the way to South Carolina away from my family, and had not even started basic training when President Eisenhower issued an order to the Defense Department directing them to stop drafting fathers. That almost made me sick.

I was assigned to Company A, Third Battalion, 101st Airborne Division. That division had distinguished itself in Europe during World War II, but in 1955 had been relegated to a basic training outfit. Maybe that's why all the old-timers were always mad. I will not bore you with any more of my basic training heroics because so many thousands of men and women have had a lot worse time in the armed services than I ever had.

The best part of basic was that the Christmas holidays fell after the fifth week, and I got to go home for ten days. The worst part was leaving to go back to Fort Jackson for three more weeks.

Carol had written me every day sending pictures of Wally, but none of herself. When she met me at the bus station in Birmingham I was shocked by the way she looked. She looked great, but she had lost so much weight, had developed a case of acne, and looked completely stressed out, all because of my leaving, living with her parents, and the baby constantly crying with a spastic stomach, which was finally eased by feeding him goat's milk. She had a right to be stressed out.

When I returned to Fort Jackson, the company commander sent for me. I reported, he told me to sit down, that he wanted to talk to me about going to Officer Candidate School (OCS). He said, "Private Price, you made excellent grades on the tests. In fact you scored high enough that you will have no trouble getting in to OCS and I suggest strongly that you consider it." I said, "Captain, how much longer would I have to stay in the army?" He replied, "After your eight weeks here, you will go to Fort Benning, Georgia for another eight weeks of advanced basic training then to OCS and, upon completion of the course, be commissioned a second lieutenant. You will then serve another three years on active duty." I didn't hesitate, saying, "No thank you Sir, I believe I'll serve my two years as a private and go home."

During the sixth week of basic training, each of the trainees were interviewed and told what their assignment would be after basic. Some were offered another eight weeks of basic in order to get into the Rangers or some other gung-ho outfit. I wanted no part of that. At my interview, the Lieutenant said, "Private Price, we've got the perfect assignment for you. You're going to the Micro-Wave Radio Relay Repair School at Fort Monmouth, New Jersey." I said, "What in the world is that?" He said, "You should know, it says right here on your papers that you have a degree in radio from the University of Alabama." I said, "That's right but my degree is in broadcasting on the radio and not micro-wave, a subject I'm hearing for the first time in my life."

He replied, "Apparently somebody goofed, but it's too late to change it now, have a good time in New Jersey."

After basic training, I was allowed another 10 days leave before reporting to Fort Monmouth. I went to Cullman, spending time with the family and planning with Carol how she would come to New Jersey if I could find an apartment for us and make arrangements to live "off post". Not knowing how to get to Fort Monmouth, I bought an airline ticket to Newark, New Jersey airport.

My first ride on a jet airplane was exciting to say the least, especially when the girl started talking about the emergency door, the oxygen masks falling down, and scarring me half to death. I got off at the Newark airport completely lost, having no idea how to find Fort Monmouth. I went to the information desk and asked. The lady said, "Take a bus to Grand Central Station and a commuter train south to either Redbank or Longbranch, New Jersey, the nearest stations to the base."

I thought the airport was big, but it was a chicken coop compared to Grand Central Station. I still don't know how I managed to board the right train, but before long I heard the conductor yell, "Redbank." I got off, lost again, I took a cab to the base, thinking to myself that I had already spent a month's pay and was not even past the main gate.

Fort Monmouth was the show place of the Signal Corp, with it's permanent concrete and steel three story barracks and beautifully landscaped grounds, very close to the beach and the New York area. It was a far cry from Fort Jackson, and as I would learn later, Fort Gordon and Fort Polk.

I reported to headquarters for instructions and an assignment to a company, ready to go to school. A lieutenant looked at my orders and said, "Private, what are you doing here?" I said, "I'm here to go to Micro-Wave school, it says so right there." "There's been a big mistake. The Micro-wave school is 30 weeks and men who are in the army for only two years cannot attend a school longer than 16 weeks. I said, " Well, Sir what do I do now?" He didn't know, saying he would have to find out what to do with me, but in the meantime I should report to a company and just wait till they decided."

For two weeks I just lounged around, killing time, not knowing what to do. Finally, the army after not being able to decide what I should do, and I suppose not wanting to bother cutting new orders, told me to go ahead and report to the school on Monday morning.

It was a very good school. There were 30 individual weeks of instruction, each with a different civilian instructor, all expert and experienced in the field of electronics. Students were graded at the end of the week by a test based on the information covered that particular week. A failure meant repeating that week, and another failure meant you were on your way to Germany, or worse.

Each class was very small, no more than 15 students, including privates like myself, but a good number of NCOs who were still in service since WWII. They were there to coast through until they had their 30 years and could retire with a full pension, caring little about micro-wave or anything else. I'm sure the instructors had been told to take it easy on them.

The first eight weeks of school consisted of basic electronics. I was totally and completely lost. The only thing I knew for sure about electricity was how to turn on a radio or a light bulb. When they started talking about volts, ohms, resisters, capacitors, coils, neutrons, electrons, and dozens of other terms, they may as well have been speaking Greek to me. Thanks to two friends I had made, Bruce Woods and Bob Wheeler, both electrical engineering graduates, (Woods from Clemson and Wheeler from Vanderbilt,) and a lot of hard studying, more than I had ever done at the University, I was able to keep up for the first eight weeks.

After that, when we really got into micro-wave, it was so new that I had no more trouble than anyone else. At graduation time in November, Woods, Wheeler and I finished one, two, three at the top of the class. We were all offered an assignment at the White House in Washington to set up and operate a micro-wave station. We would have a great job, wearing civilian clothes, living wherever we chose, and working regular hours. The only catch was, we would have to re-enlist for another three years. We all turned it down. For me, I couldn't see how a family of three could service in Washington on less than $100 a month. If I had known then that they have those good looking interns there at the White House I might have figured out a way.

After I was settled in school, and knowing that I would be in New Jersey for at least eight months, I started looking for an apartment . That was in January, places to live were plentiful, the paper was full of "for rents". I looked at several two or three bedroom apartments priced at $50, $60, or $70 a month. I couldn't believe it. That is, until the landlords told me that beginning in April and throughout the racing season at Monmouth Park race track, the rent would be $300, $400, $500 a week!! All those places were out of the question and I was disappointed because I could see no way for Carol and Wally to join me.

Luckily, I was at the post tailor shop and saw a notice posted saying, "apartment for rent." Asking about it, I learned it belonged to an old Italian tailor at the shop. He told me it was a small apartment on the third floor of his daughter's home in downtown Redbank. The first thing I asked was, "How much," "$65 a month, year round." "I'll take it." That's about the way our conversation went, however I did go home with him that afternoon to see the place.

Small was not the word for it. After climbing three flights of stairs, I entered the smallest apartment on the East Coast. It had one room with a bed, a chair, and a small table, a tiny kitchen with a small stove and refrigerator, with the bathroom door next to it. The bathroom really didn't even need a door at all. You didn't have room to use it if you shut the door. The one closet was across the hall next to another apartment. We would have to dress in the closet for privacy.

I paid Mr. Antonio a month's rent and that evening called Carol telling her I had found an apartment and the quicker she could load a trailer, (not too much, just Wally's bed and chest) and come on up here, the better. Don't bring the TV and washer, we won't have room for them, but please hurry. "How do I get there?" she said. "I don't know, just get a map and see if you can find a small dot in northern New Jersey called Redbank."

A couple of days later she arrived in our big old Oldsmobile 98 towing a trailer. Her daddy had come with her to help with the baby and the driving. They were exhausted, having driven all night, straight through, non-stop from Cullman. After my father-in-law helped me unload the trailer, he took a train to the airport to return home. I think he slept all the way.

That night we went to the post commissary to buy groceries. We needed everything, especially milk and baby food for Wally. We took a large basket full of groceries to the checkout counter and I wrote a check for them with enough over to buy a tank of gasoline. The man at the counter said when he looked at the check, "I can't accept this. It's on an out-of-state bank. You will have to pay cash or get your money transferred from the First National Bank of Tuskaloosa before you can write a check in New Jersey. That will take four or five or even up to ten days." I said, "Now look Friend, I don't have four or five days. My wife and baby have just arrived today from Alabama. They are hungry, I have no cash, but this check is good and I'm going to get milk for this baby if I have to steal it.

That gentleman, (a civilian, I had never seen before, but I've always wished I had asked his name,) took out his wallet, cashed my check personally, and we left with over $50 worth of groceries, that was a lot in 1956 at the commissary.

Considering our living conditions and our scrimping on money those months in the "Garden State" went very well. The biggest snow we had ever seen fell in April, but in the summer we could go to the USO beach free. Speaking of the beach, unlike those in Florida and Alabama, all areas of the beach in that state are privately owned. Owners of the beachfront houses run fences all the way down to the water, making the only sand available to the public those places designated as "public."

If we had money for gas we went for rides in the car. Wally loved that. One Saturday afternoon, just going for a ride, we

116

found ourselves on the Garden State Parkway headed north. There were six lanes north and as many south separated by a barrier. I kept looking for a place to get off and turn around, but there was none, and soon the highway separated so that we couldn't see any traffic going south.

Arriving at the entrance to the Holland Tunnel, there was nothing else to do but pay the man at the toll booth 50 cents of the one dollar I had in my pocket.

Exiting the tunnel, I knew we must be in downtown New York City. A policeman was standing on the corner, so I stopped, holding up traffic, with what seemed like a whole convoy of yellow cabs behind me blowing their horns and cussing. I'm sure he could tell we were lost, so he asked, "Where do you want to go?" I said," If I can find the other side of that tunnel, the one going toward New Jersey, I'm going home." He gave me directions as to how to find the tunnel, I paid the toll booth operator my last 50 cents, while praying that we had enough gas to get home, we headed south.

Although we lived less than 50 mile from New York City, that was our only visit to the "Big Apple." and that time we didn't even get out of the car. Come to think of it, maybe I should go back and run for the U.S. Senate from New York. After all, I've spent more time there than has Hillary Clinton. (Excuse me, the temptation to write that was just too great.)

My mama wrote that her uncle Charlie Defoor, my great uncle was living someplace in New Jersey and that I should try to find him. To our surprise, uncle Charlie and aunt Ida were listed in the Longbranch phone book. They were living on a vegetable farm not more than 20 miles from us. I think they were as glad to see us as we were to see them.

That summer we visited them often and ate many suppers with them. Aunt Ida was a good southern style cook, and they kept us supplied with fresh tomatoes, beans, corn, peas, or whatever was in season at the time. Although I barely remembered Uncle Charlie, then in his eighties, it was good to see and talk to someone from Alabama.

One day on the way to their place we came up behind a

station wagon with a Tuscaloosa tag on it. Soon they turned into a motel, and when they did, I followed right behind, pulled up beside them and said, " You are the first folks from Tuscaloosa we've seen in a long time, we just want to look at you and say "Hello." As it turned out, they lived in Northport and had been regular Syrup Sopper listeners. We had a great time visiting with them.

Talking about food, on Thanksgiving day 1956, I drew what I thought was an unlucky duty, KP at the officers mess hall. We cooked 20 turkeys with all the trimmings. Just a very few officers showed up to eat, and there was so much left I took a whole turkey, dressing and vegetables home with me. Carol, Wally and I had a feast for several days. After all, that day on KP was well spent.

I finished school in November was promoted to SP3, and by that time not having enough time left in the army for a tour of duty overseas, I was assigned to Fort Gordon, Georgia at Augusta.

If Fort Monmouth was the showplace of the Signal Corps, Fort Gordon was the place they would put it if the world ever needed an enema. It was hot in the summer, cold in the winter, and had the biggest, bitingest population of gnats I'd ever seen. We left New Jersey with everything we owned in the car, and a U-Haul trailer, Wally riding on the clothes piled in the back seat. We drove all night, arriving at Augusta shortly after daylight. We bought a newspaper and started searching the classifieds for a place to live. Great! We found a perfect little one bedroom house not very far from the base for only $75 a month.

We unloaded the trailer and car, turned the trailer in at a nearby service station and in a little while were back on the road from Augusta to Cullman. Now, that seems very stupid, but then we were young and so anxious to see the folks at home and wanting them, to see how much their grandson, Wally, had grown we didn't think about staying at least one night in our new house we had just rented. By the time we reached Cullman we had been traveling more that 30 hours without sleep. I don't think I've been that tired since. I had a ten day leave before reporting to Fort Gordon.

After all that extensive training, I never saw a piece of micro-wave equipment until the following January. The only micro-wave equipment at Gordon was locked up tight, sealed in a warehouse just in case our company should be called for overseas duty.

From January till the end of May our company participated in maneuvers in Louisiana. Our mission was to set up a micro-wave communications link between just north of Lake Charles and Jonesboro, Arkansas. We had main terminals at each of the two locations with relay stations about every 50 miles in between, much like our cell phone system today, only we could carry 16 telephone conversations at one time, whereas now they are capable of thousands. Along with 15 other men I was assigned to the southern terminal near DeRidder, Louisiana.

During the time I was there Carol and Wally stayed with her folks in Cullman. We had to give up our pretty little house, and hook up another trailer. She drove to Cullman, and I drove an empty 2 ½ ton truck in a convoy from Fort Gordon to Fort Polk, Louisiana, taking three days to get there.

During the time I was there, I arranged to have most weekends off and would drive the 1200 mile round trip back to Cullman just about every weekend stopping only twice for gas and a cup of coffee, passing right through Tuscaloosa. It surely did make me homesick. The company remained in Louisiana from January till June, then loaded everything on trucks, going back to Fort Gordon. I was allowed to drive my car, stopping on the way to pick up Carol, Wally and another U-Haul in Cullman, loaded with our washing machine, TV and a few bare necessities, bound for Augusta.

We rented a small three-room apartment until I could serve out my last five months. A micro-wave team consists of a lieutenant, a master sergeant, three staff sergeants, and eleven privates or SP-3s to do all the work. Our company consisted of 16 teams. I'm telling you this in order to explain that from June until my discharge on November first, my life was total misery.

After the maneuvers were over, our personnel numbers had been allowed to dwindle to a bare minimum, in fact most of the time we had more lieutenants and master sergeants than the ones of us left to pull the KP and guard duty. It was so bad that some days I would pull KP that day and guard duty the same night, or vice versa. I even volunteered to teach truck driving at the trainee driving school for a while, placing my life in the hands of kids who had never driven any kind of vehicle much less a 2 ½ ton truck. Fortunately the driving course was in the woods. The only wreck they could have was hitting a tree, which some of them did.

When the supply clerk was discharged I applied for that job, thinking that would keep me out of the kitchen duty, but to no avail. I still had KP at least twice a week and guard duty at night.

I realize this all sounds so trivial to those brave men and women who fought, risking their lives in those far away places with strange sounding names, like Guadalcanal, Midway, Luzon, Guam, Iwo Jima, North Africa, Sicily, Italy, Belgium, France, Germany, Korea, and Vietnam. However, many books have been written and movies made about those places, but I think it's time for me to write about the real battles, the ones at Fort Jackson, Fort Monmouth, Fort Gordon and Fort Polk.

I was discharged at Fort Gordon, getting out of bed with the flu to pick up my papers, refusing to see a doctor that day fearing I would be hospitalized and miss being discharged.

I had contacted Ruth Harris, then the manager of WNPT about my old job. She was anxious to have me back, but I was worried that my Syrup Sopper listeners might have forgotten me after two years. Thankfully, the program picked up right where I left it with most of the same sponsors. With our final U-Haul, we left Augusta on the afternoon of November 1, 1957, drove a worn-out Oldsmobile, not to Cullman, but directly to Tuscaloosa and to a small three bedroom house we had previously rented in the Beverly Heights section of Alberta City, across from Partlow State School.

My military obligation consisted of two years active duty,

one year active reserve, and two years inactive reserve. I joined the National Guard at Fort Brandon Armory to serve my year of active reserve. Our regimental commander was Col. Rainy Collins, battalion commander Maj. Beasor Walker and company commander Capt. Catlin Cade, all veterans of WW II. Later, Collins was elected mayor of Tuscaloosa, serving two terms, and Walker served 26 years as Tuscaloosa County Sheriff, both of them are still good friends of mine.

To my knowledge, in the history of the U.S. armed forces I am the only combination country deejay, soldier, truck driver and laundry man. It all happened this way. The National Guard unit went to summer camp at Fort McClellan near Anniston, Alabama. I had no one to do my Syrup Sopper show for the two weeks I would be at camp. So, Col. Collins our commander also being owner of Tuscaloosa's biggest laundry made me a deal. Instead of staying at Ft. McClellan for the entire two weeks of camp, I would drive a truck around to all the company headquarters each afternoon, pick up the troops laundry, drive to Tuscaloosa that evening, arrive in time to grab a few hours of sleep, get up at 4:30, go on the air at 5:00 a.m., get off at 8:00, go unload the laundry, then drive back to Ft. McClellan to start the whole process over again. I did that for two weeks, and remember that was before the interstate highways were built. That, Friends and Neighbors, was the end of my brilliant military career.

Carol, Wally and I had managed to live on the money we had saved for a house, and the meager army pay without going into debt, but when I was discharged we were flat broke. The house we rented in Beverly Heights was unfurnished. We borrowed $700 from Carol's aunt Lela Bailey to buy our first real furniture after six years of marriage. Living room, bedroom, and kitchen furniture along with a new refrigerator were finally ours.

Chapter 9

HOME AGAIN, AT LAST

The last statement of the previous chapter is misleading. I failed to say that we had ordered our living room and bedroom furniture from a furniture direct sales outlet in Decatur, Georgia.

Until its arrival in Tuscaloosa two weeks after we moved in at our place in Beverly Heights, Carol and I slept on a mattress on the bedroom floor. That was fine. We would gladly have slept on the ground if necessary, we were so happy to be home again. Two year old Wally had his baby bed, and except for the small dinette suite we bought for the kitchen, that was all the furniture in the house.

I went back to work the second day after I was discharged from the army. I had a great time that first morning on the air, seemed almost like I hadn't been away for two years, with listeners flooding the phone lines saying good things like "Glad you're back." "Welcome home." "We missed you." It made me feel really good. Some listeners wanted to know about "Mama Syrup Sopper and Little Syrup Sopper."

That morning was when Wally got himself a new name that stuck with him until he outgrew it.

Things had changed somewhat at WNPT. Mr. Tom Todd had sold his interest in the station to Ruth and Bill Harris, she being the manager and he the engineer. Keith Barze had gone to WBRC-TV Joe Langston was still there. Jack Hamm who had held my seat while I was away moved to other hours. But with the office staff, Evelyn Tidmore bookkeeper, and Betty Bailey copy writer, everything was about the same.

I was really busy those first few days, getting organized, calling on all of my old advertisers, and a bunch of new prospects that had gone in business while I was gone. I still don't know why Ruth Harris made me the same compensation deal I had before I left. Tom Todd told me later that the week before I got my draft notice, the board of directors had met and the Harrises, Mr. Gilliard, Mr. Jordan and Mr. Thielans had demanded that he do something about that Syrup Sopper. They said he was making too much money, and if he didn't fire me or reduce my pay, they would fire him. He said he had worried for a week about the unpleasant task they had given him, and had mixed emotions when I came in and told him I'd been drafted, thinking he hated to see me go in the army, but relieved that he didn't have to carry out the firing ultimatum. He told me that the next day he called each one and told them, "You don't have to worry about the Syrup Sopper any more. We'll be rid of him the first of next month. He's been drafted."

We have remained friends with the Todd family through the years. The night we visited the funeral home where Tom's body lay in state, I had forgotten he had a twin brother in Washington, D. C. He was there and I almost fainted when he came and spoke to me, thinking Tom had risen from the dead. Carol and I both loved Mrs. Allie Todd. She had been almost like a mother to us when I was in school and we were starving. Their son Tommy, Margaret his wife and their children Thomas III and Debra were neighbors in Claymont for more than twenty years.

As I was saying, I was surprised that Mrs. Harris offered me the same financial arrangement, 50% of all I sold and collected, especially after Mr. Todd told me about the firing situation before I had left. There was one little catch. She had Gordon Rosen, her attorney draw up an elaborate contract, with a whole bunch of "where as's, what ifs, and therefores" in it, but when I read the fine print, it looked to me like it was a lifetime contract. It specifically stated that I would NEVER work for another radio station. I said, "I hope my forever is going to be a long time and there's no way I can sign that kind of contract. Mr. Rosen if I were your client would you advise me to sign that?" He said "No I would not." So, without a contract, I stayed at WNPT, with the Syrup Sopper show for about four more years.

During that time, everything at the radio station, my selling, air work, and promotion were mostly routine, the morning and afternoon programs continued to gain in popularity and I was beginning to be more involved in civic activities.

At home, we were settling in, becoming a family in our little rented house, next door the pastor of Alberta Baptist Church, Dr. J. B. Maxwell and his wife Grace.

When I was in school we had attended Calvary Baptist which was located on 10th street, in the shadow of Denny Stadium and catered to students. When Dr. Maxwell came over from next door the day we moved in to greet the new neighbors, there was no way we could tell him we would not join his church. We attended Alberta Church for many years. I was an active choir member and Sunday School teacher, and Carol worked with the children's choir, Cub Scouts and the many other activities as a volunteer.

Soon after we returned to Tuscaloosa, we had a pleasant surprise. Dr. James Brown told us that Carol was expecting our second child to arrive around the first of August. We were so sure the baby would be a girl, we didn't even consider it just might be another boy.

Throughout the pregnancy, we were telling Wally that he was going to get a baby sister, and I insisted that the baby must be the milkman's because, after all, I did leave for the radio station every morning a 4:30. I had selected a name already. The little girl baby would be Patricia Price, and we'd call her Patsy for Patsy Cline, my favorite girl singer. Early in the morning on August 9, 1958 I drove Carol, by appointment, the one mile from our house to Druid City Hospital to deliver the baby. Would you believe, when we drove up to the emergency entrance, the only vehicle in sight was a Perry's Pride milk truck? I said, "I don't believe it. That milkman had not only figured the date but the exact time of day the baby would arrive."

About an hour after checking in, Ronald Blaine Price was born, obviously not a girl's name. It must have been a boy and Wally would be disappointed that he did not have a baby sister, but we decided by a vote of two to one we would keep him. Ron, as we called him, was a baby that cried all the time. It seemed he must be hurting somewhere, but the doctors could not find what the trouble was until they discovered he had been born with a hernia. They postponed the operation until he was six weeks old, our first experience with a really sick little baby. After the surgery he was fine, but when Carol's mother and daddy came to visit their new grandson, my father-in-law became sick with an illness for which the doctors, including specialists in Birmingham, could determine no cause.

For about two years, his condition gradually worsened as he became weaker and weaker, unable to work and in and out of hospitals. The last three or four months of his life he was confined to home and the hospitals. Carol spent most of that time in Cullman giving care and sitting with him. He died on July 31,1960 at the age of 51. The autopsy revealed that he died from a rare kidney disorder.

It was during this time that we noticed Wally's right eye was beginning to turn in, and in a short time the left one began to turn also. In a near panic we started trying to get medical help, not knowing that "crossed eyes" could be corrected by surgery. Our pediatrician, Dr. Peter Trice, recommended we take Wally to Dr. N.E. Miles, a specialist in that type of surgery in Birmingham.

Dr. Miles was one of the kindest old gentlemen we had ever met and he was extremely comforting and professional in dealing with a young couple who were so upset at the prospects of having a child with permanently crossed eyes. He said, " Now don't worry, I can fix those eyes, possibly with one operation, maybe two, or even three, but when I'm through, they will be perfectly straight." However, with Wally being only two years old, it would be better to wait until after he is three to operate."

I can still almost see little ole' three-year-old, cross eyed Wally, with his little "suitcase" in one hand and dragging that worn out, tattered, stuffed "dog" in the other marching into the Children's Hospital the day before the first surgery.

When it was over, he had to wear black patches on both eyes for several days, and splints on his arms so he could not tear the patches away. The first surgery was partly successful, but it was necessary for Dr. Miles to operate again about six months later. Complete success that time, thanks to God and the skill of Dr.

Miles, Wally's eyes were perfect. Years later I had a young university student, James Ellington, working for me whose eyes were extremely crossed. James was a good boy, from a good family, but like mine, they had very little money, his eyes having been crossed all his life. He had the worst inferiority complex I'd ever seen. I told him about the miracle that Dr. Miles had performed on Wally, that if he would have the surgery, I would pay for it. He did and I did, needing only one operation. After his eyes were fixed, James's whole personality changed. He changed from an introvert to an extrovert almost over night. He got his degree in engineering at the University of Alabama, then A great job with NASA in Houston, Texas.

I often wondered why country singer George Morgan, the father of modern country entertainer Lorrie Morgan never had his crossed eyes fixed. Although he had one of the best voices, was a really fine man and a pleasure to know, I never saw a picture of him except in profile.

After about two years of living in our rented house, we decided it was time to buy one of our own. We were doing well financially, and were at the point where we could afford it. Richard and Iris Mallet had just built a nice-looking redwood and brick, three bedroom house with living room, kitchen den combination with pegged hardwood floors throughout, located in the Alberta City area of Tuscaloosa. It was on a cul-de-sac just off 31st Avenue East, called Third Place East. Richard worked for Alabama Power Company and built houses on the side. We bought the house and enjoyed living there for seven years, at which time, with the help of architect Howard White, we built another house at 1326 26th Avenue East in the Claymont subdivision, where we lived until 1995.

Now I'm going to back up to January of 1955. I had just graduated form the University. Carol had invited our families and friends to our apartment on Reed street for a celebration party, which I appreciated very much, and things couldn't have been better. That was her first experience at entertaining a large group of people, but she did a great job, just as I've seen her do many times since.

A week or so later we stopped at Sam McGee's Snappy Gulf Service Station at the end of Reed Street on University Boulevard to buy gas one Sunday afternoon. While we were there a 1948 Ford convertible with a black top came roaring in, stopping by the side of our car. In the convertible was a young looking whipper-snapper with a Ben Hogan cap on his crew-cut head proclaiming in a loud voice, "I'm Hank Holman from Ozark, Alabama, I'm in Tuscaloosa to start school at the University and work at a radio station, but right now I'm looking for a place to live. Do any of you know where I might find a room?" When I heard "radio" naturally I was curious. I asked "At which station will you be working?" I knew there was one chance in three it would be WNPT. Indeed it was. He was to report to work the next morning. As I learned later, he had been working for Bert Bank at his station in Tallassee, Al. Bert didn't need him in Tuscaloosa, so Hank had called Tom Todd at WNPT.

Carol and I took him down the street to Mrs. Bert Ward, to see if she had a room for him. She did not, but she knew of a neighbor who had a room. Hank moved in and started to school and to work with us the next day. By now you must be thinking, "What has all this to do with my story?" Since that day at the service station the lives and fortunes of the Price's and Holman's have been pretty much entwined.

Hank and I worked together at WNPT until October of 1955, when I got, by now, the famous draft notice. He inherited the Syrup Sopper show, not calling it that, when I left. Soon after, he decided to leave Tuscaloosa for advanced Military Officers training at Fort Benning because of the fear of losing his Lieutenant's rank in the Alabama National Guard if he did not.

It wasn't long after we met Hank that he brought a pretty little blond cutie from Ozark to see us, his high school sweetheart, named Janice Frush. The only problem with Jan was she didn't talk good English like us, being from California. Her father was an officer at Fort Rucker in Ozark. She was smart, about the size of a butterbean, and pretty as a puppy. I don't blame Hank for marrying her in May of that year. If you stay with me, you will read a lot more about Hank and Jan later.

Keith Barze, Joe Langston and I used to sit around and day dream about the possibility of starting our own radio station, but would always come to the same conclusion that the city could not support another station. There would never be more that the three AM and one FM stations that were currently on the air. We were very wrong.

In 1958 two new stations went on the air. First, there was WTUG, with an all "black" format, owned by the Roden Group from Jasper, and then on September 5, 1958, three fellows from Meridian, Mississippi, John Primm, Joe Carson and Eddy Holiday hit the local airwaves with a bang. Tuscaloosa's first and only "rock music" station was on the air. They ran a lot of give aways, and promotions, having a really good sound if you happened to like it, which very few people who bought the advertising did.

WACT (great call letters from Alabama Crimson Tide) had plenty of listeners but practically no advertisers. Remember we're talking 1958. Rock and roll was just getting started. A "pop" or "country" station would not be caught dead playing a "rock" record. Even Elvis Presley was off limits at that time. He had been refused an appearance on the Grand Ole' Opry, and anyone not good enough for them was certainly not going to be heard on the Syrup Sopper show.

WACT had been on the air for almost three years, having never shown a profit for even one month during that whole time, when I was approached by Eddy Holiday about the possibility of leaving WNPT, doing the Syrup Sopper show and replacing a lady named Jo Stevens as general manager at WACT. I told them the only way I would consider it would be if they let me share in the ownership of the station. After several trips to Meridian and much discussion between the three of them, with their attorney, accountant, and me, we reached an agreement that I would come to WACT with the same deal I had at WNPT plus an override of 5% on all profits and 24% of the stock which they would sell to me for $4000, but providing everything was satisfactory, and I remained with the station for a minimum of three years, the stock would be mine free and clear.

Throughout the negotiations I had informed Ruth Harris that I was talking with the Mississippi folks, but would keep her informed and would certainly give her adequate notice in case I decided to leave. Carson and Holiday did not want Jo Stevens to know they were talking to me, but of course she knew, being a good friend of Ruth's. On January 31,1961 I told Ruth that the deal at WACT was just too good to turn down and knowing my ultimate goal was ownership, I must take it. I offered to work a notice, a week, two weeks, or a month if she wanted me to. Her response was exactly what my own would have been under the circumstances, "If you are going you might as well go now."

I left WNPT, went home and started calling each one of my sponsors, telling them that in two days I would be on the air at the same time only on WACT at 1420 on the dial. I continued to make the calls all the next day and at 6:00 a.m. on February 2, 1961, Ground Hog Day, I was on the air at WACT.

I was so happy that every sponsor I had went with me. I told them all to be sure to call WNPT and cancel because their contracts were with the station and not me. Only one, Jimmy Harrison, at Central Drug said, "I'll stay on with them for a while, but start running us with you now."

The day I went to WACT, Jo Stevens went to work for Ruth Harris. The two of us never even saw each other during the transition. Having never been in the place before, I almost went into shock when I saw it. The station was located on 10th street, now Paul Bryant Drive, directly across from the University tennis courts, in one half of a duplex owned by Dr. Keller. His office was in the other half of the building. His mother had lived in the apartment, which was now the radio station, until she died. I never knew, or was afraid to ask, how Keller managed to find and rent the place to three men from Mississippi for a radio station.

The living room was the front office where Nan Basinger was the only person in bookkeeping and traffic, and my personal secretary. My office next door had been a bedroom. It had a worn wooden desk, a wood desk chair that I'd better not lean back in or it would turn over, a four drawer filing cabinet that was leaning so badly the drawers would not go all the way in and my personal filing cabinet was a wooden box about 2 1/2 feet long, with a lid that opened from the top, painted green. I have always kept that little box as a reminder of how it was then. Next to my office was the studio, another bedroom, Norm Beebe, the news man thought it was still a bedroom. That's where he entertained his many girlfriends late at night. Down the hall was the kitchen, which was now the control room, the heart of a radio station, where everything happens that goes on the air. We stored our records and supplies in the kitchen cabinets. We had very few country records because the station had programmed that other kind of music. I brought enough records from home until I could contact the record companies, telling them that WACT was now country and to please put us on their mailing lists for free records.

WACT was the only small radio station I've ever heard of with a full size bathroom, complete with a tub and shower, which would come in handy later on. The bath was located next to the control room. Finally, the back bedroom, the largest, was used as a sales office, and news room, with the old United Press wire service news machine running 24 hours a day.

That same room would be used in 1963 by ABC -TV and Radio news personnel as their headquarters for coverage of the infamous "stand in the school house door" by Governor George Wallace. Our station was only two blocks from Foster Auditorium where the prearranged "stand" took place. I'll have more about that later.

Chapter 10

TROUBLE IN T-TOWN

My transition from WNPT to WACT went very smoothly, with Syrup Sopper listeners willingly switching from 1230 to 1420 on their radio dials. That first day Jack Hamm signed on as usual at 4 a.m. I went on the air at 6 with what must have been a ragged program, not being familiar with the equipment and the all together different surroundings. For several days I mostly talked, not having very many "country" records. The best part was from the first day, and for the next twenty-nine years, until I sold it in 1990, the station was in the black because I had taken enough business with me to accomplish that. So many things happened in that twenty-nine years, some good, some bad. It would take me almost that long to write about them all, but my intention here is just to record some of the highlights.

The staff at WACT was very small, but quality was not lacking. Jack Hamm had been in Tuscaloosa radio in one way or the other since he returned from the navy at the end of WWII. Don Rollins, now with NBC in New York, was an excellent announcer but he had a problem. He knew nothing about country music and really didn't care to learn, but he stayed with me until I could complete the staff as I wanted it to be. Norm Beebe was one of the best news men I've ever known. He was great at covering and reporting news of all kinds, even riding with the sheriff's deputies at night going out in the county to destroy moonshine stills.

One event in particular, stands out. When President John F. Kennedy came to Huntsville to witness the first firing of the giant Saturn engine which would eventually take men to the moon, I told Norm he could go if he would bring back an interview with the President.

I will never know how a news man from a little old radio station in Tuscaloosa even managed to be anywhere around Kennedy, but Norm was standing right beside him and when the engine fired Mr. President said, "WOW!!" Norm came back, played the tape for me and said "Boss there's your interview."

As I said, he was a good news man, but he had so many personal problems I had to replace him before very long. A couple of years later, I had a call from the manager of WMAL-TV in Washington D.C. Norm had applied for the 6 p.m. news anchor position and given me as a reference. I told him "Norm is good. I hope he has his life straightened out by now. If not, he has three problems, alcohol, women and bad debts." The manager said, " He is so good I'm going to hire him anyway." I replied, "I hope you will." He did and Norm only managed to keep what has to be one of the best local TV jobs in America for six months. I never heard from him again. I wish him well.

Back to WACT personnel, Jerry Brophy, Eddy Holiday's brother-in-law was the only sales person beside myself. He was good, but before long he decided to go back to the Meridian station, WOKK. Jerry almost ruined my life. Being an avid golfer, he talked me into going with him one afternoon to the nine hole Meadowbrook course on Hargrove Road. That was the first golf I had actually played, and throughout my days since then I've enjoyed playing as my favorite form of recreation.

Do you remember the name Hank Holman? Well I did. Every time I thought about building a new staff at the station, his name kept popping up. Having lost contact with Hank for the past two years I started looking for him. Someone said he was working at WCOV-TV in Montgomery. I almost didn't even bother to contact him, thinking he's down there making all that big TV money. He'd laugh at the very suggestion that he come back to Tuscaloosa to work for me.

However, on a Sunday morning Carol, Wally, Ron and I went to Montgomery on what was pretended to be a social visit and maybe a good Sunday dinner. Jan served us some leftover shrimp creole. I'm thinking we have better stuff at home than this, he may not be getting rich in TV after all, I'll just mention that I am now at WACT. Hearing that, Hank said, "Do you need any help?" I said, "Well, I could use someone on the air and in sales. Do you know anyone you would recommend?" Hank said, "How about me?" I said, "There's no way I could afford you. You're making so much big television money, all I could pay you would be about $60 a week and commission on sales." Hank said "I'll take it."

Within the week Hank, Jan and two babies, Hank Jr. and Karen had moved to Tuscaloosa, and he was helping me make my WACT venture a success.

Hank and I were a good team. We both liked selling and both dearly loved to be on the air. I was on in the mornings and Hank in the late afternoon. We came up with some really innovative ideas in programming. Having no mobile unit for remote broadcasting, we had Howard Smith our engineer build a wooden box, mount a turntable on top and with a small amplifier and microphone, Hank was on the air from the front yard of the station with the "Going Home Show." As I said before, we were on a heavily traveled street, so the slogan to passing motorists was "Honk at Hank." Most of them did. And he had a great view of the female students playing tennis at the courts across the street.

The only hotel in town at that time was the Stafford, a seven story building with dining and banquet space for several hundred people. The Stafford was built, during the two years I was away, as a community project, paid for by selling stock to local folks. Just about everything that happened in Tuscaloosa took place at the Stafford, civic club luncheons, meetings, parties, meals in the dining room and certainly anybody that was anybody from out of town stayed at the Stafford.

We started a daily, Monday through Friday, radio program called "Breakfast at the Stafford." 9-10 a.m. From the dining room of the hotel. Hank was the host, along with Tappy Folts, wife of a university professor and a well known personality, interviewing guests having breakfast. Most of the time the guests were booked in advance to have a cup of coffee a Krispy Kreme donut and be on the radio, talking about whatever the topic happened to be for that day.

Other hosts throughout the years included Joanne Walker, Martha Ellen Johnson and The Rev. Robert Spence, now

President of Evangel College in Springfield, Missouri. We had a phone installed at the table so listeners could call in and ask the guests questions.

The staff of the Hotel, especially the desk clerks, were alert to any celebrities checking in, and there were a lot of them, considering the Stafford being the only place for visiting speakers and entertainers at the University to stay. There were always plenty of local, state and national politicians anxious to be guests on the show. Just a few of our guests included Governor George Wallace, movie actor Jack Palance, U. S. Senators, and Congressmen, county and city politicians, sports personalities, visiting coaches in town for games with Alabama, one of the most interesting being the late coach Adolf Rupp, basketball coach from the University of Kentucky.

Late one afternoon we got a call from the Hotel informing us that Mr. H. L. Hunt Senior had checked in. It seemed he was traveling through Alabama, having never seen his Hunt Oil Co. refinery here, and decided to stay overnight. Hank immediately called his room and talking with his aide, arranged to tape an interview with Mr. Hunt that night in his room.

I told Hank, "I'm going with you. I've never seen a billionaire." Of course, Hank hadn't either. Not knowing what to expect, we took our Ampex 601 recorder, an hour long tape, and a speaker and went to Mr. Hunt's room. Our first surprise, he was not in a suite of rooms with a bunch of people around. Instead, he had two adjoining rooms, a male companion secretary, and a pretty, much younger woman than himself, who was his fifth wife. At that time Mr. Hunt was in his 80s.

He was a large man, with thin grey hair, a pleasant, friendly face and voice as he welcomed Hank and me into the room. The first thing I noticed about him was something I had never heard or read about one of the richest men in the world. When he began to speak, he stuttered. It was more of a hesitation in his speech than a Mel Tillis type of stutter. He would start to speak, his head slightly bobbing up and down, his tongue seemingly tied, hesitating for several seconds, but when he got going he could talk all right.

Before the interview, he handed Hank two lists, one the things he would talk about, and the other, things he would not talk about. Among things he would talk about was politics, but he would not talk about money, which, of course, was what we were there for. Who could interview H. L. Hunt and not talk about money?

Before long, due to Hank's skill at interviewing, the lists had been discarded and they were talking about how Mr. Hunt had bought his first oil lease in Arkansas for $50, struck oil, and begun to accumulate one of the world's largest private fortunes. Hank asked him, "Mr. Hunt how much money do you have?" His reply after a pause was "I don't really know. Besides, if I did, by the time I got through telling you, there would be so much more the figure would not be right anyway." He went on to say, "A man with $250,000 is just as wealthy as one with $250,000,000. A man with $250,000 can own a nice home, a car, plenty to eat and a pretty wife, after that it's only bookkeeping." Remember that was in 1962. He would probably have to revise his numbers now. Another key question was, "Mr. Hunt what would you personally like to be remembered for?" He said, "I would like to be remembered for the No Third Term Amendment to the constitution of the United States, limiting the president to only two terms in office. That's mine, I bought and paid for it myself, my greatest accomplishment." We didn't ask who he paid, one can only guess. He did express his very strong conservatism and his dislike for President Roosevelt's new deal and the ever increasing size of the government.

When the interview was over, he said he would like to listen to the tape. As it ran, he sat with his eyes closed listening intently, then after the hour was over, the old man made a statement I will never forget. He looked at Hank and said, "I'd give anything in the world if I could talk like you do." In the elevator on the way down I told Hank, "That should be a lesson to both of us. That old man has the money to buy anything in the world he wants except the one thing he wants most, and that's the ability to speak."

In 1961, before the advent of specialized programming with all news and talk formats as we know them today, an hour of nothing but talk from 9-10 a.m. was unheard of, but it worked for us and really helped promote WACT, and fulfilled, to a great extent, our public affairs obligation. Hank and I developed a number of new programs and promotions which I will discuss later, not the least of which was "Ask the Authority." That program deserves it's own chapter.

I titled this section "Trouble in T-Town" because my intention was to get right into the subject of integration, not only of the University, but the entire community.

In 1956 an attempt was made to integrate the University of Alabama by a young lady, Autherine Lucy. I was in New Jersey at the time, but I still remember picking up a copy of Life Magazine containing a big spread about Tuscaloosa, the University, riots and big trouble in my adopted home town. That attempt at integration failed, but everyone, including our little governor, George Wallace, who preached segregation now and segregation forever, knew that segregation had to end soon. We returned to Tuscaloosa in 1957, in time to witness some of the most frightening times one can imagine. The KKK with it's Grand Dragon, Bobby Shelton, was very active with rallies, cross burnings, and hanging Negroes in effigy. There was a complete feeling of unrest in the community. The other side was marching, conducting sit-ins at lunch counters, and theatres, worship-ins at previously all white churches, strikes and boycotts of local businesses.

Almost all of it would eventually culminate in the now famous and much ballyhooed "stand in the school house door" by George Wallace.

It seemed at the time WACT and my staff were always involved in the situation, regardless of whether we chose to be or not. By that time, my buddy Joe Langston from WNPT days had come to work for me at WACT. Captain Hank Holman was company commander of the Northport National Guard unit, leaving for summer camp at Fort McClellan on Sunday before the stand in the door only to return to Tuscaloosa on Tuesday.

As I learned later, orders to return had already been cut when they arrived at camp.

As a member of the local chamber of commerce and owner, manager of WACT I was involved in the entire situation. Our town was full and running over with network TV and radio personnel, journalists from the world over, Klansmen, White Supremacists, NAACP, SCLC and hundreds of on-lookers. Our radio station was located only two blocks from Foster Auditorium, where the stand was to take place.

Foster was not a school house, but an auditorium, gymnasium combination used for student registration for the summer quarter. As the day approached, the day for the Governor's stand in the door, conditions were at a fever pitch. Automobile traffic through the University was completely shut off, and all streets in and out were barricaded.

One night Joe and I attended a Klan rally at the gym of Holt High School, just outside of Tuscaloosa. It was an event staged especially for the national news media (all of the major networks, ABC, NBC and CBS had TV crews there). The rally, sponsored by the KKK featured such "noted" speakers as Birmingham's police chief "Bull" Connor and others.

The leaders of the city, mayor, council and civic leaders Frank Moody, Lewis Manderson, Charlie Snider C. J. Hartley and George LeMaistre called a public meeting one afternoon at the Stafford Hotel, the week before the Tuesday that Wallace was to "stand in the door." They presented a petition which in effect said to Governor Wallace.

"Stay in Montgomery, We don't need you here. Your presence and protest will only serve to heighten tensions." A vote was called on the petition, with at least 90% of the attendees standing and voting in favor, but when it was passed around for signatures, only about 15 people actually signed it. I was one of them, and you know, the Klan distributed to their members that list of signees. I had threatening telephone calls . They tried to organize a boycott of our advertisers, but got nowhere with it. On that morning June 11, 1963, I witnessed Governor George Wallace standing on the front steps of Foster

139

Auditorium surrounded by hundreds of national guardsmen, state troopers, sheriff's deputies and university security as Nickolas Katzenbach, Assistant U.S. Attorney General, escorting James Hood and Vivian Malone, demanded they be allowed to register and attend the University.

He let George make his little prepared speech, then General Graham ordered him to step aside and let the students in, which he did.

Shakespeare could not have written a better play for a southern demagogue than the performance of all the participants that morning. I have always maintained the entire event was prearranged between the Kennedy brothers, President Jack and Attorney General Bobby and Wallace. He would stand in the door to fulfill a political promise, make his speech, and move aside right on cue, just as his own National Guard arrived to force him into submission. The Governor was not only a great politician, his followers believed him all the way. He was an excellent actor.

For years after the so called stand, if I mentioned anything on the radio like that, there would always be some little old lady, that Wallace had deceived, calling to say "Well he tried." During that time the security people did a great job of sealing off the campus and preventing trouble such as had occurred just before that at 'Ole Miss. I'll describe one more incident, then I'll move on. On Monday night Joe Langston and I were at the radio station when we received a call from Col. Floyd Mann, the State Public Safety Director, asking us to come out to Mary Burke Hall, a ladies' dormitory on campus. We had to walk in the dark to the place where we were met by Mann and several officers. They led us to a room where they had set up two beds and on the beds were dozens of hand guns, shotguns, rifles, bayonets, machetes, knives and even a hay hook.

The officers had been stopping and searching suspicious-looking people and cars headed for Tuscaloosa. Those weapons were a sample of what they had confiscated. It was scary just thinking about what could have happened.

On the way back to the station it was even darker. I'm sure

Joe and I must have held hands, expecting an attacker to jump out from behind every tree. My, how times and events have changed not only in Tuscaloosa, but the entire south since those terrible days. And, I must say, " for the better."

Thank goodness!!, all of that was becoming history and we could get on with the business of running a radio station. Joe, Hank and I worked together for a while before Keith Barze hired Joe away from us to anchor the news on WBRC-TV. I was very proud of Joe. We began making plans to move the studios to a better and more suitable location.

Do you remember my experience at Vinemont school, the night I danced with Polly. Well, Hank was working the Saturday afternoon shift at the station, all alone in the building, when he had a pain. He grabbed a long play record, put it on the turntable, ran down the hall to the bathroom that I described earlier, but didn't make it. He left a trail all the way down the hall.

After stripping off his clothes, he took a shower, but had nothing clean to put on. He called Jan at home telling her his predicament and to bring him some clothes. She said "You've got the car." He said "Do something." Jan put some clothes in a brown grocery bag, called a cab, and told the driver to deliver the bag to the back door of WACT on 10th street, knock on the door and place the bag in the hand that will reach for it, from behind the door, and don't ask any questions.

In the meantime Hank is playing records and talking on the radio, buck naked, hoping no one will come by. Finally the mysterious knock on the back door. Hank barely opened it, reaching around as the cab driver placed the bag in his hand. I've often wondered if the driver looked to see what was in the bag or if he is still wondering what he delivered to WACT that day. A footnote concerning Hank and Jan, by that time they had FIVE babies, two in one year. There was Hank Jr., Karen, Carol, Paige and Patricia. They used to come to our house with all five stacked like cordwood in the back seat of the VW Beatle.

We had a wonderful old black maid and babysitter named Lilly. Jan and the kids came over one day while Lilly was there.

141

When she left, Lilly said "Miss Carol, them babies show is close together, ain't they?" Carol replied, "They really are, she had two in one year." Lilly said, "That Miss Holman ought to get her a DIAGRAM." We've kidded Jan about that.

Chapter 11

THE NINETEEN SIXTIES

In the early 60s Hank Holman and I were searching for ways to promote WACT, in fact, I made a fun type "rule" that every member of the staff come to work each day with an idea for a contest or promotion. Out of that came the "Breakfast at the Stafford" program, as mentioned earlier, the "Going Home Show" and the most successful and long-running program of all, "Ask the Authority."

We ran contests, give-a-ways, stunts, such as, the race from our studios downtown through the University campus and ending at Druid City Hospital, a distance of about three miles. It was not an ordinary race. Hank rode a bicycle and I drove a tractor from the Ford Tractor Company. In the late afternoon, heavy traffic, Hank, the rabbit on the bicycle ran away from me, the tortoise on the tractor. But, when we made it to the east side of campus, on University Boulevard, going up the hill past Fort Brandon Armory, I caught and passed him just before the finish line, proving once and for all a man on a tractor is faster than a boy on a bicycle.

There was the hot summer day we put 1000 pounds of ice from Tuscaloosa Ice Company in the parking lot of Leland Shopping Center and invited listeners to come to the Center, guess the exact time the ice would melt, and become eligible to win prizes. The Center merchants liked the extra traffic that little contest drew for them.

A really important innovation at the time was our buying a mobile unit for remote broadcasting. Our first "ACTion Wagon" was a converted Volkswagen bus, equipped with a Marti transmitter, turntables for playing records, a console and outside speakers. On the top it had a yellow flashing light to indicate we were on the air and to draw attention. We used it for remote broadcasts from the locations of sponsors, such as car dealers, shopping centers, grand openings, sporting events and political rallies. It was also used for covering news "as it

143

happened" and it really made Hank's Going Home Show mobile. He could not only talk about traffic, he was part of it.

Just about every radio station in the country has mobile units of some kind or other now, but in 1965, ours was quite unique, drawing crowds just to see us broadcast and to get a free coke or whatever we were giving away on that particular day.

In 1967 our license for WACT-FM was granted. I purchased all new equipment, including a new Gates transmitter and a 300 foot tower, previously owned by my friend and former boss Tom Todd for his small TV cable company, for $500. We began simulcasting our FM and AM, except at night because the AM was designated as "daytime" only meaning we had to sign off at sundown.

At that time there were still very few FM radios in homes and practically none in cars. It was hard to sell FM because there were just not many listeners. Therefore, most FM broadcasters only programmed continuous music, no news or commercials. Shortly after WACT-FM went on the air the Tuscaloosa American Legion Post 34 baseball team, coached by my friends Jerry Belk and the late Jones Tubbs, won the local, state, regional, and finally the national championship. We broadcast all games live on the FM. By the time the team got to the World Series in Oklahoma City, every FM radio in Tuscaloosa had been sold and people were calling the station trying to find where they could buy one. It was great for the promotion of FM.

I made a really big mistake when I applied for the FM license. There are three classifications of stations, classes A, B, and C based on power and coverage. A class A station has a maximum power of 3000 watts, class B 50,000 and a class C up to 100,000. Thinking that 3000 watts would provide ample coverage of our trade area, and the more power the more expensive to purchase and operate the equipment, I short sightedly applied for a class A license. No one at that time, certainly not me, could look ahead twenty years and predict the dominance of FM over AM and the 100,000 watt regional stations covering half the state or more.

Most of the class C operators did not turn on that much power due to the expense. However, about 1980 the FCC ruled that they must increase power to the maximum and install 1200 foot towers or more. Most broadcasters complained, but that ruling was the best thing that ever happened to them. As I said, it created the super stations, and in just a few years made them worth millions on the market. I figured that if I had asked for a class C license in 1966, instead of a class A, WACT-FM would have sold for three or four time what I sold it for in 1990. Oh well, that was not the first and certainly not the last mistake I ever made.

There were so many things going on at the same time in the lives of the Prices it would be impossible to record them all in chronological order, so, if I seem to wander, please forgive. I will try to cover as much as I can, realizing some of the dates and times may not be exactly correct. Besides, I am not a professional writer and have not had very many New York publishers knocking on my door as yet, but I'll try to put it down so that it may make some sense, if you just hang in there with me.

Things were going well at the station. We were having fun, doing what we liked best, visiting with the friends and neighbors in "radio land," selling and servicing our advertisers and becoming an important part of our community. We were making money and paying our debts. What else could one ask?

I always encouraged the staff to become involved in the community, working with civic and charitable organizations as well as the church. I was involved in the Civitan Club, as President and District Governor. Later, due to meeting schedules, I joined the Tuscaloosa Exchange Club, serving as President in 1972. At one time or the other I served on the board of directors of the YMCA, Chamber of Commerce, Ad Club, Tuscaloosa Country Club, Stafford Hotel, and was very active in the Alberta Baptist Church.

Carol and I both enjoyed our many years of membership in the Alabama Broadcasters Association. Through that organization we created many lasting friendships with in the

Alabama radio and television community. There were so many friends I would not attempt to name them because I would surely leave some out. I served as President of the Association in 1972, and in 1974 was honored to be named Broadcaster of the Year in Alabama.

I was kept very busy performing as master of ceremonies at banquets and other events, too numerous to mention. I was much in demand, I suppose not because I was so good, but I worked cheaply. There were a couple of conventions I still remember very clearly.

One was a convention of the Alabama Nurses Association at the Stafford Hotel. The ballroom was arranged in typical banquet style, round tables, with a long elevated head table about three feet above the main floor. With me at the head table were officers of the state association, the main speaker, a Dr. Hodges from Birmingham, who incidentally had been elected that day as President of the Alabama Medical Association at their convention in Mobile.

At the very end of the table was the local nurse who had been in charge of the arrangements for the meeting, including hiring me. It would be difficult to describe her, but to say she was over weight would not do her justice. She was a very nice sweet lady with oodles of personality, about as big around as she was tall, what papa would call "short and stocky".

Everything was going real well. After the invocation and some brief remarks, we enjoyed our usual roast beef, mashed potatoes and English peas, followed by my introduction of Dr. Hodges. He made a very inspiring speech, if one cared about nursing and doctoring, which I didn't at the time, thinking I would never need their services. How wrong I was, as you will learn later.

When the good doctor finished his talk, I got up to thank him and wish everyone a good night. When I was just about to say something, I heard a voice coming from my right and noise sounding like "tromp, tromp, tromp, tromp. Looking around I saw it was our heavy hostess making her way from the end of the table to the microphone, while saying "Wait a minute Syrup

Sopper, don't adjourn yet. I want to say something." Naturally, I stepped aside to make room as she pulled the mike down to her level and exclaimed, "Dr. Hodges, from the heart of my bottom I want to express my appreeeeeeeiiii," realizing what she had said she almost fainted. Totally embarrassed, she went back to her seat, leaving me standing there.

The audience fell into a deep silence. No one said a word, they were feeling her pain. I had to say something fast, so, I said the first thing that popped in my mind, "Honey, if your heart is as big as your bottom, that's a whole heap of appreciation." That broke the silence. The crowd had a good laugh and everyone left smiling except her, I'm sure. Needless to say I was never invited back to the state nurses convention.

Another gathering at the Stafford was the state convention of the Rural Letter Carriers of Alabama. They had hired me to be their emcee and my big buddy Harry "Buckshot" Blevins, along with his band, to play for an after dinner dance. It came time for the dance, and even though the lights were lowered and music was good, nobody was dancing. After several songs were played and still no dancing, I got on the mike and said, "It's obvious ya'll don't want to dance. Buckshot and I are here on your nickel, what do you want to do?" Somebody said "Let's sing." I said "Sing what?" Someone else said "Sing hymns." I said "OK if that's what you want. Buck can the band play them?" He said "Man we can play anything." Having no hymnbooks we sang everything we could remember, like "Amazing Grace," "When the Roll is Called Up Yonder," "The Old Rugged Cross" and others. We all had a good time, but that was the only dance I've ever heard of that turned into a hymn singing.

Harry "Buckshot" Blevins, from now on I'll simply call him Buck or Buckshot, few people actually knew his name, was one of the most likeable, talented, extraordinary individuals I've ever known. He was a great entertainer, emcee, singer, musician, disc jockey, promoter and a wonderful person who not only worked for me, but was my friend.

Ruth Harris at WNPT had hired him from a station in

Birmingham, to be her early morning man, to compete against The Syrup Sopper for the early morning audience, and I must admit he was pretty strong competition.

When Hank left to work for the new television station WCFT-TV, remembering Buck had indicated that he was not really happy at WNPT, I called and offered him a job at WACT doing our afternoon show. He accepted immediately. I had a new right arm. Like with Hank, Buckshot and I made a good team, Syrup Sopper in the morning and Buckshot in the afternoon. Buck was in the army about the same time I was, only he was in what they called "Special Services" because of his musical abilities, stationed at Third Army Headquarters, Fort McPherson, Georgia.

His duty was to front the country music army band called the Circle A Wranglers, traveling over the country entertaining troops and recording recruiting programs for the army. Some well known country artists spent time with the band including Faron Young and Roger Miller. According to Buck, a judge had given Roger Miller a choice between the army or jail for stealing a guitar. He chose the army. Buck let him join the band and they became lifelong friends. The day Buck died, Roger called me from California for details, after hearing about it on the radio.

Buckshot Blevins was the perfect country deejay. He knew the music and the performers, some personally, was a good "on the air" salesman and most of all, his audience loved him. He organized and managed a fine country band, playing every Saturday night at the Jaycee fairgrounds park exhibit hall and on special occasions such as grand openings, mobile home shows and remote broadcasts for the radio station.

Buckshot was the only person I've ever known that actually ate himself to death. When he was discharged from the army, he weighed 175 pounds, but by the time he came to WACT I would estimate he had gained to more that 250. It seemed that his weight just exploded. Eating constantly, he would bring large bags of potato chips, jugs of pickled eggs, cucumber pickles, pickled pig's feet, sometimes some of each with him when he reported for his 3 P.M. show. He would eat while on the air indifferent to my warning him about it. He gained so much weight, he couldn't drive the Action Wagon, could not sit in an ordinary chair, requiring me to buy specially built chairs for the control room. He was obviously short of breath, breathing hard and chomping away while on the air.

I talked to him about it so many times, finally saying "Buck, you are killing yourself eating. Bring no more food into the radio station, and above all no more eating while you are doing your show from 3-6 p.m.." He complied but I began to notice that he would park his car in the station lot, but before coming in, would go to the back, open the trunk, and stand there for several minutes.

One day I just happened to stroll past his car and saw that he was punching food into his mouth with both hands. He had so much junk food in the trunk of his car he could have started a small grocery store. Buck would get up in the morning, eat a big breakfast his wife Sue had fixed for him, then go to his mother's over on Orange Street, eat another breakfast, then to Garners restaurant downtown for another, all before coming to work. The process was reversed at lunchtime. He was as addicted to food as an alcoholic to booze or an addict to drugs. He just could not control his appetite.

At the insistence of Dr. John Todd, he tried one time to lose weight, checking into a hospital in Birmingham for 10 days. They put him on a no-calorie diet. He lost 50 pounds. The first week all they fed him was one lemon. Buck told me "I swallowed that lemon whole I was so hungry." That was all to no avail, he gained the lost weight right back.

The week before my mama died on Saturday night I had asked Buck to stop by my office. My mind was made up, something had to be done and the only solution I knew was to let him go, especially since his work had become so bad, not only the eating but he had started falling asleep on the air. Buck came in the office that morning, tried to sit in a chair, only one "cheek" would fit.

As we talked about his wife, Sue, divorcing him, how he

hated being so large, but just could not control his appetite, I knew I could not do what I had intended to do. Buck said "What did you want to see me about?" I said, "Oh, nothing in particular, just wanted to see and talk to you awhile."

Mama died on Saturday night, her funeral was on Tuesday, I returned to the office on Wednesday. Buckshot came by that morning looking so bad, his face almost purple, I said, "Buck you don't look good at all, come on I'm going to take you to a doctor." He said "I don't feel good, but I can drive myself over to Dr. Todd's office." I told him, "Don't waste any time, get on over there as soon as you can." He left the station, but as I found out later he never went to the doctor, instead he went to his mother's house and went to bed. About 3:30 the next morning I got a call from Morgan Brown at Memory Chapel Funeral Home informing me that my buddy, Buckshot, had died. He was 31.

At the time I was part owner of the funeral home, so the family depended on me to help them with the funeral arrangements. Buck was so large, we had to special order an oversize casket from Birmingham Casket Company. Cement Products Company said to make a vault that large would be cost prohibitive, so I decided to have my friend and advertiser, Rufus King, the cabinet King make a wooden box that would serve as a vault. After all that's what people used to do.

I called Rufus and asked if he could build a cemetery box? He said, "How big is one?" I said, "A regular size is 30 inches wide, but I need one 44 inches. Rufus said, "What the hell are you gonna bury, a mule?" I said, "No, Buckshot." He built the box, the funeral was the following Saturday. I loved big Buck.

When I was a student, I had bowled a few games at Red Swanson's Bama Bowling Lanes on University Boulevard, where he still used "pin boys" to reset the pins. When I returned to Tuscaloosa in 1957, a brand new bowling alley, Leland Lanes, had been built in Alberta City with automatic pin setters, creating a lot of interest in bowling. I decided to sponsor a team, The Syrup Soppers, which in 1961 became team WACT. We bowled one time a week in league play, and if I do say so we were pretty good, winning several league championships.

Bowlers on the team were Ray Boozer from Boozer Motor Co, Hale Armistead from Armistead Brothers Supermarket, Joe Hendricks, a postman, Dr. John Todd, physician and me, with Stan Stanczyk, State Geologist, as a substitute.

When I left for the army, one of my sponsors was Quality Motors, owned by George Fowler and Ade Faulkner, located at the corner of Greensboro Avenue and 14th street. When I returned, they had moved to Northport and the corner was occupied by Boozer Motor Company, owned by John Boozer and his brother Ray.

Even before I got around to calling on them for advertising, Ray called and asked me to stop by and talk to him about it. That call was the beginning of a long relationship, both in business and pleasure. Our families have been friends since that meeting in 1957, going on numerous vacations, to football games, golf tournaments and just visiting in each others homes. Ray and Gail Boozer have three children, Tanya, Trent, and Todd almost the same ages as our Wally and Ron.

One of our most memorable trips was to Disney World the first year it opened. Our two families, along with Billy and Mary Angelyn Tinsley, their four children Angelyn, Peggy, Eddy and Joe, Bill and Martha Strickland and their two, George and Lea, Guy and Beverly Elmore along Lee, Laura and Kevin loaded the cars and drove to Orlando, checked into the Polynesian Village and stayed three days and four nights.

When we arrived, I don't know whose eyes "bugged" out the most, the grown-ups or the kids. None of us had ever imagined a place so wonderful. All old folks like me like to compare prices of things then and now. Here's one. The first, second and third years the group went to Disney World, they had a family package, including room, two meals a day, tickets to the Magic Kingdom and all the golf you could play at the two courses, the Magnolia and the Palm for only $268.

Today, admission to the park is more than that for a three day pass per person. My purpose here is not to try to describe Disney World, but if you have been there, you can imagine our reaction to the wonders the first time we saw it.

Ray Boozer came to Tuscaloosa from a small town, Rainsville, on Sand Mountain in Northeast Alabama. He and Gail had gone to college at Jacksonville State University, then moved here to go into the automobile business with John.

Just before the 1963 bowling season was to begin, Ray said to me, "I've got an old buddy here in Tuscaloosa from up on the mountain that likes to bowl, could we use him this year?" Dr. Todd had told me he was too busy to continue on a regular basis, so I told Ray to bring his friend on out, which he did. That was how I met Leroy McAbee.

Leroy was from Route 3, Henagar, Alabama, and a classmate of Gail Boozer's at Sylvania High School. He too had been in the army, going to Korea for almost three years. After his discharge, he enrolled at the University, majoring in mechanical engineering, on the G I bill. If anyone ever went to the University poorer than I was, it was Leroy, but I tell him he had it easy "The Government" was paying him to go. We had a good time bowling together, but that was only the beginning of a long and cherished friendship that is still strong today.

While in school Leroy rented a small mobile home just off campus and before he realized what was happening two other good old mountain boys, Morrell and Reese, had moved in with him. He worked some odd jobs, one of which was selling cars for John and Ray Boozer.

As he tells it, he was driving down Broad Street one day and noticing a cute little blond strutting down the sidewalk, said to himself, "I'm going to marry that girl." I'm not familiar with every detail. All I know is that in just a short time, Babe Ruth Barger and Leroy McAbee were married. His buddies refused to leave the trailer, so Leroy and his bride Ruth had to find another place.

Over the past more than thirty years Carol and I have spent more time with Ruth and Leroy than anyone outside of our immediate family. Hardly a week goes by that we don't visit or go out to eat with them. We have traveled so much together that when Carol and I go alone we always comment about how much we miss them.

A few years ago we chartered a twin engine plane, large enough to carry fishing gear and luggage for Carol and Ruth to last a week, and flew to Lake Okeechobee, Florida. Leroy had heard how the big bass were jumping in the boat down there. The deal was, he would pay for the plane, I'd pay for the rental car while we were there and we'd split all of the other expenses. We stayed at a small motel in Okeechobee.

I didn't know that he had already made arrangements for two bass speed boats and guides from a supplier of fishing equipment and such. By the time we were ready to go fishing early the next morning, we had bought more equipment and buckets of large minnows, met our individual guides before sun-up and headed for the lake in the guide's pickup truck.

I think that must have been the coldest January morning ever recorded in central Florida. Carol and I got in that boat, the guide driving, and when he left the dock he was running all 225 horsepower of engine wide open. As we left, my mouth flew open and I couldn't close it till we finally stopped about five miles later. I looked at Carol, she was turning blue from the cold, and catching bugs between her teeth just as I was. When he stopped the boat, he said "O.K. lets catch some fish." I said we're going to have to wait until the sun comes up and thaws me out so I can move my hands. I'm frozen stiff.

After sunup, we fished all morning catching a few bass, but the thing I could not understand was, when I caught the first one he took it off the line and threw it back in the lake. I said, "Man, what are you doing? That was a keeper; why'd you throw it back?" He said, "Here at Okeechobee we practice catch and release." And I said, "Where I come from we practice catch and eat. Don't you do that anymore." But he did, we would catch and he would release.

We went back to the marina for lunch at the same speed we had run before daylight, not quite as cold, and by that time he had wrapped Carol in his emergency rain gear but when I tried to step out of the boat onto the floating peer my legs wouldn't work, from being so cold and sitting in the boat for about five hours. The dock tilted, almost throwing me in the lake. It would have if I hadn't fallen on all fours and held on.

After lunch we went back for more fishing, but about 2 p.m. I asked the guide what his normal hours were. He said he had to quit at 4 p.m. I said, "It's two hours till your quitting time, so while you are on my time let's head back at a slower speed." He cranked the boat and roared back to the marina just as before covering 5 miles in no more than 5 minutes. The next time we go to Florida, we're taking winter clothes.

That day, with the help of the guide, Carol and I, mostly Carol caught 26 bass, but we came home with nothing to show for it. We had thrown them all back for somebody else to eat later. What really broke my heart was, I found out when we settled up the expenses, that I had been paying a dollar apiece for the minnows. I told Leroy, "We should have eaten the minnows."

The next day we rented a small pontoon boat from a local fellow and went crappie fishing, catching only two. We felt so sorry for them we threw them back in the lake too. After several hours of crappie fishing, Carol and Ruth started complaining about needing to go to the bathroom. Since we were at least a mile from shore, the only thing for them to do was hang over the back rail of that little old pontoon boat like two crows on a limb. They raised the level of Lake Okeechobee considerably.

The McAbees and Prices have eaten in some of the strangest places, high classed, high priced and low classed, high priced, but the most low classed has to be a place out in the country from Okeechobee.

It was located about twenty miles out of town on a highway that runs beside the lake. We were just driving late one afternoon when about suppertime we noticed a small frame building with a sign in front that read "Our Place Restaurant". Leroy was driving, so he wheeled into the unpaved vacant parking lot and said, "We're going to get some fine country cooking".

You can bet that when you enter a restaurant at suppertime and nobody's in there but the waitress, something is wrong. She said "Y'all set any where you'ens want to."

We all ordered steak, knowing it would be hard to mess up a grilled piece of meat. We were wrong. The steak was as tough as shoe leather, and about as thin. The salad tasted like pure vinegar. The black eyed peas tasted like kerosene. The strangest thing, during the time we were trying to eat, we kept hearing all sorts of noises, clanging and banging, coming from the direction of the kitchen. I asked the waitress what it was and she replied, "Oh that's just daddy the cook, washing the pots and pans."

After a while, just as we were about to leave, "daddy" came out of the kitchen, to speak to his only customers. He had a very bad hair lip and speech impediment, wanting to know if we enjoyed our meal. We lied, saying it was fine. He suggested we try his cocoanut pie, everyone declined except Ruth. She ordered it and as the other three waited while she dawdled over it, I said, "Ruth, if you don't hurry up, we're going to leave you." Daddy said, "Don't leave that blund headed woman wi me. I ain't takin' her to my house, my cat wooden eben like her." Since that day, every time I get in an argument with her I tell Ruth, "My cat wouldn't eben like you."

Another trip was to Las Vegas. At a Mexican restaurant, Leroy ordered chili. The waitress brought him the typical Mexican variety, so thick he could stand his spoon up in it. He called her over and told her to take it back to the kitchen and have them put some "pot licker" in it. The little Mexican waitress had no idea what he was talking about.

When it was time to leave Las Vegas, neither of us were ready to fly straight home. We rented a station wagon, loaded the ton of luggage that Carol and Ruth had taken along and headed south. We stopped for the night at a pretty little town, Lake Havasu, Arizona where the famous London Bridge is now located.

The next day, after Leroy and I had played golf we drove on to Phoenix and Scottsdale. Leroy and I played thirty-six holes of golf at the McCormack Ranch (both eighteen hole courses) while the women shopped. We flew home from Phoenix the following day.

The time that Leroy and I went to Vegas without the women, we discovered the shopping mall called The Forum Shops between the Mirage and Cesar's Palace Hotels. We entered a men's clothing store, just looking around for nothing in particular. The only other person in the store was a sharp-looking Yankee dude, the salesman for the evening. Leroy took a sports jacket off a rack, put it on and looked in the mirror to admire himself. He said, "Hey, this looks pretty good, Syrup Sopper, what do you think?" I said, "Yeah, I like that, looks good on you." He said to the clerk, "Lad, how much is this jacket?" The reply was, 1995. Leroy said, "Man, that's a bargain. I pay more than that at J.C. Penny's." The man said," That's $1,995.00." I've never seen a jacket go back on a rack as fast. He asked about the prices of the suits and was told, "They start at $3500." Leroy asked, "Lad, do you ever sell any of them? He was told that they indeed do sell a lot of them. We became friends with the clerk and went back the next two nights. Leroy finally got the price of the jacket down to $1100 if he paid cash. When he still would not buy it, I told him, "I'll bet you've some coats in your closet at home that Ruth paid more than that for." The last night we were there, feeling obligated to buy something since we'd taken so much of the dude's time, Leroy bought a $250 shirt and I paid $150 for a tie, the cheapest thing in the store.

As we were leaving the men's store I remembered it was Carol's birthday, and told Leroy I'd better find her a gift. We went into a jewelry store, again the only customers, being greeted by a beautiful, tall, lady with her blond hair pulled back and up on the top of her head, the longest reddest fingernails I'd ever seen and fingers loaded with diamonds and bracelets on her wrists. When I looked at those hands I knew right away, they had never picked cotton. She greeted us with a great big smile and asked if she could help us. Leroy said, "Yes, Ma'am, my old buddy, the Syrup Sopper here, needs to buy his wife a birthday present."

As she took the keys and began to open the show cases, she was asking what kind of jewelry my wife liked, rings, bracelet, necklaces, or ear rings . I said, " Oh, she'll like anything, just as long as I remember her birthday." The lady said, "You are in luck, I have some very nice pieces on sale, how do you like this diamond bracelet? It's only $30,000 tonight." I said, "She's already got one of them." After I turned down the $25,000 ring and the $40,000 diamond necklace, with similar excuses, she reached back in the case and brought out a pair of earrings, saying, "Here's something I know she doesn't have. They are one of a kind." They were sorta pretty, shaped like a poke salad leaf with a big black pearl in the center. She said, "These are also on sale. I know your wife will just love them. Their regular price is $15,000 but tonight I can let you have them for only $12,000, plus tax. I looked at Leroy and said, " You know what? I think I'll go back and get her that Las Vegas tee shirt we looked at a while ago."

Neither of us had ever seen a beautiful woman cramming expensive jewelry back in the case and locking it up so fast. I learned one thing from that experience. When they call jewelry "pieces" it's going to be expensive.

I apologize for jumping so far ahead of myself, that trip was in 1996, but I thought I'd better tell you about it before I forgot. Now, lets go back to the sixties.

When Leroy graduated with a degree in mechanical engineering, he, along with his brother Harold, started a small shop on River Hill just off Broad Street in Tuscaloosa. From that small beginning McAbee Construction Company Inc. has grown to be one of the largest industrial and mechanical companies in the country. Put your finger on a map of the United States and some foreign countries, including the Soviet Union, and it will be near a place where they have done a job, are doing a job or will be, before very long. There is more I could say about the company, but I'll save that for Leroy to write someday when I can convince him to do it.

There are so many things I like about LeRoy, not the least of which is his ability to run a large company, with hundreds of employees who would kill for him, be involved in more civic work than anyone I've known, be a good husband and father to Ruth, Leah Ann, Lisa, and Leroy Jr., and a good down-to-earth person who has not changed one bit since the first night I met him at the bowling alley in spite of an unbelievable net worth for an old boy from Henagar Route three. I have no idea what his net worth is, and I don't care. I would love him and be proud to call him my friend if he were a pauper.

When their younger daughter, Lisa, graduated from the University of Alabama, she went to San Diego, California to visit friends, where she stayed for several weeks. While there she met a very fine young man named Bruce Peckham. Bruce was from an old San Diego family, one of the most prominent and well respected families, his ancestors having settled there many years before. Among his fathers holdings were downtown real estate, a large marina, A ranch out in the country from San Diego, and a piece of the Padres baseball team. After dating a while and several more trips back to Tuscaloosa Lisa and Bruce decided to marry.

When it came time for Bruce to ask Leroy's permission to marry his youngest daughter, he was very nervous, but he got up the courage to ask Leroy's blessing. His comment was, "Lad, you know that girl has been used to living pretty high on the hog, do you think you can handle that?" Bruce's response was, "Mr. McAbee, I don't know exactly what that means, but if it's what I think it is, I believe I can."

I've told Leroy many times that he is the luckiest man I know. Just think what Lisa could have brought home from California instead of a fine young man like Bruce Peckham. Lisa and Bruce still live in San Diego and have three daughters, Babe, Carol and Leah.

Ruth and Leroy's other daughter is married to Ted Sexton. Ted has been our Tuscaloosa County Sheriff for about six years. They have two sons, James and Edmund. Leah Ann works at the company headquarters. After they had been married for several years, I asked Ted how he was getting along with Leroy? He said, "Just fine I guess, even better than when we first married." I said, "How's that?" Ted replied, "Well, he used to call me Piss Ant, but now he calls me "Lad."

Leroy is just the same today as he was in 1963. Sure, he and Ruth live in a big house on twenty-five acres of land in the city limits, have everything they could want in the way of luxuries, hundreds of acres of land, condominiums at the beach, and two airplanes, but he still wears his khakis and brogan shoes to the office, chews Beechnut chewing tobacco constantly, and would "cut your throat" on the golf course for a quarter. I have often wished I could be a fly on the wall during labor union negotiations, or high level meetings with some of his customers.

Speaking of Beechnut, occasionally when we go out to eat, he will want to drive the big Mercedes, with less than 10,000 miles on it, just to keep the battery charged. Recently we went to the Cotton Patch Restaurant about thirty miles south of Tuscaloosa, at Eutaw, Alabama, off I-59. Leroy had forgotten to bring along a "spit cup," so every four or five miles he had to pull off the highway to the shoulder of the road and spit out the window, Ruth had warned him not to spit while the car was moving. I told him that he must be the only fellow in the world driving a $140,000 car and stopping every few miles to spit.

Ruth and I argue all the time about everything and anything. I tell her she would argue with a stump on fire. We just enjoy disagreeing with each other, but she knows I dearly love her and wouldn't have her any other way. Leroy has been tremendously successful in business, but he would be the first to tell you he couldn't have done it without "Ruby" as he affectionately calls her. She has managed the office personnel, bookkeeping and banking the whole time they have been in business, still going to the office every day.

Several weeks ago when I mentioned I was writing this, Ruth asked me, "Are you going to say something good about me?" I replied, "If I can think of anything." I will say that besides being good to look at and a good cook she loves animals. At last count she had three dogs and 27 cats, several game chickens, guinea hens, and three horses, two of which are at least thirty years old. She never takes any animal to the vet unless it's an emergency. Dr. Conant comes to her house. I haven't known a vet that made house calls since old man Yeager used to come to our place at Nebo and treat papa's cows for the "holler tail."

One of my favorite animal stories is about her rooster. Late one afternoon, Carol and I went to the McAbees' house to pick them up. I got out of the car and heard a weird sound coming from the direction of the chicken house, sounding like a rooster trying to crow, but choking. I asked what that noise was and Ruth said a terrible thing had happened that day. Her big Rhode Island Red rooster had gotten in LeRoy's bird dog pen and the dog had broken the roosters neck. Instead of taking an ax, putting the old rooster out of his misery, by chopping off his head and having baked rooster and cornbread dressing for Sunday dinner, she grabbed him up and took him to a veterinarian. The vet constructed a cast for the rooster's neck out of bamboo strips, the only trouble, his head had to remain up-right She had to hand feed and water the old bird for the three months it took to heal. When the big day finally arrived for the removal of the cast, the doctor came and took it off. The rooster lowered his head for the first time in three months, crowed a couple of times and strutted down to the hen house looking for some female company.

He made one big mistake. He got himself too close to the dog pen, the bird dog grabbed him, and finished the job he had starter three months earlier. After a proper burial, that was the end of that old rooster. I still think we should have eaten him.

There are so many stories I could tell about the McAbees and the Prices but time and space will not permit more than a few. I like the one about the time Ruth had been out of town and came back unexpectedly about 1:00 a.m. just a few minutes behind Leroy's return from a night on the town.

Wouldn't you know it, just like a woman, as she walked by his Jeep in the parking area, she felt the hood and it was still warm, but entering the house she couldn't find him, he was not

160

in the den, kitchen, or living room. So, she went to the bedroom. There was Leroy, all snuggled in his bed with the cover up over his head. She yanked the cover back, exposing him. There he was with a chaw of Beechnut in his jaw and with his boots on.

Leroy and I have had lots of fun and won many local golf tournaments, including the first we ever played at Indian Hills Country Club. Ray Boozer had helped me get started playing golf. I, in turn with Ray had persuaded Leroy to start. At the time Leroy and I won the first tournament, I called Dan Patton, the pro, asking about Leroy's handicap. He said, "It's 36 strokes and he needs every one of them." The thing our opponents didn't realize was that Leroy is a true competitor, in a game, in business and in life.

Or, I could tell about he time he and I went to Las Vegas, without the "girls," Carol and Ruth, and how it took us 23 hours to fly home on Delta.

Or the day the four of us, along with their daughter Lisa and her husband Bruce Peckham, went to a football game at Legion Field in Birmingham in my custom van, and how as I pulled out of the parking lot Leroy's "spit cup" turned over spilling the entire day's accumulation of "juice" all over my shoes and the floor of my van. I told him "Someday I'll get even with you for that."

Several years later the opportunity for my revenge came along. Leroy developed a condition that caused him problems swallowing.   After a thorough examination the doctors determined he had a tumor in his chest, of some considerable size and that surgery was required immediately. Of course, all of us were concerned, fearing the worst but praying and hoping for the best.

The morning of the surgery, Carol and I sat with Ruth, Lisa, Leah Ann and Leroy Jr. in the waiting room at DCH for about three hours, when finally the surgeon, Dr Olivet, came in to report that the operation was over, Leroy was fine, they did remove a tumor about the size of a grapefruit, it was not malignant, it was not attached to his heart or lungs, just sorta floating around in his chest, that he shouldn't have anymore problems and the family could visit him in a private recovery room in about an hour.

We all went to his room, but only Ruth and the girls went in, staying just a couple of minutes, seeing that he was barely awake. As we stood outside his door, Dr. Olivet came down the hall and as he started to enter Leroy's room, I said, "Doctor I want you to do me a favor". He said, "What can I do for you?" I replied, "You know Leroy as well as I do, he's going to want to know all the details about the operation, how big was the tumor, what was in it, what caused it, what it looked like and as an engineer, what it was made of. What I want you to do, doctor, is tell him you cut it open and it was full of tobacco juice."

Knowing how meticulous and humorless Olivet is, I sincerely doubted he would do it. However, when he went in the room we could hear Leroy, in a shaky, sleepy, drowsy, voice asking the doctor the very same questions, the doctor telling him the tumor was not malignant and that he would be OK in a few days. When Leroy said, "Doc, what was in that thing, did you say it was as big as a grapefruit?" The doctor said, "Yes it was Leroy, I cut it open and it was full of tobacco juice". Leroy said," TOBACCO JUICE", just as the doctor left the room without further comment. Early the next morning, I went to the hospital to see Leroy, taking the morning papers and hoping to cheer him up a little. When I went in the room the nurses already had him sitting up in a chair, and as he saw me he said "Syrup Sopper, dang your time, where have you been? I'm dying and you don't even care, you haven't been to see about me." I said, "I was out here all day yesterday, you just don't remember." His next words were, " I want to know what's going on here, they won't tell me anything, what did the doctor tell y'all was wrong with me?" "Leroy, the doctor didn't tell me anything, but I did hear him tell Ruth that it was a grapefruit size tumor, with a long name that I can't remember, it was not attached to your heart or lungs and best of all it was not malignant." Leroy said, "That SOB told me it was full of BEECHNUT." That's all he could remember from the day before. He still doesn't think that trick was funny, but I like it and besides I got my revenge for the van incident.

Harold McAbee, Leroy's brother, five years younger, was a good man and Leroy's right arm in the business. Harold loved everybody and I never heard anyone, especially those men who worked for him say an unkind word about him. He went about doing good in the community and never asking for or receiving the credit he deserved. He loved country music, and was a pretty good "picker", one of his good friends was Charlie Louvin, of Grand 'Ole Opry fame.

We were all shocked in September of 1996 when a numbness in his right hand was finally diagnosed as being caused by a brain tumor. After months of treatment Harold died in April of 1997. He was 60 years old.

His was the only funeral I've ever attended where the people leaving the church commented that they enjoyed it. About twenty minutes before the service Jack Marshall, former pianist for the famous Blackwood Brothers Quartet started playing gospel songs one right after the other including a medley of patriotic songs in honor of Harold's military service.

The music during the funeral was provided by a McAbee family quartet from Georgia, and the minister did a wonderful job. That night about twenty of us gathered at Harold and Opal's house for a good old gospel singing. The only thing missing was Harold. I wish he could have been there to sing with us. Another much younger brother, Wendell, is an engineer with the company, and has assumed much of Harold's duties.

About the time we moved the radio station to Office Park, Carol and I began talking about building a new house, trying to decide between the Alberta area and some new sub divisions opening up on the Northport side of the Black Warrior river, Indian Hills and High Forrest.

Because of the traffic on the two lane draw bridge, the only link between Tuscaloosa and Northport, and the fact that we were already in Alberta, we decided to buy a lot in the newly developed Claymont subdivision between University Boulevard and 15th street. We bought a nice, sloping back to front, 145 ft. lot from Harry Pritchett the developer for $4500.

As luck would have it, next door to the station in Office Park was an architectural firm, Fitts and White. I told Howard White I would be needing some house plans before long, so he and I started working on them over coffee in the morning or at lunch time. Finally completing our plans, we submitted them to three contractors for bids, A. C. Whitley, Marco Visconti and Bob Morrow. Morrow was the low bidder at $36,000. His builder and foreman was Roy Hubbard.

In the spring of 1965 construction was started, and in November Carol and I along with the boys and "Big Boy", our English bulldog moved into our brand new house, with it's three bedrooms, living room, large pecan paneled den with a fireplace, a downstairs playroom, a utility room larger than the den at our old house, dining room and kitchen.

It was about half way between Alberta Elementary School and Eastwood Jr. High. Wally and Ron could walk to school all the way through the eighth grade. We lived in that house at 1326 26th Avenue East for more than thirty years, before moving to our present place at the North River Yacht Club. Thinking about that place still brings back some wonderful memories.
Our family life was pretty much typical of a four person family.
The boys were involved in little league baseball, extracurricular school activities, Cub Scouts, church choirs, and school, just being boys.

All of the neighborhood boys, Bill Lavender, Eddy and Joe Tinsley, Ted and Greg Gryska, John Ricks and the Kent brothers liked to come to our house because we had a basement playroom with a pool table and ping pong table, a refrigerator loaded with soft drinks and Carol would always make sure there were plenty of "goodies" for them to eat.

It was about that time that Carol got a new name. Because she always insisted that the kids behave themselves and threatening to, as she said, "jerk a knot in their tails", and because she broke up so many Junior High parties, they nicknamed her "Woof". That name has stuck with her for all these years. Even now our grand children hardly know she has a real name. She's just Woof.

Wally and Ron earned extra money for themselves by cutting grass for the neighbors and eventually "graduating" to cutting the grass at Memory Hill Gardens Cemetery, and the ultimate job for two strong boys, digging graves, out in the rural cemeteries in places where a backhoe could not be used. I'm afraid some country folks in Tuscaloosa County are buried in mighty shallow graves. Carol would see that the boys were driven to wherever they were supposed to be, usually taking "Big Boy" along too.

One of my regrets, as for as the family is concerned is that I never saw the boys go to school and very seldom saw them return. The years they were in school I was on the air at the radio station from 6 to 9 a.m., requiring me to leave the house about 5:15 in order to stop for breakfast at the Waysider Restaurant and make it to the station about five minutes before 6 o'clock. Very often I did not arrive home at night before they went to bed. I don't know how I could have, but if I had it to do over again, I would try to find more time to spend with the boys.

Shortly after we moved to Claymont, Ed and Nell Wright built their house around the corner, our two back yards joining. Before long they sold their house to a couple from Belgrade Yugoslavia, Dr. Milan and his wife Natalie Djordjevic. Dr. Djordjevic had been employed by the University of Alabama to teach in the graduate engineering program, his specialty being mechanical engineering and a further specialty in internal combustion engines.

A few years earlier he had been allowed to come to this country on a sabbatical from Belgrade University, where his older brother was the president, to teach for a year at Duke University. While here he made plans to return as soon as he could,, only the next time he would bring Natalie. The two of them returned to Duke with plans to defect, asking for asylum and finally, citizenship in the United States. They never returned to their native land.

The day they moved in, even before we had a chance to meet

them, Ron came running into the kitchen telling his mother that someone had written all over the new neighbor's mailbox. Of course, it was their name, looking so strange to a young boy, and me too. Natalie and Milan were great neighbors, although their customs, food, language, religion and ways in general were opposite most of ours.

Being Greek Orthodox, they celebrated Christmas and New Years holidays two weeks after ours, using our Christmas tree after we had finished with it. For years we celebrated with them and they with us, two Christmases and two New Years. The most sacred day of the year to them was their family Holy Day called Slava. Natalie, being an excellent cook, would begin preparing the food weeks in advance. She made a special bread from flour she had ground by hand, then on the special day a priest from Birmingham would come to "bless" it.

The bread would be the center of the feast and each guest was expected to break off a small piece and eat it. She would have a table loaded with food, vegetables, cheeses and meats while in the center was always the baked whole suckling pig with an apple in its mouth.

Her deserts were unbelievable for their taste and attractiveness. Her specialty was torts, many different kinds. She taught Carol how to make some of them, but she must have forgotten how by now, I haven't had one in a long time.

They would invite our immediate neighbors and friends of theirs from the University to the feast. Milan was one of the most interesting men I have ever met. He was a teenage soldier in the Yugoslav army, when Hitler attacked and conquered his country in 16 days. Being captured by the Germans, he spent most of WWII in a German prison camp. I called him the Yugoslavian "Captain Hogan" after he told me about how he organized a communication spy link between the prison and the underground, being involved in espionage and the destruction of as much German war machine as possible.

Upon his release by the Germans, the Russians put him in prison when they took over Yugoslavia. I really don't know how, he tried to explain, but I never understood how he managed to acquire a doctorate in engineering.

Natalie grew up in a small town, her father being what we would call the "mayor" only he was more. They had a very large house with servants, lots of money, jewelry, furniture, and everything a family of five could ever want. However, after the war, when the Russians occupied Yugoslavia, the party made the Popovic home their headquarters, after forcing the family out.

They managed to escape with their lives and a few possessions, the most prized was Natalie's baby grand piano, which was later shipped to the United States for her. She was an accomplished concert pianist, a very talented lady.

Natalie and Milan was granted American citizenship in 1969, being sworn in at New Orleans. When the happy couple returned home, Carol had arranged a Welcome Home new citizens party for them at our house, with an old fashioned American menu of hot dogs, hamburgers, chips, cokes, apple pie, and home made ice cream. All of the neighbors attended, the Brownings Cones, Todds, Steagalls, Tinsleys, Ricks, Bahars and Gryskas.

In 1972 Milan was granted a one year leave from the University to go to Vienna for a year of teaching there. Natalie and Milan insisted that we visit them in the spring, which we did. They were living in a small one bed room apartment, so we stayed in a hotel nearby. We enjoyed the sights of the old city, but one trip was enough for me.

When we checked in the hotel, and went to our room, I discovered right away that my first impression of Europe left a lot to be desired. In the bathroom there were two facilities I had never seen before, a commode with the hole at the front instead of the back, and a bidet, which as I found out later was not for the purpose of washing your feet. I called room service, asking for a bucket of ice, instead, I got two small glasses about the size of the famous "coke" glasses each with two small ice cube in it. Worn out from the trip and jet lag, I flopped down on the bed and it felt like I had flopped on the floor. The bed was plywood with a piece of foam rubber on top for a mattress.

So far, things weren't going so well, but I was sure they would get better. The food was not to my country boy liking, especially the rolls they served at every meal. I told Carol "The next time I come over here I'm going to bring me a ball peen hammer to bust the bread." One thing I did enjoy was their fabulous deserts of all kinds. The trip was made enjoyable by Milan and Natalie showing us all the sights of the city and the surrounding countryside. They could speak the language and were very familiar with all the sights.

We saw a performance of the famous Lippazon Horses, the Vienna Boy Choir, and one day Milan and I took a street car out to the city cemetery, the largest I had ever seen, it was two miles square. I enjoyed looking at the dates, going back for centuries on the head stones. One section was devoted to gravesites for the world famous composers, Mozart, Schubert, Liest, Beethoven, and others.

Natalie and Carol insisted that I go with Carol to the opera. After much coercion I agreed to go. The Viennese Opera house is one of the most beautiful building in the world. We were seated down front about four rows behind the orchestra. When I checked out the program, I said "Good, it has an English translation along with the German". The translation was a waste of time.

When the opera started they turned out the lights except for those on stage. I knew absolutely nothing about what was going on, with folks all over the stage dressed in funny looking costumes yelling at each other, and now and then somebody would swing on a rope or as we used to do at Nebo, when we swung on a scuppernong vine yelling at the top of their lungs about something. In the midst of all the hollering, somebody else would start to sing, then be joined by some others.

Not understanding a word, none of it made the least bit of sense, I was so bored and sleepy but when I would doze off, the fool on the big kettle drum would hit that thing, making it sound like real close clap of thunder, causing me to think it was time to run and get the milk out of the creek and wake me.

Finally after what seemed like an eternity, the house lights came on, the entire packed house of people stood and clapped for a long time. I got up thinking the thing was over and I could get out of there, but I discovered it was only half-time.

They served a buffet of some fancy food upstairs, which we enjoyed, but after about 20 minutes they announced it was time for the second part of Mozart's The Magic Flute to begin. I learned the name when it was light enough to see the program.

I told Carol, "I am not going back for the second half". She said "I've got to go back, I left my fur coat in the seat." I said, "You go back, get your coat and stay if you like, but I'm not going". By the time she got down to our row, it was dark again. Stumbling over some of the most highbrow feet in Europe, she retrieved her coat, met me in the lobby and we went across the street to a restaurant for a cup of strong coffee. She was not at all happy, but as yet she hasn't mentioned wanting to go back to the opera.

The next day when Natalie asked me how I enjoyed the Opera, I told her it was wonderful, not mentioning that we had left early, not wanting to hurt her feelings because she was so delighted that we were able to get tickets. I wanted to tell her that I would have been much more comfortable at "The Grand Ole' Opry."

Milan taught at the University in Tuscaloosa for 15 years before retiring and moving to Tarpon Springs, Florida. We continued to visit regularly, Carol helping plan their 50th wedding anniversary and my acting as emcee for the very special occasion. Natalie died about three years ago, Milan is still living in Tarpon Springs, but in very poor health. The Djordjevics were good neighbors, and friends. By the way they were Serbs.

One of my very special memories of trips I made during the nineteen sixties was at the invitation of NASA to visit the space center at Cape Canaveral, Florida. You remember that in 1961 president Kennedy declared that before the end of the decade the United States would put men on the moon. I along with most Americans thought that would be an impossible feat to ever accomplish and surely not before 1970. NASA invited me along with a few other broadcasters to come to the cape in 1965 for a briefing and to see what was actually going on.

They showed us the construction of the gigantic vertical assembly building, the launch pad, the huge multi-tracked vehicle that would transport the rocket from the assembly building at four miles and hour to the pad. They gave us a complete briefing as to how they proposed to do the seemingly impossible, but they convinced me that we were someday actually going to the moon. I came home and told Carol that, "Those people down there are really serious about going to the moon. They think it is possible."

As it turned out, Kennedy's prediction came true on July 20, 1969, when Neil Armstrong stepped out of the Lunar Module and set foot on the moon for the first time. Too sad that president Kennedy did not live long enough to see this great accomplishment for our country, but I personally think that former president Richard Nixon was never given the credit he deserved for continuing to finance and promote the goal of Kennedy, to put men on the moon.

Another interesting trip was provided several members of the Tuscaloosa Chamber of Commerce, to Omaha, Nebraska. We were permitted to visit the real center of the country's defense system, the underground headquarters of the strategic air command at Offut Air Force Base. It was during the height of the "cold war" between the USA and Russia. They gave us a two day tour of the facility and an extensive briefing about the state of readiness of the country, in case we were attacked. They told how the B-52 bombers, with atomic weapons on board were constantly in the air. They showed us a mock up of and actual command plane to be used in case Washington were ever destroyed.

They showed us actual "spy" photos that had been taken from as high as 60,000 feet by the U-2 jets. They even had pictures of Tuscaloosa, in such detail we could count the pipes on the Central Foundry storage yard. I decided then that our great country was in deep trouble, but was more confident about our readiness to retaliate a sudden strike.

Chapter 12

RADIO AND REGULATION

From the first morning I walked into WACT, I was determined to relocate the studios as soon as I could afford it, and could find a suitable location. In the spring of 1964 my friend Lloyd Wood, a real estate developer built an office complex downtown, at the corner of 6th Street and 27th Avenue. I leased space in Office Park from him, bought and installed some new control room equipment, using our old equipment in our new production room. Thanks to David Peacock our engineer at the time, the move was accomplished overnight without any loss of broadcast time.

Mr. John Primm, a retired Gulf Oil distributor from Meridian, Mississippi was the financial backer for Joe Carson and Eddie Holiday. He had helped them to acquire stations in Biloxi, Laurel, West Point and Meridian, Mississippi and in Tuscaloosa. When I joined WACT the stock was divided four ways, but not equally, Carson and Holiday retained 26% each with Primm and me 24% each.

Mr. Primm was a fine old gentleman, one of the best I've ever known, but having nothing else to do, he liked to drive over to see me about every other week. I felt obligated to spend time with him, taking him to lunch and going over the books, time that I could have spent more wisely doing the station's business.

We were at lunch one day at the Tuscaloosa Country Club when he asked if I had met his son-in-law, Graham Hildebrand. I said, "Yes Sir, I have met Graham He's a great guy," knowing all along that Graham was a professional student and had never had a real job. He had a degree and commission from West Point Military Academy and an engineering degree from Georgia Tech. I sensed right away Mr. Primm had a reason for asking if I remembered his son-in-law. Finally he said, "Graham is thinking about moving to Tuscaloosa and going to Law School at the University, and if he does, he can help you run the radio station." I said, " Mr. Primm, have you ever thought about selling your interest in WACT?" "No," he said," but I would if someone wanted to buy it." I replied "What would you take for your 24%?" Without hesitation, he said "$25,000." "That seems a little high to me, how about $10,000 was my response." He said "I'll take $15,000." I said "How about $12,000?" He said I think that's fair enough, I will sell it to you for $12,000." My next question was, "Now will you finance it for me?" He agreed, and before lunch was over, I had bought his stock, and he had financed it for 3 years at 6%, giving me 48% ownership without even signing a note. We did not have to apply to the Federal Communications Commission for approval of our deal because with 48%, I was not acquiring control.

All was well for awhile, but as time went by, the station making more money and increasing its leadership in the Tuscaloosa market my partners became more and more greedy. When we had money in the bank they would come over and vote themselves a payday. Of course, every time they took out $52 I would take out $48, which I didn't need. I was making enough already. Sometimes these drainages on the bank account were detrimental to the operation of the station, leaving me with no reserves, and occasionally having to borrow money for routine expenses, even the payroll.

In 1966 Joe and Eddie were in my office. We were discussing the situation my telling them that I believed it was time for them to buy me out or vice versa. Even though I had more stock than either of them, they always voted their 52% as one. Whatever Holiday said, Carson would agree, resulting in the two of them over ruling me. I must say though, we never had any serious disagreements and they gave me total control of the operation of the station, the change of locations, and the decision to put an FM station, WACT-FM on the air, which we did in 1967. That day when the subject of a buyout came up, Holiday indicated he thought it would make more sense for me to buy them out. I agreed saying, "How much would it take?" The result was, after much discussion with offers back and fourth, we agreed on a price of $100,000. They wanted cash, that day.

I didn't have the money and was afraid if I let them leave without it, they might change their minds. So I called George Shirley, at The First National Bank, told him I had just bought out my partners in the station and needed a loan of $100,000. He said that sounded like a good deal to him, "When do you need the money?" I said, "Right now, they want the money before they leave town." George said "Go ahead and write them a check, I'll put the money in your account to cover it, and when you get a chance come by to sign a note."

My secretary, Pat White, was so nervous writing out the check, she made it for $1000 instead of $100,000. I was so nervous signing it, I didn't notice the mistake either. Joe and Eddy were halfway to Meridian, when they decided to look at the big check one more time and discovered it was short by $99,000. They turned around and came back in a hurry for another check.

I went home that afternoon not knowing exactly how to break the news to Carol, that we were the sole owners of WACT. She was not really surprised. I remember telling her, "If I could ever get the radio station billing to $7000 a month, we would have it made. We would have no financial worries." When I sold it in 1990, it was costing an average of $100,000 a month just to open the doors. I think she had been expecting something like the buy-out for a while before it actually happened.

People used to ask me, "Syrup Sopper, how do you get up so early every morning?" I would always reply, "George Shirley calls me every morning making sure I'm still alive and telling me to "Get Up and go to work." Before the buy-out could be finalized, we had to apply for approval of the transfer of stock from Holiday and Carson to me, which was approved without question by the FCC in Washington.

During the 1920s radio was in it's infancy, considered a toy to be experimented with by all sorts of people, with very few even realizing they were on the cutting edge of a whole new industry. Radio "stations" were springing up all over, in attics, basements, barns or any place one could hook up a homemade transmitter to an antenna. Obviously something had to be done toward regulation of frequencies, power and coverage of radio stations, so Congress established the Radio Commission to help solve the problems.

That designation was changed to the Federal Communications Commission, FCC, with the passage of the Communications Act of 1928. It set fourth a series of rules and regulations regarding frequency allocation, power, locations, qualifications for, and transfer of ownership, and granting of Federal licenses to broadcast. Nowhere in the act did it authorize the FCC to regulate programming . It required that stations east of the Mississippi river use four letters in their call sign, or as we say, call letters, beginning with a "W" and those stations west of the Mississippi would begin with a "K". Someone will say "How about the three letter stations like WSM, WLS, WSB, KDKA, in Pittsburgh or WFAA in Dallas? They were already on the air when the communications act was passed and were grand fathered.

The act also established what was known as 50,000 watt clear channel stations, almost every one of which could be heard, especially at night, through out most of the country. Every radio listener back then was familiar with WCKY, Cincinnati, WLS, Chicago, WSM, Nashville and KMOX in St. Louis, just to name a few. All station were on the AM band because FM was not perfected until the 1940s.

The makeup of the FCC is seven people, a chairman and six commissioners, appointed by the President, approved by the Senate, with hundreds of employees in a nine story building on M street in Washington. For about three decades no one heard much about the FCC, as it went about doing the jobs it was authorized to do by Congress, mostly granting new licenses as a steady stream of applications were pouring in.

With the development of television in the late 1950s, responsibilities for its regulation also went to the FCC. Then came along the 1960s and 70s, and as the country was changing, the government growing, expanding, and assuming more and more regulatory powers over all phases of American lives, drastically changing as the FCC began to exert more control over broadcasting. Still regulating license assignments and things technical, the Commission, on its own began passing a series of rules and regulations, exerting controls over programming and personnel for which it was never intended. Technically, not regulating program content, the commission passed rules, with the approval of Congress, designating the amount of time a radio or TV station must devote to the different types of programming, for instance, music, news, public affairs, politics, public service announcements and commercials.

They even had rules about things we could not do. One was no program length commercials were allowed. If that rule were still in effect today, the world would have never known about Gensu knives, Moulis, Salad Shooters, Flobies, Tater Peelers, George Forman Grills, how to make millions of dollars in real estate working only part-time, numerous kinds of exercise equipment, and Homecoming Friends video tapes by Bill and Gloria Gaither, all program length commercials. The commission considered any program over three minutes sponsored by the same product or company to be a program length commercial.

Few people outside of broadcasters ever realized that broadcasting was the most regulated industry in the country beside the airlines, and very few cared. The 1960s were years of extreme turmoil in our country. There were the Civil Rights Movement, the assassinations of President John Kennedy, Robert Kennedy, Dr. Martin Luther King Jr., student demonstrations against the Vietnam war, the Kent State massacre and the rising crime rate, just to mention a few.

During those years there were some really weird appointments made to the FCC by Kennedy, but more so by President Johnson. The commission itself was loaded with very liberal, big government minded men and women, one a long haired hippie, named Johnson, who each morning, I was told, while barefoot, brought his cat to his office with him.

To my knowledge, in the entire history of the FCC, there have only been two broadcasters appointed to the commission.

175

Mr. James Quello, from Michigan, still there, has served as somewhat of a buffer between idiocy on the Commission and the broadcasters. Mr. Quello had never heard of preparation "H" until Carol told him about it. He still thanks her for solving one of his biggest problems, which was probably caused by "sitting" on the FCC for 25 years.

The other broadcaster was Robert Wells from Garden City, Kansas. Bob served two terms, leaving because, as he said, he just couldn't take it anymore. Bob and I served together on the Associated Press board of directors beginning in the1980s. He and Kay, Carol and I became really good friends and still correspond regularly. They have visited us twice, Bob and I playing in our club's annual member/guest golf tournament.

You may wonder why I'm taking so much space and your time with all of this, but I believe by the time I'm through you will understand that this too is a big part of "my story." Under these rules that I mentioned were requirements that a radio station had to be all things to all people, not necessarily expressed but implied. An entire book could be written on that subject, but I will not attempt to list all of the absolutely insane rules and regulations the, as George Wallace called them, "wild-eyed liberals" or as Rush Limbaugh calls them "the environmentalist wackos" imposed upon broadcasters during that period.

What were the penalties for not following the rules to the letter? Penalties were primarily fines, as the FCC called them, forfeitures, or license revocation or both, depending upon the nature of the "crime."

A station had to renew its license every three years. No sooner would we finish a renewal, than we had to begin working on another. Licenses are now renewed every seven years.

Renewing a radio station license was very different from a renewal of your drivers, hunting or fishing license. We were required to keep a daily program log, a listing of everything that was broadcast each day, programs, news, music, public service announcements, commercial announcements during the entire license period. In addition we kept what was called a public inspection file, available for inspection by any member of the public during business hours. In that file, which at WACT was a three drawer filing cabinet in the front office, we kept all correspondence regarding programming, the three previous, and current renewals, the original application for license, engineering information, all other information about the station including our annual EEOC reports and a separate political file which contained a form called "Requests for political time."

If a candidate, one of his supporters or his ad agency even called inquiring about rates and availabilities, a form had to be filled out and kept on file, whether or not the candidate actually bought advertising. Speaking of EEOC, the original Equal Employment law, passed by Congress required that a company with as many as 25 employees had to adhere strictly to the guidelines, but the commissioners said that was not good enough. They raised the standard for compliance by radio and TV stations to those with as many as five employees, based on the percentage of minority population in the coverage area. I certainly don't mean to imply that all licenses expired at the same time.

Expirations were staggered by state, year and month so that licenses were expiring every month. In Alabama our licenses expired on April 1, every third year. That meant the renewal application had to be filed before January 1. The three months between January and April we had to run announcements on the station to the effect that our license renewal application had been filed with the FCC, and any member of the public could come by the station to review it, or if they so desired, could contact the FCC with comments regarding the stations performance during the past three years.

Of all things a broadcaster dreaded most was a petition to deny, even though he might be totally innocent of wrong doing, the commission would accept a petition in any form from anyone. The greatest problem was the time and money required to defend against a denial petition. If one were set for a full hearing before the Commission, the cost to the broadcaster could run into millions of dollars.

A petition to deny a license could be a hundred-page document drawn up by a battery of lawyers or a simple postcard to the FCC requesting a denial of a stations license. It really made no difference to the Commission. Not every renewal was inspected by the Commissioners themselves. That was done by the more than 700 lawyers and their staffs, employed by the government for the FCC. If the staff felt it was necessary, they would refer them on up to the ninth floor.

The Commission used "catch phrases" like "equal time" meaning if you editorialized or presented one side of a controversial community issue, you had to present all sides, which sounded good, but there was no way to present all sides. Just as soon as a broadcaster thought he had done a good job in that regard, some off the wall, far-out person or group would complain, resulting in a letter from the FCC.

Another phrase they liked was "Promise vs. Performance.". About six months before renewal time the FCC would issue a list of seven days during the previous three years cycle, called the "composite week" on which a license renewal was based. Those days were meant to represent the period in question, with a Sunday in January, a Monday in May, a Tuesday in September, etc. It was always amazing to me how a random drawing could always pick unusual days like the day before an election or the day before Christmas.

The broadcaster had to take those seven logs, analyze them not only as to the percentage of time devoted to each type of programming he had performed, count the number of spot announcements in each hour, both public service and commercial but compare what he had done with what he had promised to do when he filed for renewal three years previously.

I know that sounds rather complicated. It was. We were telling the FCC what we had done during the past three years, comparing that to what we said we would do, and at the same time telling them what we intended to do for the next three years. Woe unto those whose promise did not match performance.

Another big item for public inspection was the

178

"ascertainment" file. I called it asinine ascertainment, the silliest rule the commission staff ever devised and imposed upon broadcasters and the public. The rule at first was very simple. Each station was required to periodically interview certain community leaders asking their opinions as to how the station could serve them or their organization better. The ruling was suggested by Commissioner Cox, who told me later that in his opinion it was the worst mistake he made as a Commissioner, not having any idea at the time he was creating a monster.

The Commission staff developed a list of nineteen different groups among which were blacks, Indians, Asians, Spanish speaking, religious, civic, political, educational, medical, business, governmental, student, legal, agricultural, law enforcement, women and even homosexuals groups which we were supposed to interview at least once a quarter to determine what their problems were and what the radio station could do to solve them. Should there not be a particular designated group represented in the station's community of license, for instance, there were very few if any Native Americans in Tuscaloosa, the broadcaster was allowed to substitute but had to prove that he was not doing that for the purpose of omitting a group.

I know to you that all seems so ridiculous that I must be making it up. It is absolutely true. These interviews must be conducted in person ,no phone calls. Furthermore they must be one on one, meaning two or more stations could not interview the mayor or anyone else at the same time.

A written record of each interview, had to be kept on file including, the interviewer, interviewee, their position, date, time, place, along with the questions asked, answers, and signature of the interviewee. These had to be kept at the station for three years and then all filed with the FCC at license renewal time. That must have made the paper shredders work overtime in Washington.

One result of that foolishness was, some of the community leaders got mad and upset with broadcasters taking up their time with questions about their problems, and when told it was a requirement of the government, that we must do the survey, some started writing and complaining to their Congressmen about it . Our mayor, General Rainey Collins told me once, when I asked what the problems were at City Hall, "Hell, Syrup Sopper, I don't know what the problems are. I listen to you every morning to find out what they are."

It was bad enough in Tuscaloosa but can you imagine in a city the size of Atlanta, Chicago, New York or Los Angeles, the mayor, police chief, or sheriff being asked, by as many as five dozen radio stations, every three months what their problems were. No wonder they complained.

Back to petitions to deny licenses, a bunch of lawyers were getting rich off of broadcasters by encouraging citizens to let them file petitions on their behalf. Other lawyers were getting richer by defending the broadcasters, and the FCC lawyers were lining their pockets at the expense of the taxpayers by keeping the money pot boiling in Washington and their soft government jobs. In the case of a petition to deny, the only losers were the broadcasters.

The mother of all petition filers was an outfit in Washington, with a misleading name, the Citizens Communications Center, headed by a lawyer named Kramer. That outfit, being financed by tax free foundations, one of which was the Ford Foundation, was turning out petitions to deny wholesale. The Center didn't cull anyone. They filed petitions against small, large, small town, big city, independent and network owned stations. The only ones they did not bother were the "black" owned or "black" programmed stations.

At the time all I knew about them was what I read in Broadcasting magazine. However, in 1972 I would meet Mr. Kramer in person. Before I bore you anymore with problems, I need to return to the more pleasant aspects of the Syrup Sopper family and WACT.

Chapter 13

MORE SIXTIES & JOE DICK

Programming a radio station in the 1960s was much different than today. Due to FCC regulations regarding programming and the small number of stations, mainly FM, a broadcaster had to provide a much greater variety. Music, news, talk, religious, public affairs, and sports were all included in the government "guidelines," although the Commission was never authorized to regulate programming. With the proliferation of stations, and the deregulation of broadcasting, which began in 1981 during the Reagan administration, stations are much more free to program as they choose. The goal was to find a niche and try to develop a loyal audience for it. Today it is not diversity of programming but diversity of individual stations, such as news, talk, sports, country, soft rock, hard rock, classical, oldies, oldies but goodies, rap, or whatever the current fad may be.

In 1961 when Hank and I were trying to change the image of WACT from a rock format to country, we wanted it to be more than just a music station. I am a firm believer that a radio station should be more than just a juke box with commercials. We, as I said before, were looking for a variety of programs, Breakfast at the Stafford was one. Others included southern gospel music, news, Calvary Baptist Church live on Sunday morning, little league baseball, high school football and, of course, country music. Without the benefit of a large research staff and an abundance of audience survey information that larger stations had, we just sorta programmed "by the seat of our pants". Try something, if it worked fine, if not, try again.

One idea of mine turned out to be the best. That was a program on gardening. It was early spring 1963, when I talked to a man I had met, but didn't really know very well. His name was John Robert Spiller, his friends and family had nick-named him "Joe Dick." I don't know if it was because of his heroics on the football field at County High, his big grin, showing all 32 teeth, his wonderful personality, certainly not his good looks, being short, fat, and bow legged like his mama, but everything about him and his extensive knowledge of the subject as the owner and operator of Spiller Field and Garden Shop, made him the perfect candidate for the program I had in mind.

Due to the type of merchandise, his was mostly a spring business, February through April. I approached him with the idea of sponsoring a gardening and farming program from 7:10 to 7:25 a.m. right in the middle of the Syrup Sopper show.

The plan was to have listeners write in questions. I would get with John Robert sometime during the day, record his answers and then play them back on the air the next morning. After only two days of that, we both saw it just wouldn't work. He was so busy, I could never get him to sit down with me for fifteen minutes without being interrupted by a customer, salesman, telephone or numerous other things.

So, we implemented plan number two, sounds complicated but was really very simple. I had three phone lines at the station. John would be at home, drinking his morning coffee. I would call him on the phone leaving two lines open for the friends and neighbors to call in with their questions. Putting John on hold, I would put the caller on the air, John would hear the question on the radio, I would punch him back up, he would answer the question. Later with a more sophisticated phone system the caller could talk directly to him, both on the air at the same time with me in the middle. That's the way it went. John contracted for the program to run for three months. "Ask The Authority" was on WACT and WACT-FM every day, Monday through Saturday for the next twenty three years. John always joked that the only reason he bought the program was that he felt sorry for me.

In order to understand the program, you must know more about John Robert and the Spiller family. Earnest and Kate Spiller raised four girls and three boys, John Robert being the middle son between James and Jack. The family lived on a farm just south of Tuscaloosa in what was known as the Taylorville community, now one of the fastest growing, commercial, residential, cultural and educational sections of the city known as Hillcrest. The Spiller farm is now a residential sub-division. John's widow, Eileen still lives in their house on old highway 69 south. The widow of his brother James, Jackie, still lives across the highway and John's sister Mary Jean, the widow of CPA, Winston Way lives next door. His nephew, Mike, and Connie live about a half mile up the road. James made his fortune in the furniture business, with stores throughout west central Alabama and east Mississippi. His son Mike and family are carrying on the tradition. Spiller Furniture was also a very good customer of ours at the radio station. That area where the Spillers lived, John and I called "goat hill", but as the Spillers prospered and built new houses, painted their barns and started eating catfish instead of possum, we changed the name to "Angora Heights."

John Robert used to sit and talk about growing up in a family of seven children, telling about funny things that happened with a hearty laugh and maybe just a little exaggeration. Like the story about the time the family was going to visit kinfolks in Birmingham. Jack, being the youngest and most spoiled, refused to go unless he could take his pony along.

So, with Earnest and Kate in the front seat of the T model Ford, the seven youngun's and the pony, with his head hanging out one side and tail out the other side, they set out on an all day trip to the big city.

Or, he would tell about the batch of elderberry wine he and James made. They put it in the attic over the kitchen to ferment, and how when the family arrived home from church bringing the preacher with them for Sunday dinner, they found the jugs in the attic had exploded and the purple liquid had stained the kitchen ceiling, walls and floor. No one could figure out how the wine happened to get in the attic, least of all, James and John.

One of his favorite stories was about the day his older sister, Eileen, pronounced, E-leen, (John's wife Eileen is pronounced I-leen) was baking cookies for her boyfriend. She had burned to a crisp the first batch, but had several more good ones that she wanted to save for her boyfriend. Little John Robert was slipping around and eating the good ones as fast as he could.

She told him, "John if you want some cookies, eat the burned ones and save the others." To which he replied, "I've eat so many burned cookies, I'm farting soot now."

Growing up on a farm, with a large family, John and I had similar backgrounds even though he was about 10 years older than I, and lived much closer to town. I used to tell him he was close enough to town to hear the oil mill whistle blow, which we couldn't at Nebo unless the wind was just right, or that goat hill was like downtown Atlanta compared to where I came from.

John Robert got his sense of humor from his mother whom everyone called Miss Kate, or Big Mama. She was a fun loving person, always wearing a big grin, welcoming one and all to visit and eat, a wonderful personality. She was short, large around the middle, with the most bowed legs I've ever seen. During the "hot pants" era, somebody gave her a pair for Christmas. Carol, the boys and I were at John and Eileen's house with the rest of the Spiller clan, for Christmas dinner, when after we had all gathered back in the living room, Miss Kate came in just a grinning, wearing the hot pants, leaving no question about her legs, a full grown hound dog could have run between them.

John used to laugh about the night he broke loose and was running for a long touchdown in a game at County High. Crossing the goal line, he looked and saw Big Mama running stride for stride with him just outside the fence. His first experience at selling was going with his mother to sell produce at the county curb market, located on the courthouse grounds in downtown Tuscaloosa. The best I could tell, most of the farming by the Spillers was vegetables, or as we say truck farming under the supervision of Miss Kate. She loved flowers and she would sell them along with the vegetables.

John Robert joined the Alabama National Guard while still in his teens, being assigned to the 31st Dixie Division. The unit was mobilized in 1941 even before our country became actively engaged in the war. The survivors of that group of men who left Tuscaloosa for Fort Blandon, Florida in 1941, still have an annual reunion, which I used to attend and emcee, at John's request, until some of the old fellows started asking me what unit I was in. I told them, "Man, I was only nine years old when Ya'll went to war."

John left Tuscaloosa as a private in the guard, saw combat in North Africa and in the battle of Italy, received a battlefield commission, a 2nd Lieutenant's rank, and two purple hearts for wounds. He returned home in 1945 as a U.S. Army Major. After all those years in Italy, I used to tell him that I'll bet it must have been really sad to leave behind little Sophia and Antonio.

The smartest thing he ever did, shortly after returning from the war, he married Eileen Springer in 1945. Soon after, they went into business on 7th street with Spiller Field and Garden Shop.

They had three children John Jr., Fran and Ellen. From the time John and I started the program, our two families were always very close, spending a lot of time together, especially the Prices visiting them. Eileen being such a wonderful cook, and with freezers brimming with meat and vegetables and two catfish lakes, there was always plenty to eat at their house. I don't remember ever turning down an invitation to eat fresh vegetables, fried squirrel, gravy and biscuits, catfish, chicken, hamburgers, home made ice cream, or anything else.

John Robert was the one person I've known who never saw too much of anything. When he would go to the curb market in Birmingham, he would bring back a bushel of onions, ten bushels of corn, peas, beans or whatever he could load on his pickup. Then he and Eileen would spend several days canning and freezing, as if there would never be any more grown.

The four of us took a lot of trips together, especially to football games. There was one in particular, to Mobile for the Senior Bowl game. The night before the game we ate at Wintzel's famous seafood restaurant. John ordered himself a salad, gumbo, shrimp cocktail, crab claws and red snapper, washing it all down with three bottles of beer. Eileen, Carol and I had a normal dinner, and when it was over John said, "You buy the supper and I'll get the breakfast in the morning." I said all right, but thinking as I paid the check, "I'll fix him."

185

The next morning we went to The International House of Pancakes for breakfast. I told the waitress to bring me some of every kind of pancakes on the menu. There were buttermilk, blueberry, apple, strawberry, buckwheat, whole-wheat, regular, half dollar, and even some with fruit and whipped cream, along with eggs, bacon and sausage. When John went to the counter to pay, the cashier looked at the check and said, "There must be some mistake, four people can't eat $40 worth of pancakes". John said, "He didn't eat them, the SOB just ordered them."

Back then, to go from Mobile to Tuscaloosa you took highway 43 all the way, about a three hour drive. When we left Mobile that Sunday morning, John said, " I'm going to show you a shortcut." Sometime that afternoon we wound up in a lumber yard in Frisco City, Alabama, further from Tuscaloosa than when we left Mobile that morning.

On another trip to Jackson, Mississippi I was driving. It was a dark, rainy night during the construction of I-20, with lots of detours, on and off ramps, and construction barriers, when I took a wrong turn and we were stopped by a dead end at a place called Lost Gap. For years John Robert kidded me about going to Lost Gap, but I would always remind him of Frisco City.

In the very beginning, "Ask the Authority" was intended to be a serious, question and answer session between John, the expert, and the listener calling in to the program, but after awhile it became much more relaxed, humorous, and sometimes ridiculous. The personalities of Joe Dick and Syrup Sopper were a perfect match themselves, but throw in the personalities of some of the regular callers, and the show developed a personality of its own and a large audience.

It has been fifteen years now since I was on the program, but I still have people mention how much they miss me and John Robert in the morning. Or the younger people will say, "My grandma used to listen to you and Mr. Spiller every morning." When either of us were at the mall or a restaurant, even at church, someone would always say, "Where is John Robert?" or to him, "Where is Syrup Sopper?" They assumed that we were together every day even though we might not have seen each other for a couple of weeks.

Besides answering legitimate questions about planting, cultivating, fertilizing and harvesting of fruits, vegetable and row crops, the program was full of some of the best "country comedy," provided primarily by some regular "characters" who called, not necessarily to be funny, but their very nature was comical.

There was the old fellow who would always call to predict the weather, according to how his reumatis' was feeling that particular day. We called him, "The Groundhog Man." He was so disappointed when, after winning one of our little contests, we announced that he had won a garden hoe. He almost cried, saying, "I don't want something to work with, my wife will make me use it." Then there was the "fig man." Old Mr. Hayes over on Prince Avenue had a fig orchard in his back yard, and during the season would call, knowing we didn't allow "for sale" announcements on the program, with some kind of irrelevant question, and before I could cut him off would always say, "Y'all don't forget, I've got figs for sale for $2.00 a gallon."

One old gentleman, Mr. Barger, living on Hargrove Road, out in the county, was a regular caller. He would argue about everything. Regardless of the way John would answer a caller's question, the old man would call and say that John didn't know what he was talking about. "You plant them beans when the "signs" ain't right, and you won't make nothing but vines, no beans, you put that fertilizer on them taters, you'll kill em or I ain't never seen a city feller that knew the first thing about farming," were some typical comments from him.

One day on a different program, the WACT Action Hot Line, my guest was a dentist, Dr. Carol Clements, talking about National Children's Dental Health week. She was stressing how important it was to take care of a child's teeth; brushing, flossing, avoiding sweets, regular dental check-ups etc. The old man called and said to her, "Young lady you don't know what you are talking about. I was raised over in Pickens county, never saw a dentist till I was grown, the only brushing we ever done was with a hickory twig, we eat syrup and biscuits and anything else we wanted." At that I broke in and said, "When did you lose your teeth?" He said," I ain't lost em, they're in that glass over yonder on the sideboard." Dr. Clements didn't know what to say after that exchange.

Then there was "Aunt Samanthy," as I named her, a just about every day caller. She lived 20 miles north of Tuscaloosa in the Samantha community. She very seldom had a gardening question, but she too, had the answer for everyone else's' problems, most of the time disagreeing with John Robert. Finally there was "Granny", Mrs. Velma Gammons from out at Romulus community. A feisty little widowed octogenarian, always with her opinions and the most natural sense of humor and way of genuine "country talking" I have ever heard. She was so genuinely funny, that people used to swear that I paid her to call, but of course, I never did. I called her a poor man's Minnie Pearl.

There are dozens of stories I could tell about Granny, but one of my favorites was the day she called to ask John if he had any pole cat pea seed at the store. Before John could answer, I said, "Granny, there's no such thing as pole cat peas, you're just making that up." She said, "Yes, they is Syrup Sopper, they is pole cat peas. I've planted em ever year, but I forgot to save the seed last year. They was so good I eat 'em all up." I came back with, "I'll tell you what Granny, if you'll plant em, work em, pick em and cook em, John will furnish the seed and I'll furnish the side meat to go in them and we'll come to your house to help eat them." She said, "I'll shore do that, Syrup Sopper, but you be shore to cut the titties off that sow belly 'fore you bring it over here." As a result of the program Granny got her a new husband. An old preacher Wheat, after hearing her on the radio so much, called her, they got together, and were married a short time later, both in their 80's. John and I felt like cupids.

It would be impossible to adequately cover twenty-three years of fun and foolishness that transpired on the Spiller program. We always had something going between the two of us and the listeners, and best of all it was commercially successful for John's business. When he would recommend a specific pesticide, insecticide or seed, feed, fertilizer, plant or even tropical fish in the pet department, the items would sell quickly that very day, because the listeners believed in John Robert and Syrup Sopper.

After DDT was taken off the market, we sold truck loads of an insecticide called Diazinon 25E. We sold so much of it that Standard Oil Company, the manufacturer sent a special representative to Tuscaloosa to see what John was doing with the stuff and how he was promoting it. Another popular product was a rat killer called Warforat, containing the chemical warfarin made for killing rats around barns and out buildings on the farm.

I was working on the air one Saturday morning. Pat White, my secretary, was at the front desk in the reception area of the building when Mrs. Patrick and four of her young'uns came in, carrying a large paper grocery bag. The visit was not unusual. The Patricks were pitiful, almost homeless, just roaming the streets scavenging whatever they could to eat, or junk to sell for a few pennies. They would often stop by the radio station to use the bathroom or just to rest.

That Saturday morning, though, as I looked down the hall toward the front office, I knew something was wrong. I saw Pat hurrying down the hallway and into the control room where I was, looking like she had seen a ghost and muttering something about rats and Patricks all at the same time. I asked what was wrong, and she said, "You've got to come see what's on my desk."

I went up front and looked in the bag on Pat's desk and saw it was almost full of the biggest, meanest looking dead gopher rats I had ever seen. The old lady said, "Syrup Sopper, you and John Robert said that thar rat killer would kill em' and hit shore did, thar they air. I even killed one in my oven." I suggested she take her bag of rats, show them to John and Eileen and then find some place to bury them right away. Pat White, the Baptist preacher's wife, almost passed out as cold as the sack full of dead rats.

John being the generous, fun loving person he was, loved playing Santa Claus at Christmas time. He had a beautiful Santa suit, long snow white beard and hair, looking exactly like an ideal Santa. He required no padding under the suit because his stomach was already built for it. Every Christmas Eve afternoon, he would hitch his old pony named "Varooom," (because he snorted with every step he took) to a two-wheel cart loaded with fruit, candy, nuts and toys then walk along behind the cart as they went all over the south side of Tuscaloosa, passing out goodies to children.

With all those kids following Santa, the cart and pony he created an unusual Christmas parade. One Christmas he and the pony came all the way from goat hill, down Greensboro Avenue, 15th street, and 26th avenue to our place in Claymont to bring gifts to Wally, Ron and all the kids in our neighborhood, a distance of at least five miles. It was difficult to tell which was more worn out, Santa Claus, or Varooom the pony.

For many years it was customary for the Tuscaloosa Exchange Club members to give a Christmas party for the mental patients at what was known as The Boys Colony, a division of Partlow State Mental Hospital. They lived in a large two-story building on the Brice Hospital farm, where they worked raising food and fiber for the hospital, before Federal Judge Johnson decreed that the state could not require patients to work. It was time for the Christmas party, so in the early evening the members of the club gathered at the hotel, our regular meeting place, packed individual bags of treats and two gifts for each patient. We all boarded buses and went to the colony for the big celebration, taking with us Santa Claus, John Robert.

The recreation room was on the second floor and as we were climbing the long stairway, Tommy Moore, club president, in the lead, was yelling "Hey boys, here comes Santa Claus," with Santa right behind him ringing his little bell, ding, ding, ding, and shouting "Merry Christmas, Merry Christmas, Ho, Ho, Ho." There was much excitement with all the ding, ding, dings, ho, ho, ho's and merry Christmases. It was beautiful. Suddenly one of the patients jumped up and yelled loud enough for all to hear, "F--- Santa Claus, I want to see Syrup Sopper." I never let John forget that incident which proved once and for all that Syrup Sopper was more popular than Santa Claus.

One Fourth of July, John came up with the idea of barbecuing a goat. He managed to buy a fresh slaughtered, full grown goat for us to cook on a temporary pit of concrete blocks in his front yard. That morning he told the radio audience about our plans and invited everybody listening to come to his house that evening to help us eat the goat. We worked all afternoon keeping the coals hot under the meat, the fire as hot as we dared without burning it all up, dabbing the goat with marinade to keep it moist, and when the people began to arrive about sundown, there was no indication the goat would ever be tender enough to eat.

By dark the Spiller yard was full of cars, parked all the way around the house to the barn. They were lined up on both sides of the highway in front of the house for at least a quarter mile. Two state trooper cars stopped to see what the excitement or trouble was at the Spiller house. The officers stayed for supper too.

John hurried up the road to Gas Island, a country filling station, grocery, and meat market to buy steak, chicken, hot dogs, hamburger, ribs or whatever he could find, along with bread rolls, potato chips and soft drinks, brought them home, put them on our grill and in a few hours, we had enough cooked to feed the multitude.

In the meantime Eileen was in the house looking out the window, not knowing John had invited the public for goat supper, and seeing all those hungry people arrive, almost lost her mind wondering what she was going to do to feed them. She and Carol started making tea and serving it. When the tea bags ran out, they just kept adding water to the tea pitchers.

About 10 p.m. the crowd started leaving. We tested the goat again, John, Jack, myself and Slim, the hired man hoping to somehow find enough tender parts for our supper. No luck, we still could not stick a fork in that tough old "billy". We just left him on the grill and the next morning disposed of our "burnt offering". Invariably, every year after that, on the Fourth of July morning someone would call inquiring if John and I were going to have another goat supper that evening. We would all have a good laugh about "old billy" that refused to be cooked done enough to be eaten.

Before "Ask the Authority" ran it's course, it became very much a Spiller family show. When John was unable to be on, his brother, Jack, his son John Jr. or Eileen would fill in for him. They each did a great job, but I just always felt more at ease with John because he was never at a loss for words, and if by chance he didn't know the answer to a question, he would make up one. He continued to do the show with Wally for two more years after I was forced to cut back on my work schedule in 1984 due to heart problems.

We all cried when in 1986, the doctors discovered John had developed prostate cancer. To my knowledge, he had never been seriously ill. He put up a gallant fight against the disease, but died two years later. I went to visit him at the hospital the day before he died. It broke my heart to see him in such pain and just a shell of the man he had been only two years before. He opened his eyes, took my hand, and whispered something I could not understand, but I'll bet it was some smartass remark about me. That was the last time I saw my friend Joe Dick alive. I still miss him.

Some other program ideas we started on WACT included twenty five minutes of Southern gospel music from 6:30 - 6:55, featuring all the popular groups of the day, Blackwood Brothers, Statesmen, Cathedrals, Stamps, LeFevres, Florida Boys, Chuck Wagon Gang and many others. We broadcast the funeral announcements live from Memory and Hayes Chapels followed by an appropriate hymn, every morning at 6:55, probably the most listened to five minute segment of the entire morning.

I almost had a running fit one Sunday morning when at home, I heard one of our weekend, part-time student announcers follow the funeral announcements with the country song "Rusty Old Halo." The kid apparently didn't know what a hymn was, but I explained it to him the next day. That was almost as bad as the words spoken by the singer and emcee for a local country band. It was customary at the time to close the program with a religious song. I heard Hurdis Lake and the Lake Brothers one Saturday evening close their show with Hurdis saying, "Now Boys it's time to take our hats off and dedicate our last song specially to all of our sick and shut-in friends, "The Rosewood Casket." I laughed about that because that slip up was on the local TV station.

The 7:30-7:45 segment of the show was what I called my Syrup Sopper's almanac and star for the day. I featured two songs by a "star" who was celebrating a birthday on that particular day. Besides the music, that quarter hour was when I announced local birthdays, anniversaries, weddings, hospital discharges more in depth weather, today in history and a thought for the day.

One of my fondest memories of childhood on the farm at Nebo was listening to our first radio after we finally got electricity. One of our favorite programs was Lum 'n Abner, featuring two old codgers, Lum Eddards and Abner Peabody owners of the Jot 'em Down Store in a small town, Pineridge Arkansas. It was one of the most popular radio programs of all time.

In 1969 I served as convention program chairman for the Alabama Broadcasters Association meeting here in Tuscaloosa. Searching for some interesting speakers, I read somewhere that Chester Lauch, known as Lum, on the famous old show was working in public relations for Continental Oil Company, traveling over the country and making speeches to groups such as ours and of course plugging Conoco gas and oil.

I contacted the office in Little Rock, and they were happy to book Lum to speak at our meeting. I didn't know what to expect when I met him at the airport, but I just knew that one of my all time idols of radio had to be very nice. The second he stepped off the plane, I knew him. Then in his seventies he looked as if he had just stepped out of one of the Lum 'n Abner movies, which he and Abner had made in the 40s. He was tall, thin, grey haired, with a small grey mustache, real then, but fake in the movies.

Lum was the hit of the convention, having a great time himself, entertaining the broadcasters who appreciated the old, true radio pioneer, an inspiration to all of us. He told about how in 1928   after he and Tuffy Goff, Abner, had grown up on farms in Arkansas, they heard about this new thing sweeping he country called radio. They went to the only station in Little Rock to apply for a job. The manager sat them in front of a microphone and said, "Do me a radio program."

Without a script, they just started talking like two old men sitting around a wood heater at a country store. After several minutes of dialog, the manager offered them a job for $ 2.00 a program. They continued daily on the Little Rock station until in the mid thirties they were invited by a radio network to come to Chicago and go nationwide.

That was the beginning of their phenomenal popularity. Lum told me the hardest thing for them at the network was they had to write a script and timing on and off had to be precise to the second. On the local station they never used a script, and sometimes the program would last for fifteen, twenty or even thirty minutes, depending on what time they were through.

To me the most amazing thing about the program was that Chester and Tuffy did every voice on the show for it's entire duration, from 1928 until it ended in 1951. The other characters besides Lum and Abner played major rolls, but only two people were ever actually there. There was Dick Huddleston, a grocery store owner and competitor across the street, a good level headed friend, who was always getting Lum and Abner out of trouble. Squire Skimp, a big mouthed, scheming country gentleman pretending to be a lawyer, but always trying to bilk Lum out of money. Grandpappy Spears, a cantankerous old man, coming by the store every day, always fighting with Abner over a checker game or any subject under discussion, always taking the other side. Cedric Wehunt was the town clown, not quite having all his marbles, but he was a good boy always helping Lum and Abner any way he could. Finally there was

Elizabeth, Abner's wife, called LizzyBETH by Abner, a very important character, but she never spoke on the program. In reality Elizabeth did not exist, her character being created entirely on the old,, hand cranked, operator type telephone, from the store to the Peabody home. Many a stage was set for action, by the one sided conversations between Abner and 'LizzyBETH.

I believe one of the secrets to success of the show was, from beginning to end, it was only meant to be funny. The only message they ever tried to send was during the forties, World War II, they would sometimes plug the importance of buying war bonds.

On the way back to the airport the next day after his speaking to the broadcasters, I asked Lum if they had ever thought about syndicating some of their old programs. He said, " Yes, believe it or not there's a company in Little Rock working on that now. The first years were not recorded because there was no recording equipment available in the late twenties and thirties, but we will be able to reproduce on tape about twelve years of daily fifteen minute programs." I said, "When they are ready, be sure to let me know, because I want to run them during the Syrup Sopper show." Before long he called to tell me the shows were ready for distribution, so I leased them and programmed Lum 'n Abner from 7:45- 8:00 a.m. Monday through Friday. They would ship one month of programs at a time, with us returning the previous month's supply. The shows were brand new to the children and young people, being familiar to the older folks, bringing back a lot of fond memories.

I had many carpool mamas call to say they appreciated Lum 'n Abner because on the way to school the program kept the children quiet while listening in the car. One university professor called, saying he had a complaint about Lum 'n Abner. Thinking to myself, "What now? What could possibly be wrong with a country radio program, featuring two old men and their friends," and besides in the sixties and seventies we had never heard about sex, violence or foul language on the air. His complaint was Lum 'n Abner's program ending at 8:00 made him late for his first class, because after he arrived in the parking lot at the University, he would sit and listen till the program was over. He wanted me to begin the program earlier, at 7:40 to fit his schedule.

That, as I explained to him was impossible. We aired the Lum'n Abner show for about 15 years with a few reruns thrown in. That pretty much winds up the schedule for my Syrup Sopper Show. To recap the schedule—

6:00 News
6:05 Country Music
6:25 Sports
6:30 Gospel Music
6:55 Funeral announcements
7:00 News and weather
7:10 Ask the Authority
7:25 (when I could get John Robert off on time) Sports
7:30 Almanac, With local birthdays, anniversaries, hospital discharges, weather, today in history, two songs by the star for the day, and a thought for the day.
7:45 Lum 'n Abner
8:00 News
8:05 Country music and calls from listeners with requests for songs to be played, lost dogs to be found, charity suppers to be eaten, or just to talk about anything on their minds.
8:30 News headlines and weather.
8;32 More music
9:00 End of Syrup Sopper and news

It seems a little strange now to recall how during the entire morning show I was all alone at the station, after Jack Hamm left at 6:00. Before we joined the Associated Press Audio News Network, I had to personally pull the news and sports copy from the teletype machine, edit and read it live, pull and play the records on the two turntables, answer the phone and the front door, do all the commercials live or play them on tape, read and record certain meter readings on the transmitter every hour and hope that no emergency, like having to go to the bathroom, occurred. Just in case though, I always kept Marti Robbins recording of "El Paso" or Jim Reeves, "Shifting, Whispering Sands," or Ray Steven's "Shriner's Convention," handy because they were the longest country records, about four minutes.

Our local news man or woman would be out gathering the local news from the sheriff's office or the police station until just before time to report local happenings on the 7:00 newscast, then spend their time writing, editing, or gathering by phone more news for subsequent news programs.

I spent most of forty years in a radio station, but I would be completely lost in a modern station. There are no records to play, music is delivered by satellite, as is news, sports, weather and network commercials.

Local commercials are not live, recorded, or on anything you can see and feel. They're all somewhere in a computer, with the machine deciding when and where they will be aired. Even with all the sophisticated hardware, some stations will have many more employees on duty than I did, but some have no one there at a studio, they are all "automated." I still like my way the best, and besides it was a lot more fun then.

On the subject of commercials, one of my greatest pleasures from broadcasting was to start out with a small or a brand new business and through my advertising and promotional efforts, a lot of hard work on their part, and see them grow large and prosper.

My local advertisers were not only customers but we were good friends. I appreciated every one of them, and still do.

Chapter 14

GOLF

I was a freshman at Auburn University in 1950, when I tried to hit a golf ball for the first time. The next time was shortly after I went to work at WNPT in 1953. Tom Todd, my boss asked me if I played golf. I said, "Sure, I had a whole quarter of golf at Auburn," not mentioning that I had never actually played a round of golf. He invited me to join him for his regular Saturday morning round with M. E. Grant and Jimmy Thompson. I know he must have been really embarrassed before the game was over for having asked me to play. I found the actual game was not at all like the driving range. I don't remember what I shot, but I'm sure it must have been the all time high score for Tuscaloosa Country Club. He never asked me to play again.

The next time I tried the game was in 1961, the year I went to WACT, and my sales manager, Jerry Brophy asked me to go with him to Meadowbrook, a nine hole course on Hargrove Road. Using some of his clubs, I hacked the ball around the nine holes. For some reason, Jerry never asked me to play again either.

In 1966 Charlie Monk was working at WACT and going to school at the University, when he decided he just couldn't support himself, his wife, Royce and son Chip, that's right Chip Monk, and pay school expenses on the salary I was paying him, but I couldn't afford to pay more, so he took a job in Mobile, his hometown, at WUNI. Needing money for the move he asked me to buy his golf clubs, saying he would take $25 for everything, which included a small bag a partial set of rusty old   Sears clubs, 6 balls, and a few tees.

After I bought the equipment, I thought I had better get serious about the game. Carol and I had joined the Tuscaloosa Country Club shortly after we returned from the army, so a place to play was no problem. I took a couple of lessons from the club pro, Bill Burton, but the one person most responsible for me developing a love for the game and developing as a player, good enough to play with just about anyone without being ashamed of my game was Ray Boozer, my old bowling buddy. When we first started, he spent a lot of time coaching me, spotting me one stroke a hole on the par threes and fours and two strokes on the par fives. Gradually, I was able to lower the gap between his game and mine.

One great thing about the game of golf is the handicap system, used by players worldwide, enabling a poor player to have a chance to beat a good player using the system. What I like most about the game is the way it affords one the opportunity to meet and share with friends or total strangers the one thing they have in common, that is, the love for the game. Some of the best times I've had were with people that I met for the first time on the first tee. Someone said the best way to really get to know a person is to spend the four or fives hours with them that it takes for eighteen holes of golf. I was able to develop long and lasting friendships through golf that would probably never have happened otherwise.

At the local club I normally played with the same group, depending on the day of the week. There were those who could only play on weekends and some who played on week days. I played at every opportunity, generally on Wednesday or Saturday, in the early days and later on just about every day.

In 1968 C. M. Newton was hired by Dr. Frank Rose, the president of the University, to coach the men's basketball team.

C. M. was an athlete, himself and a great coach, having played basketball at Kentucky for coach Adolph Rupp. He consistently shot golf scores in the seventies, occasionally shooting par. Not only was he a good golfer, he was every bit a true gentleman and a person I really enjoyed associating with both on and off the golf course.

I don't remember exactly how it happened, but Ray Boozer, Bill Drake, coach Newton and I started playing every Tuesday afternoon, even during the basketball season, because that was the day the players all had labs and could not practice until late in the day. We played in all kinds of weather, rain, wind, heat, cold and even one time with snow on the ground.

One of my favorite golf stories, and one that illustrates his temperament better than anything, is about the day C. M. and I were playing a twosome. I always said that he was so unemotional, that he could win or lose a basketball game by 20 points and you would never know the difference from his actions, but losing really tore him apart on the inside. The day of the story, neither of us had been playing very well, then while teeing off on number 16 at the Country Club, a downhill par four, C. M. almost missed the ball, whiffing it dead left into a kudzu patch just off the tee, losing the ball ten feet from where he was standing. He played another ball and then on the tee at number 17, a short par three, about 125 yards, with a lake from tee to green, he shanked his tee shot into the lake, taking his putting ball out of his pocket, he teed it up, took a swing and it too took a mighty dive into the lake. I had already hit, my ball resting safely on the green, and I was sitting in the golf car waiting for him. After the second ball went in the lake, he turned to me and said, "Give me another ball." I said, "I'm not going to give you a good one", as I pitched him an old ball the mowers had run over leaving it cut in several places. I said, "Here, hit this one." Another shank, another splash, I'm about to burst out laughing but, held it back, while he got in the golf car and crossing his long legs, said, "I'm going home and beat the hell out of Evelyn." I said, "If you don't hit her any better than you did those last three golf balls she'll never feel it." We both had a good laugh.

That event was never mentioned again except the times I would tell it while introducing him as a guest speaker. There was another time, on number 12, one of us had pull hooked a ball left into deep sedge grass, and as we looked for the ball we realized we were being eaten alive by fire ants. We were in the middle of some really big mounds. By the time we ran out of there, we were completely covered by the stinging little varmints, they were in our shoes, shorts, underwear and shirts. We both stripped off all our clothes right there in the middle of the fairway. Luckily it was a slow day on the course, and we got the ants out of our clothes and them back on before anyone else came along.

Yet another day, I got into a big red wasp's nest near number 3 green, getting stung three or four times on my back, and really in pain. C. M. said, "Here chew some of my pipe tobacco, put it on the stings and they will never swell." I said, "Man I'd rather swell than to chew that stuff", so he chewed it and rubbed it on my back. It did prevent swelling. Remember that next time you get a sting. After incidents like those I used to come home and tell Carol, "Yeah, you thought I was out there having fun, what if you had to go through all that misery?"

Another quickie about C. M. We were riding together in one of coach Bryant's tournaments, when he discovered he had lost his pipe, Insisting we go back looking for it, we headed back trying to retrace our route. I told him, "Don't worry about it, if we get within a hundred yards of it we'll smell it."

A most memorable day for me was June 20, 1970. Coach Paul "Bear" Bryant always had a two day golf outing and his annual summer press conference, talking about the prospects for the upcoming fall football season, for the press and radio people of the state. The event was held at Willow Point, Indian Hills, or on this occasion, at Pine Harbor near Pell City. The first day was for practice, the second day was the actual tournament, followed by dinner, breakfast and the press conference the next morning.

I was scheduled to play a practice round on Sunday afternoon with the basketball coaches, C. M. Newton, Wimp Sanderson, and Jock Sutherland. As I waited at the pro shop for them, to my surprise coach Bryant and coach Johnny Vaught, famous, long time coach at the University of Mississippi walked up. Coach Bryant asked if I had a game. I replied, "Yes sir, I'm supposed to play with the basketball coaches." He said, "We need you to play with us." I said, "Yes Sir". No one said "no" to the man. About that time Sam Bailey arrived, the big coach said, "Sam we need you to play with us to make a foursome." Sam, his head assistant coach, a man who had been with Bryant for years even a Texas A&M, said, "Coach you know I don't play golf." Bryant said, "You are playing today, borrow some shoes and clubs from the pro and meet us on the first tee".

Playing golf with the two greatest legends of the game, especially in the south, I will admit I was so nervous on the first tee I could hardly draw the club back, but after making pretty good contact with the ball, I settled down, having an enjoyable afternoon. Sam and I beat coaches Vaught and Bryant, winning a dollar from each of them. I still have those two one dollar bills, no, they are not for sale.

I remember the date so well, because that evening during the meal I received a call from Carol saying my sister, Lela, had called and told her Opal had taken a turn for the worse and was not expected to live much longer. I caught a ride home after supper with coach Jack Rutledge. Carol and I packed and left Tuscaloosa early the next morning, picked Louis and Maggie up in Athens, Alabama, then on to Anderson, Indiana. Opal died the next morning. I don't believe she ever knew we were there.

Coach Newton was at the University of Alabama for 12 years, then moved on to Vanderbilt University as head basketball coach for awhile and then to Lexington where he is still Athletics Director at The University of Kentucky, a perfect spot for him. Carol and I used to travel with the team to most of the out of Tuscaloosa, Southeastern Conference games, Athens, Ga. Baton Rouge, La. Gainesville, Fl. Knoxville, TN, Lexington, Ky. And Nashville, TN.

One time in Nashville, after an afternoon Vanderbilt game, I had arranged with my friend Ralph Emery for front row tickets to the Grand 'Ole Opry for the entire team. Most of them were not impressed to say the least.

Talking about Coach Bryant, I would not even try to write very much about him, so many books, movies and stories have been told, but later I have a few that you may not have heard. I will say here that he was probably the most unique individual I ever met. The kind of person who could walk into a crowded room and everyone in there would immediately know that somebody special had entered. I have several mementos from him that to me are priceless, plaques, certificates, a Bulova watch with his famous hounds tooth hat printed on the face, all from the golf tournaments, but I especially prize the picture of him and me together at the last of his golf outings in 1982.

When our boys were growing up, playing little league baseball, usually the night or morning after the end of the season, several family friends and their children would form a caravan headed for the beach, Disney Would, Calloway Gardens, Six Flags, Panama City, Destin or Daytona. I won't mention all the children, but the adults were, Bill and Martha Strickland, Tommy and Peggy Belk, Billy and Mary Angelyn Tinsley, Ray and Gail Boozer, Guy and Beverly Elmore, and of course, Carol, Wally, Ron and me. Sometimes the kids would take along a special friend. Greg Gryska, son of coach Clem and Alice Gryska, liked to go with Ron. We men would play golf during the day and the women would take care of the children then all go out together to eat at night. We almost gave several waitresses and cooks heart attacks when they saw the mob moving in.

I enjoyed playing golf regularly at the Tuscaloosa Country Club with both Ray and John Boozer, Bill Burton, John Henry Suther, John Gresham, Bill Koeppel, Bobby Dugins, and his dad, Dr. Rufus Partlow, Coach "Red" Drew, Vance Miles, Henry Rice, Steve Sturgis, Guy Elmore, Bill Strickland, Ray Perkins, Bill Drake, Walt McCracken, and coaches Wimp Sanderson Jock Southerland, and let's not forget my buddy Leroy McAbee. Coach Wimp Sanderson and I went together and bought an old golf cart, actually, I bought it and he was to pay the club the monthly storage fee. We never got to use it very much because it was always broken down. There's a funny story about Wimp,

C. M. Newton's assistant, and later the head basketball coach at the university. Those who knew both men will agree that there were never two more different personalities in the same profession. As I said earlier, C. M. was easy going, not getting excited, win or lose, but Wimp was very motivated, and emotional to say the least, during a game pacing up and down the floor, tossing his plaid sports jacket, ripping his tie off, and if he thought a call was really bad, he was on his knees begging.

For every call he didn't like he had a special scowl on his face toward the official, you might say he was really involved in the game. He was the same way on the golf course, missing a shot got to him in a big way. I was in a foursome with Wimp, playing in a tournament, a crowd had gathered at the first tee to watch the golfers hit their first shots. Wimp was on the tee, his shot hit a big pine tree just to the left front of the tee box, bounced back on top of the pro shop, bounced down to the concrete porch, then back on the tee right at Wimp's feet. Without taking a step, he hit it again only when he got off the tee, he was lying two. That was the only time I've ever seen his temper subdued, Wimp did not say a word for two or three holes, and neither did I.

When John Boozer sold Boozer motor company to Bill Barkley, he visited Bill's summer home at Lake Toxaway, North Carolina. John bought a house there on the Lake Toxaway Country Club golf course and moved up there permanently. For several years, Ray, Leroy and I along with Carol, Gail, and Ruth would go there every summer for their annual Member/Guest tournament. Ray and John were partners, as were Leroy and Bill and my partner was a friend of Bill's named Courtney Quinn who lived at Lake Taxiway in the summer and Naples, Florida in the winter. We always had a good time at Lake Toxaway, high up in the mountains of North Carolina. Speaking of North Carolina, our traveling group would usually make a fall trip to Maggie Valley, not only to play golf, but to view the fall colors, and every other year to attend the Alabama vs. Tennessee football game the third Saturday in October.

And speaking of traveling, Jess Reid, and some of his friends from Anniston formed a "Dirty old Men" group of sixteen who would take a trip to Pensacola, Destin or Gulf Shores for three or four days of golf, eating and story telling. Sometimes we would have as many as twenty-four in the group. In our Tuscaloosa delegation we had too many for me to try to remember all of them but some unforgettable ones were Charlie

York, Bobby Dugins, Mutt Shirley, Henry Rice, Dr. Frank Patton, Dr. Dudley Davis, both of whom were dentists, Bill Koeppel, Dr. Bill DeShazo, Cookie Barlow, J. B. Williamson and me.

On one of these trips I was driving my brand new BMW 735. Dr. Dudley Davis who always liked to ride with me and Max Morton were in the back seat, while Charlie York was in the front next to me. During the first several miles, they were all bragging to me about what I fine car I had purchased, and I was enjoying showing off all the things the computer would do and was so proud of it. By the time we had gone about 40 miles or less I kept noticing Charlie was becoming restless, squirming around in his seat, like he couldn't relax and enjoy the trip in my car.

When we reached Thomasville, 100 miles south of Tuscaloosa, Dudley again said some nice things about the car. Charlie couldn't take it any more. He said, "This is a nice car all right, but my ass is burning up". When we left Tuscaloosa that morning Charlie had accidentally pushed the "high" button that controlled the heated front seat. He had ridden 100 miles with the seat heater on "HOT".

The late Dr. Dudley Davis, a long time dentist in Tuscaloosa was a good friend of mine, one of my favorite people. He looked forward to that golf outing like a child looking for Christmas. His wife, Josephine would not let him smoke at home, so, on the golf trip, he would smoke a whole carton of cigarettes in four days, then quit till the next year. One year, at the last minute, she decided he couldn't go with us, absolutely heartbroken he stayed home. The next year, as usual I picked him up anxious to get started to Gulf Shores. Right away I asked, "Dudley, "How did you manage to get permission to go this year?" He replied with that big grin on his face. "It was really easy this year, she was so nice to me, even insisting that I go with you, I think it may be because I've got her on tranquilizers. She thinks they're vitamins." Some years Carol would arrange to be at our condominium at Orange Beach and would invite the "dirty old men" to our place for a party, which they all enjoyed.

In the early nineteen seventies, Jack Warner, president and CEO of Gulf States Paper Corp, one of the largest privately held corporations in the world, which his grandfather had established in Tuscaloosa, in 1919, developed what he called North River Yacht Club on the east side of the newly built Lake Tuscaloosa. No attempt will be made here to describe the facility which began with a small dog-trot cabin on the edge of the lake and developed into one of the most fabulous country clubs in America. With two beautiful club houses, tennis courts swimming, one indoor and outdoor pool and one Olympic size pool, marina and water sports and a great golf course designed by Gary Player for members and guests to enjoy. The whole facility, with the famous Warner art collection, is indescribable. You will just have to see it. We joined North River in the early stages of its development and I started playing golf at both clubs when I could. Carol played some, but she was never addicted as I was.

I should have died on the North River golf course the afternoon of August 11, 1984. I was playing in a tournament when on hole 11 a pain hit me like a ton of bricks in the chest. Telling myself that it was only indigestion from the hotdog I had eaten at the end of nine holes, I finished the round, tied with Max Gathings for the lead in our flight but was still in terrible pain and sweating, hardly able to make it to the car. I don't remember much about driving myself home, passing right by the hospital, but when I entered the back door Carol said, "What's wrong with you?" I said, "I've got the worst case of indigestion I've ever had."

She tried to get me to go to the emergency room, but I refused until our neighbor Tommy Todd, who had had a heart attack a few years before, came by and recognized that I was in deep trouble. He convinced me to go, but my stupidity made me take a shower, and get dressed before Carol drove me to the hospital.

The last cigarette I ever smoked was on the way to the

hospital. It did not taste good. I indeed had a heart attack and another one in the emergency room. Young Dr. Charles Gross in the emergency room treated me with morphine and hooked up all the monitoring equipment before cardiologist, Dr. Bill Hill arrived. I was so "knocked out" by the drugs by that time I can vaguely remember him saying, Mr. Price you are having another heart attack now, and we need to perform an angioplasty I had no idea what that was but it would not have made any difference if he had told me that he intended to run a tube from my right groin through an artery all the way up to my heart, then blow up a balloon and try to open a clogged spot.

At that time I said "Sure, go ahead, I don't care what you do, run two of them, cut my head off if you want to, I don't care." During the procedure, as I watched the television screen showing the tube as it made it's way to the exact spot on my heart, I became so nauseated that I began throwing up all over the doctor, nurses and that expensive equipment. Even after I was moved to intensive care, I continued to be sick. My male nurse kept busy all night changing me and the sheets on the bed. About the only other thing I remember about that night was when the young man leaned over the bed and said, with his mouth under a mustache, Mr. Price, my name is James and I'm your nurse for tonight." I said, "No, you're not my nurse, son you're too ugly to be a nurse". I apologized to him later. He was wonderful to me, I couldn't have had better care.

They discovered much later that I was allergic to morphine. I remained in intensive care for two or three days. When they moved me to a private room the first person I saw was a nurse who said, "Mr. Price, do you realize you are in the room that coach Bryant died in? I said, "Hey, tell me somebody that LIVED in here, not somebody that DIED." I suppose she thought I'd feel it was an honor to be in that room.

After I sold the radio station and retired, we bought our present house at North River Yacht club overlooking the number 6 tee and a beautiful lake between the tee and green. As I write this, I'm looking out the window at a wonderful view of the lake and golf course. When we moved to North River, we left the

Tuscaloosa Country Club, but we still go back there to see friends and for the good Sunday buffet.

I played golf with Tom Davenport, Max Gathings, Steve Sturgis, Dr. Floyd Fitts, Richard Keshen, Norman Bobb, Wiley McCleod, Lloyd Bridger's, Jim Briggs, Woody Browder, Dr. Pete Snider, Harry Sherritt, Jim Cole, Bill Rose, Dr. Joab Thomas, a Tuscaloosa native, and former President of both The University of Alabama and Penn State University. my next door neighbor C.D. Tatum and others

The Tatums, C.D. and Margaret Ella, are wonderful neighbors and good friends. He was in charge of the athletic ticket office at the university all the time that Coach Bryant was there. He is now in LaRocca nursing home suffering from Alzheimer's disease, but she still lives next door. She and Carol visit just about every day.

In July of 1997 I had to give up the game for reasons I will discuss later. After almost two years, I still miss the golf and the association with my friends. and I must admit I'm a bit envious of them as I sit on the back deck of the house within spitting distance of the tee, and see my friends enjoying playing. Some day I hope to join them again.

I have been privileged to play golf on some of the great courses in the country and a few in Mexico that I would not call great, but even at it's worst golf is still good. I have played courses from Hyannis, MA to San Diego, CA and from Rochester, MN to West Palm Beach, FL. Some of the more famous were Pebble Beach, Laguna Niguel, Indian Wells, PGA West, and San Diego Country Club in California. There was Columbia in Memphis, Calinas in Dallas, The Las Vegas Country Club and Desert Inn in Las Vegas, PGA in West Palm Beach, Disney World, Palm, Magnolia, and Buena Vista, Quail Creek in Naples, Florida. I've also had the good fortune to play Congressional, Columbia and Burning Tree in the Washington D.C. area, and many of the finer courses closer to home. Some of the finer Southeastern golf courses are on the gulf coast, at Destin, Panama City, Fort Walton Beach, Mobile, and Gulf Shores, along with the Montgomery Birmingham and Huntsville clubs and the famous Robert Trent Jones courses throughout Alabama.

As I said before, golf and my involvement in the boards of The National Association of Broadcasters and the Associated Press have provided me an opportunity to meet and enjoy the company of many men and women all over the country, some still friends today. When I turned 55, Buddy Walker of Tuscaloosa, was president of the Alabama Seniors Golf Association. He insisted that I join that group my first year of eligibility. Carol and I both have enjoyed the association with between 400 and 500 members from throughout the state. We have four tournaments a year, and sometimes five, at different locations in Alabama and some are held at Jekyl Island, GA, Hilton Head, SC, Biloxi, Ms., or Destin, Fl. I have served on the board of directors, and as president of the seniors organization. From all of the above, one would think that I never worked at all, but I did manage to squeeze in some work between rounds.

Chapter 15

THE NINETEEN SEVENTIES

The decade of the seventies was in some ways the most rewarding and yet the most frustrating of my entire life. It began with the radio station doing very well. We had paid all debts, had an excellent staff of sales, office, and "on the air" personnel. The Syrup Sopper Show was still going strong. We were involved in just about every phase of community, club, school and church activities, Carol, the boys and I were happy to be in our new house, and enjoying living in a great neighborhood. The first year, 1970, brought the death of mama. She died in her sleep on February 7th, and my sister Opal died on June 22nd.

In 1973 Wally graduated from Tuscaloosa High School and entered The University of Alabama in the fall, graduating with a degree in communications in 1978. Also Wally was married to Judy Kline, daughter of Joe and Lola Kline from Jasper, Alabama. He worked with us at the radio station part-time throughout his school years and worked full-time after graduation.

Ron finished high school at Central High in 1976, also entering the University and graduating in 1980. Ron and Terry Davidson, daughter of Buddy and Ann Davidson of Northport were married in 1981. He worked at the radio station a while before leaving to work for The Associated Press and later the National Association of Broadcasters.

More sadness came our way in 1973 when papa was diagnosed by doctors in Huntsville as having colon cancer at the age of 87. We brought him to Tuscaloosa for surgery. Our friend Dr. Floyd Fitts, an excellent surgeon, performed an operation, removing much of his colon. After the operation, Floyd told me that papa could possibly live as much as two more years, without a recurrence of the cancer, but no doubt it would return. He died, almost to the day, two years later, on June 3rd, 1975, at the Scottsboro Hospital. We buried him next to mama in the Mt. Zion Methodist Church cemetery just north of Cullman.

The day before he died, something happened I will never forget. Papa had been in a coma, not responding to family, nurses, doctors or anything for over a week. During that time he had not spoken a word to anyone, when as I stood at his bedside, he suddenly opened his eyes, looked up at me and said, "Clyde, let's sing." After I recovered from shock, I said, "Papa what do you want to sing?" He replied in a weak voice, "You know that song about I'll have a new body, I'll have a new life, let's sing that." It took me a while to remember the song he had on his mind, but I started to sing softly, "On the resurrection morning when all the dead in Christ shall rise, I'll have a new body, praise the Lord, I'll have a new life." Papa hummed along as best he could, then closed his eyes.

I have always thought, how appropriate that his last wish was to sing, because he loved gospel quartet music, church hymns and was especially fond of Sacred Harp, (better known in the South as Fa-Sol-La singing.) He was 89.

The year 1972 was both good and bad for the Prices. Throughout the latter sixties and early seventies, I had been very active in the Alabama Broadcasters Association, serving on the board of directors, representing the Tuscaloosa district. Carol and I never missing any of the semi-annual conventions. After serving as Secretary, Vice President, President elect, I assumed the office of President at the summer meeting.

That same year, I was elected president of the Tuscaloosa Exchange Club, the largest civic club in Tuscaloosa and one of the largest Exchange Clubs in the United States, so large that our officers only served six month terms so that more members would have a chance.

Two other important events happened in 1972 that changed our lives almost completely. The first, I was elected to a two year term on the Radio Board of the National Association of Broadcasters. From now on I will refer to the Association as it's known worldwide the NAB. There were actually two separate boards, Radio and Television, but both met in January and June, with committee meetings in between as called by the chairmen.

The radio board was made up of thirty five district representatives, my district being Alabama, Georgia, and Florida, and five at large representatives plus four network reps, one each from NBC, CBS, ABC, and Mutual. Those were the only networks at the time, now there are dozens of networks whose membership on the board is determined by a lottery, provided they actually own broadcast stations.

The executive committees of each board consisted of a chairman, chairman elect and vice chairman, with a joint chairman elected by both boards, rotating the position every two years between radio and television.

Those two years and five more that I would serve beginning in 1980 broadened both mine and Carol's vision of broadcasting and the wonderful people who were prominent in our industry more than anything else we could have done. Through the NAB we were able to associate and socialize with some of the very best professionals in the industry. On the board were network presidents, group station owners and officers, large and medium market station owners, each having one goal, and that was the promotion of broadcasting.

Like all national associations, the primary purpose of the NAB was, and still is, lobbying the Congress for favorable legislation and the FCC for favorable regulation of the industry. The first time I ever saw Washington D.C. was in the fall of 1971, after my election to the board. I attended an orientation meeting for newly-elected board members at the NAB headquarters building located on the corner of Connecticut Avenue and N street.

My very first trip to our nation's capitol was an eventful one. I had never flown on a jet but one time and that was in 1956 when I flew to New Jersey. I flew from Tuscaloosa to Atlanta on a small Southern Airways jet, and when I changed planes at the Atlanta airport, they bumped me off my flight to Washington National airport putting me on a Boeing 747 bound for London, with a stop at Dulles airport near Washington.

The 747 wide bodies had just gone on line for the airlines, and when I first walked in the door of that thing, I could not believe anything that huge could actually get off the ground. We took off and right away the pilot was on the intercom telling the passengers, "Ladies and gentlemen you are on the biggest thing that flies. We have 350 people on board, 40,000 pounds of luggage and cargo, this plane has 300 miles of wiring, the landing gear weighs 20 tons, etc. etc., now sit back and enjoy your flight, thanks for flying Delta."

No sooner had he finished and turned his mike off, he was back on saying, "Er, ah, ahem, ladies and gentlemen, we have just lost one of our engines, and we are returning to Atlanta, while I could feel the tilt of the plane as it was turning back. I told the fellow next to me that "I wish that fool hadn't told me a while ago how big this thing is." That is the only time I've ever flown into Hartsfield airport in Atlanta without circling. We flew straight in. They unloaded all passengers as soon as possible, and waited for about two or three hours for Delta to prepare and load another plane. After midnight we took off again for Dulles airport.

When I got off the plane about an hour later I was completely lost, had no idea where Dulles was in relation to Washington, and not knowing how to get downtown, I went to the taxi stand, asked a cabbie to take me to the Mayflower Hotel. I guess he could tell I was lost and from the country and didn't have much money, so he said the fare would be $45.00. I said, "Man! What are you talking about? I just want to go downtown." He said, "Hell, Fellow it's thirty miles. There is a bus that will be a lot cheaper for you." So, I made my way down to the bus stop, boarded the bus and asked the driver if he was going by the Mayflower Hotel. He said, "No, but I'll be going within about three blocks of the hotel." I said, "When you get as close as you will be, let me know and I'll get off."

After a while he put me off somewhere on Pennsylvania Avenue. It was about 2:00 a.m. and I, having heard so much about how dangerous it was to be out alone at night and about the muggings and murders that happen so often, I was scared to death. The driver had pointed the way for me to start walking, so, with my suitcase in my hand and a prayer on my mind I started walking down Connecticut Avenue toward where my hotel was supposed to be. Whew! I made it safely, what a welcome sight that Mayflower sign was. I checked in and got to bed about 3:00 a.m.

I was almost jolted out of bed at 4:30 a.m. by the biggest explosion I had ever heard. I thought for sure that Washington was being attacked by the Russians. As it turned out, they were building the new subway, and the construction, at that time, was in front of the Mayflower. I got up, went to breakfast. That was the first time I had ever paid $12.00 for an egg, a strip of bacon, a piece of toast and a cup of coffee. I then tried to become acclimated to my new surroundings.

That afternoon old Syrup Sopper decided to rent a car and look the city over. That was my first big mistake. I rented a car just around the corner from the main entrance to the hotel. Leaving the hotel, I started driving, looking for the monuments, the Capitol building, the White House and other famous landmarks I had heard and read so much about. I was doing fine for a while. Finding the Capitol, I decided to park, and go in to see what was going on. It so happened that I entered the House of Representatives side of the building and hearing from someone that the House was in session, I wound my way up the spiral staircase to the hallway outside of the visitors gallery. There a uniformed guard stopped me asking if I had a pass. I said, "No, Sir I don't." He said, "You must have a pass to enter the chamber." "Where do I get One?" "Who is your congressman?" "Walter Flowers." "Go to Mr. Flowers' office, they will give you a pass, then you come back, I'll let you in."

I said, "Look, Friend, I don't even know where I am or how I got here, much less where his office is. I just got to town on a big old Delta airplane this morning, never been to Washington before, I'm just an old county boy from Nebo, Alabama and all I wanted to do today was to see how them folks in there are spending all my money I've been sending up here. If you will let me in, I'll be real quiet, won't bother nobody and next time I

215

come I'll bring a pass." The guard said, "I think you are all right, go on in."

I stayed a little while but found the goings on so boring I left right away looking for more adventure in the most beautiful city I had ever seen or dreamed about, especially in the area from the Capitol, down Pennsylvania Avenue to the White House, across the way to the Washington Monument and, further down toward the Potomac at the end of the Reflecting Pool, the Lincoln Memorial.

I just had to get a better look at the Lincoln Memorial, so as I drove in the circle around it, I wove my way to the inside of about eight lanes of traffic. I got a closer look at Mr. Lincoln's statue, but when I tried to get to the outside lane, it was impossible. Traffic was so heavy by then, I had to keep circling the monument for what seemed like a very long time. When I finally broke out of the circle traffic I was headed toward the Jefferson Memorial and the Potomac river, with no place to turn around. After crossing the river, I was able to turn at Arlington Cemetery and began trying to find my way back to the Mayflower.

One thing I didn't know, but soon learned, was that Washington had a lot of one way-streets. Some even change to the opposite direction in the afternoon. It took me forever to find my way back to my hotel and the car rental place next door. I could see it, but I couldn't figure out how to get there. Finally I made it back, turned in the car and promised the Lord I would never rent another car in Washington D. C.

That evening there was a brief meeting of the new board members, and then with Vince Wasilewski, president of NAB and John Summers, Vice President and the five of us. We left the hotel in a cab for the very famous Washington Palm restaurant only three or four blocks away.

When we left the hotel it was raining, so we all piled into the first taxi available. The first time I ever met my friend Stan Wilson, a radio station owner from Fort Worth, Texas, he was sitting on my lap in the backseat of that crowded cab. As you might imagine, we became good buddies after that experience

216

and later Stan and Christine, Carol and I became very good friends, visiting and corresponding by phone or Christmas card even now.

Stan and Christine lived just off the great Colonial Country Club, made famous by the golf legend Ben Hogan. One of my favorite golfing experiences was playing that course with Stan, having lunch in the clubhouse and seeing all of Mr. Hogan's many trophies that are on display in cases there.

Two other gentlemen who became really good friends were Don Thurston and Bob Hilker. Don and Oralie still live in North Adams, a small town in northwest Massachusetts. They own radio stations in North Adams and Great Barrington. Carol and I have visited them on two occasions and they have been to Tuscaloosa twice, Don playing golf with me in our annual Member/Guest tournament.

The first time either of them were in Alabama, they were extremely nervous, not knowing how we Southerners would treat to a couple of Yankees, especially Oralie, she being originally from Vermont with a New England accent you could cut with a knife. I had told her that folks down here still blame folks like her for us loosing the war, so to protect herself and me please, keep her mouth shut, and I would introduce her as my deaf and dumb cousin from Cullman.

From talking to them before they made the trip, it was obvious they expected to find in Tuscaloosa, people living in abject poverty, a washing machine on every front porch, an old car on blocks in every front yard, goats being used for lawn mowers, good old boys with rifles on racks in their pick-ups, Bull Connor turning the dogs and water hoses on black folks, as portrayed so many times on network television.

They had been to Florida, but had never been to Georgia, Tennessee, or Alabama. Don called just before they were to make the trip, saying, "Oralie and I have decided to drive to Alabama we want to see Appalachia. How do I get to Tuscaloosa?" I said, "Don, it's real easy. Just get on the paved road up there and it comes right here to the front of our house."

Needless to say, when they got a look at Tuscaloosa, the

Yacht Club and facilities here, they dreaded going back to the North and the 30 feet of snow that usually covers the ground from September until April in the Berkshire Mountains they call home. They were anxious to come back the next year. Don was elected joint chairman of the board later and the four of us ate pretty "high on the hog" at convention time because he was on a very liberal expense account. Neither of them knew what that term means, I didn't try to explain it. Don has served the broadcasters as Chairman of the Board of Broadcast Music Inc. (BMI) for several years in addition to operating his radio stations. I liked Don, but fell in love with Oralie in 1972, and still feel the same about them.

Another one of my favorite people on the board was Bob Hilker from near Charlotte, North Carolina. Bob was a fun loving guy, always with a joke, a great fellow, always great to be around. When we first met he was single, but later married a wonderful lady, Juanita. They lived in a beautiful house on Lake Norman between Charlotte and Statesville, North Carolina. He began his broadcasting career as an engineer, but got into ownership, buying a station in a small town near Charlotte, Belmont, North Carolina. Before he was through he owned as many as eleven stations both AM and FM, but his favorite was always Belmont, where he first started and still maintained his general offices.

The terrible hurricane, Hugo, completely destroyed his station on the island of Saint Croix in the Virgin Islands. Then the storm hit Myrtle Beach, South Carolina where he owned some condominiums, destroying them. Then it moved inland to Lake Norman where it demolished his boat house and damaged the big house, and would you believe, Bob and Juanita were on a cruise of the Saint Lawrence Seaway, and had to ride out the tremendous wind and rain caused by the same storm. I told them the Lord must be trying to tell them something.

Carol and I have visited their place many times. As we sometimes drove to Washington, we would stop overnight with them, then Bob and Juanita would ride with us to D.C. and back. They also enjoyed visiting Tuscaloosa.

The first year I was on the board the Joint Chairman was one of the most distinguished looking and sounding men I had ever met. His name was Bill Walbridge, a TV station owner from Houston, Texas. Vic Deam, a former president of mutual network and a station owner in Pennsylvania, was a real "character," never making a serious statement, interrupting board proceedings with an off-color joke. To make him even funnier, he was about the size of Mickey Rooney, too short and fat to fit in a coach seat on a plane, always fussing about having to fly first class. I would tell him the seats were not too small, his butt was just to big. Now I know why he was complaining.

As I was saying Bill Walbridge was the epitome of a Texas gentleman, tall, with grey hair, deep melodious voice, with a slight Texas drawl. All he needed was a Texas size ten gallon Stetson, and he would have looked like he was right out of North Fork Ranch. He was greatly admired by the entire board and the paid employees of NAB. At his last meeting, before retiring from the board, Bill was presiding and as we came to the end, he said, solemnly, "Gentlemen, my good friends, this is my last meeting with you. Most of you I will never see again. I have enjoyed my twelve years, serving in every position on the TV board and the past two as Joint Chairman. I will miss all of you and if you are ever in Houston come to see me. However, before I go I want to say just one more thing to you gentlemen, that is F--- Vic Deam. That remark, knowing both men, and that they were actually very good friends, broke up the meeting and all of us left laughing.

Walbridge was replaced as joint chairman by Andy Ockershausen, general manager of WMAL radio in Washington. As some of us sat talking during lunch at a board meeting, Bob Hilker asked Andy "What are ya'll getting for spots in Washington now?" Andy said, "Oh, about three to four." Hilker said, "Hell, I'm getting $2.50 in Belmont."

I tried to make a phone call from my office to Andy at WMAL. When I told the operator that I wanted to speak to Mr. Ockershausen. She said, "Would you please spell that?" I said, "Honey, if I could spell it I would write him a letter." I am probably misspelling his name now, but who cares besides Andy, and I'm sure he'll never read this.

Bob Hilker was funny even without trying to be that way. Every time a waiter would bring his check at a restaurant Bob would look at it and regardless of the amount exclaim $42.00!! It might be more or less but we could always count on him to say "$42.00!!" One evening the four of us had been out to Kennedy Center and being hungry we decided to stop at Blackie's House of Beef for a snack before returning to the hotel. We each ordered a hamburger and a cup of coffee. We ate, the waiter handed Bob the check, he said, "42 dol------, Damn! it is $42.00!!"

Another time late at night we stopped by a small bar, restaurant combination next door to the Canterbury Hotel where we always stayed. We went in, the cocktail waitress, a gal much too old for the little tutu she was wearing, asked if she could help us. I said, "Would you know what I'm talking about if I said I want some cracklin' cornbread, buttermilk, and a platter of collard greens?" She said, "I shore would, Honey, I'm from Demopolis, Alabama." We had a good time visiting with her.

Bob Hilker sold his radio stations for millions, selling the one at Norman, just north of Charlotte for $16,000,000 with $8,000,000 down financing the balance. The buyer defaulted on the loan, Bob took the station back and sold it again.

About three years ago he had a stroke and is almost completely helpless now with Juanita taking care of him at home. About the time of the stroke, lightning struck their beautiful home on lake Norman while she was taking Bob to the Mayo Clinic in Jacksonville. The fire completely destroyed the house and everything in it. While living at a Holiday Inn for several months, she built another house. We call them often, but most times Bob doesn't recognize us.

Before I was elected to the NAB board of directors, Carol and I had traveled very little, the farthest from Alabama was to Fort Monmouth, New Jersey, which was certainly no pleasure trip. We had gone for years without taking a real vacation, except for the summertime outings with our neighbors and all the children. Serving on the board gave us an opportunity to go places, do and see things, meet celebrities, congressmen, senators and even presidents, in the company of some of the best in the broadcasting industry. The good part, most of the travel, food and lodging expense was paid by the Association.

Our first board meeting was in Palm Springs, California. Carol and I arrived there late at night, unable to see much of the area, but when I looked out the bathroom window, the next morning I saw something I had never seen before. Waking Carol, I said, "You have got to see what's out there, the biggest rock I've ever seen." She thought I was crazy, but sure enough, there was a mountain right behind the Canyon Hotel, the first I'd ever seen with no trees on it, looking like a gigantic rock.

The full board met twice a year, with the June meeting always at our headquarters building in Washington, and the January meeting someplace warmer, more desirable than Washington. The first summer meeting, June of 1973, Carol was anxious to go with me to continue her exploration of the city, the museums, art galleries and shopping that she had not been able to finish when we had been there briefly the spring before. She enjoyed meeting the board wives and the staff, forming lasting friendships with many of them.

It was at that meeting that I learned very quickly new board members were to be seen and not heard. Nobody said so specifically but right away we figured it out, we were there to learn and not to advise. At lunch the first day, I asked Don Thurston, "Recon it'd be all right if I asked for the salt?" He didn't know what I meant by "Recon."

Man, were we excited about going to Maui for the winter meeting in January of 1974. Neither of us had ever been to Hawaii, but having heard so much about the place, we looked forward to it for months. We were not disappointed, the island was beautiful and the Westin hotel resort was fabulous. One thing I learned at that meeting, a Mai Tai is not fruit juice, even if it does taste like it.

The National Association of Broadcasters holds its annual convention every April. Now, it is held every year in Las Vegas because no other city in the country has as many hotel rooms and convention facilities in as close proximity to accommodate the more than 100,000 broadcasters, equipment and program suppliers and old folks like me who just go to renew acquaintances with other old folks. For years the convention was held in Washington, but so many people had such bad experiences with the hotels, it was moved to Chicago, which was much better but McCormick Place exhibit space was totally inadequate.

Dallas was the next best place, but so large and with hotels scattered throughout a forty mile radius, transportation expense was just too much. The last convention in Dallas cost the NAB more than $300,000 for shuttle busses to and from the convention center and the hotels. We tried Atlanta one year, but again the city could not hold that many extra people, and since that year, Vegas has been the permanent sight of the NAB convention. I told someone, "If Las Vegas is good enough for the Southern Baptist Convention, it should be good enough for the broadcasters."

One city I did not mention, being Houston, Texas, was the sight of my most memorable convention, the one that stands out above all the many I have attended. Our convention in April of 1974 was the one, with most of the board member and staff of NAB staying at the Hyatt Hotel. The convention committee had invited, as was customary, the President of the United States Richard Nixon to speak.

We thought when he accepted that he would fly in, speak, and fly out, but the day before he was to arrive, we received word that the President would stay over night at the Hyatt and would require the top four floors of the hotel, which were already filled to capacity. The NAB staff went into a frenzy trying to find rooms for those who had to vacate the Hyatt. Even our president Vince Wasilewski had to move.

You will remember that in 1974 Mr. Nixon was under fire from the press, some members of Congress and the public for the Watergate fiasco. He was with us in Houston about three months before he resigned. He and his staff were the most paranoid folks I had ever seen. The hotel, before his arrival, was completely surrounded by armed guards. Police and troops could be seen on surrounding rooftops of buildings adjoining the hotel, across the street and those on the route to the convention center. All elevators in the giant hotel were closed one hour before his arrival. Some conventioneers who could not get to their rooms were very upset. The President was to speak on national television, more in the format of a press conference than a straight speech, at the convention center auditorium at 7:00 p.m. Our entire board was to share the stage with him and our instructions were to gather in a first floor meeting room at another hotel no later than 5 p.m. Carol and I shared a cab to the meeting place with Stan and Christine Wilson, on the way, discovering that our cab driver was actually a Secret Service agent. He showed us the real drivers picture identification on the back side of the sun visor. All regular cab drivers had been replaced by officers during that time period, in that section of the city.

Upon arrival we were not even allowed to go to a bathroom or leave the room for any reason after we had been identified and searched. Leaving would have meant we could not re-enter the room. About 6:30 we were loaded on two different buses, board members in one and spouses in the other and driven to the under-ground area of the convention center. We left the bus and had to march single file between armed guards up a long flight of stairs to the main auditorium, board members to the stage and spouses to a special roped off section down in front.

The members of the press were seated in the front rows of the center section just below the stage. The board members had arranged themselves in sort of a semi-circle behind the podium. When Vince Wasilewski introduced the President I was close enough to Nixon to almost touch his coat-tail, but I was afraid to move considering all the security forces in the hall.

During the questioning he, of course, denied any part in the Watergate burglary and cover-up. I was one of the ones who believed him, just not believing the President could actually be involved in such a scheme, especially when his re-election was

223

so obvious anyway. By the way, I was in Washington the night of the break-in at the National Democratic Headquarters, with not much attention being paid to it the following morning by the press. They treated it more or less as a political prank, until Woodward and Bernstein from the "Washington Post" began their investigation.

That occasion in Houston was when the now famous confrontation between reporter Dan Rather and President Nixon occurred. the one that by now everyone has seen on CBS They and Mr. Rather like to rerun it every time they do any kind of a story about the late President.

I don't remember the exact words, but the exchange went like this. Rather asked Nixon a question, Nixon followed his answer with, "Are you running for something?" To which Rather replied, "No Mr. President, are you?" I remember thinking at the time it was a smart-ass remark from a smart-ass reporter to the President of The United States, and I still do.

When the show was over, we marched back downstairs, to the buses were transported back to the front of the Hyatt, left the buses and marched single file like a bunch of prisoners, between two rows of armed guards across the lobby and up the hotel stairway to a rather cozy meeting room on the mezzanine floor. By the time we arrived back at the hotel Nixon and his party were already in the room waiting for our official reception to take place. As he received, shook hands, and chatted briefly with each board member and wife or husband, his official photographer took a picture, which was later mailed to us. I have had a lot of fun through the years comparing my picture with the President to that of him and Carol. In mine he is smiling looking very pleasant and happy, but with Carol he has that well known Nixon scowl, looking like he is really upset, about to cry. I named that picture of the two, "Dick, I'm pregnant again". Come to think of it, that might not be too far fetched if our present chief executive had been there. We had been warned again not to leave the room, but during the reception, you do remember my old friend Vic Deam, started to leave. The guard at the door stopped him saying, "Sir, you are not allowed to leave the room until after the President has left." Vic said, "Young man, I am 75 years old and Richard Nixon may control the country but he does not control my bladder and neither do I. Now you let me go, or I'll pee all over the President and this fancy carpet." The guard said, "That's OK go ahead."

We had a great time in Houston. One of the most unusual things I have ever had happen to me was the late afternoon Carol and I rode with Stan and Christine Wilson to the Shamrock Hotel for a party. They had driven their car down from Fort Worth. Leaving the elevator, as we walked across the large lobby, we were stopped by a small man in a green suit and green derby, accompanied by a much younger woman, who I assumed was his wife. I was thinking what kind of nut is this, or that it was some kind of promotion. Then I remembered it was St. Patrick's Day which explained the green attire, as he asked, "Are you folks with the broadcasters?" I said, "Yes, Sir, we sure are." He said, "I'm a member of the Houston Chamber of Commerce. If there's any thing we can do for you while you're here just let me know", as he handed me a simple card with the name Joe Albritton on it.

I said, "There is one thing you can do now. We are hungry, and I'll bet you could tell us the name of a good restaurant." Joe said, " Wait a minute, let me make a phone call." A couple of minutes later he was back, asking if we had a car. After hearing that we did, he told Stan to bring his car around and for us to follow him.

We followed him and his wife for several miles on the interstate, then off onto a four lane highway and then onto a two lane road. All the time I was telling Stan that I don't know who is the craziest, us or that little leprechaun in the car ahead of us. Finally after what had to be 15 or 20 miles, we pulled up to the front of a white colonial-style mansion with a small sign in front on which was neatly engraved "Court of St. James," which we assumed was a restaurant.

Joe jumped out of his car, saying, "I'm sorry my wife and I have another party to go to and cannot eat with you, but y'all go in and tell the maitre d', Roscoe, that you are the folks I called him about. We entered, and did as we were instructed. Roscoe escorted us back to one of the most unusual restaurants any one of us had ever seen, with large plants, running water-falls and real birds singing.

He seated us at a choice table where the wine was already poured, handed us menus, and called a waiter over to take care of us. Stan and I both were hoping our credit cards would not bounce when we signed the ticket for what was already shaping up to be one of the most expensive meals in the Texas. The four of us enjoyed a truly delicious meal, thinking that since we were there we might as well go ahead and blow our entire food budget for the week on that one meal.

As we finished the last course, desert, and coffee, I asked the waiter if the check was ready. To our surprise he said, "There is no check. Mr. Albritton has already taken care of it." We left but that night I resolved to see if I could find out more about this Joe Albritton.

The next morning, at the convention, I asked Bill Walbridge from Houston if he had ever heard of a character around there named Joe Albritton? He said, "Yeah, how do you know him?" I told Bill the story of the night before, and he said "Joe Albritton is one of the richest men in Texas, that all sounds just like something he would do."

That was the one and only time I ever saw or heard from Joe personally. I did send him a "thank you" note, but never received a reply. Later I read in "Broadcasting" magazine that he was buying radio and TV stations; in fact just about four years ago he and his son bought WCFT-TV Channel 33 here in Tuscaloosa and WHMA-TV Channel 40 in Anniston, moved both stations to Birmingham identifying them as ABC 33/40, owned by Albritton Communications Company.

In 1980 there was a big shake-up at the top of the NAB. Vince Wasilewski retired after nineteen years as President, the board appointed search committee was chaired by Eddie Fritts from Indianola, Mississippi, the joint board chairman. The preliminary report as reported in "Broadcasting" was that the board had chosen my good friend Don Thurston to be the new president.

In the meantime, Roy Steinfort, president of the Associated Press in Washington had convinced me to run for a southeast district seat on the AP board, which I had won. My first AP board meeting was to be in New York City. Carol and I decided to take a long drive to the New England states, stop by North Adams to visit Don and Oralie, and back to New York for the AP meeting. We drove to Charlotte, then north through Akron, Cincinnati, and finally to Niagara Falls. I don't mean to stray too far off the subject, but I must say the falls are the most spectacular sight these old eyes have ever seen. The one thing that no picture, not even a movie can not do justice.

As I stood on the Canadian side looking at the magnificent view an old fellow standing by me said, " You know, this is my favorite spot in the whole world. My wife and I came here on our honeymoon 42 years ago and we still come back every year to celebrate our anniversary. We have never missed a year." Thinking he must be from Buffalo or Syracuse, someplace close by, I said, "Where are you folks from?" He replied, "Chicago, I'm in the hardware business."

I said, "It is indeed beautiful, awesome, spectacular and a whole bunch of adjectives I can't even think of, and I would like to come again sometime ,but I don't think I would like to visit it every year for forty two years, what is it about Niagara Falls that you like so much that keeps bringing you back every year?" To which he replied, "The reason I like the Falls so much, they are always working. I've never been told they are closed for repairs, the power is off, the weather is too bad, come back tomorrow, or you should have been here yesterday. Yessir, they are always turned on. That's what I like about the falls". As I left him standing there I was thinking to myself, he's right, when the falls stop running it will probably be the end of time on this earth.

Carol and I drove across upper New York state, spending a night at Lake Placid, site of a former winter Olympics, then on to North Adams to the Thurstons. As I was congratulating Don on his being named President of NAB, he said, "Wait a minute, haven't you heard what happened?" "No what?" I had not heard any news in several days and did not know that at the special board meeting in Chicago where everyone thought Don would be selected, Eddie Fritts, chairman of the selection committee who had developed an extreme case of "Potomac Fever" dreaded to go back to Indianola, Mississippi. Who could blame him; decided to throw his own hat in the ring. After a battle between the Thurston forces and Fritts forces on the board, they gave the job to Eddie by one vote.

I believed at the time they had done wrong by selecting the man who had headed the selection committee, but I had no say in the matter since I was not on the board. Ironically, when I did go back on the board, Eddie was instrumental in appointing me chairman of the bylaws committee which proposed a change in the bylaws that prevented a sitting board member from running for president without first resigning.

The proposal was overwhelmingly approved by the full board at our next meeting.

Eddie Fritts has done a good job, and is still President of the Association, soon to be in his twentieth year. Carol and I had a great time with Don and Oralie, driving up into Vermont and New Hampshire, spending nights in bed-and-breakfasts, seeing country we had never seen before. We came back to North Adams and then on to New York City. The drive itself was an experience for me. We had been to New York the year before staying two night at the Americana Hotel before leaving for the trip to Vienna. I'll never know exactly how we found the New York Hilton, but we did, checked in and prepared for my first of many AP board meetings.

The next morning I was called out of the meeting to a phone call from the chairman of the NAB radio board inquiring if I would be willing to come back on the board to serve one year, completing the term of Bill Stakelin, our representative from Florida. He had moved up to joint chairman, due to the election of Eddie Fritts to the presidency. I agreed to the appointment, then after that year, ran for a full two year term, was elected and two years later won another term, the maximum. We had a two term limit, but because my first year was filling Stakelin's last year, I served for five years, from 1980 till 1985.

My Associated Press board time was for eight years, so for the next five years Carol and I had four very interesting places to go for board meetings and conventions, with my AP board time ending in 1988. I'll have much more to say about the eighties, but since this part is concerned with the seventies, I must confine the next segment to the period from 1972 until 1978 and show you everything was not all fun and games, why I turned prematurely grey, developed high blood pressure and lost a lot of faith in our government's regulatory processes. In order to understand the next chapter of My Story you may want to go back and read again the chapter on Radio and Regulations.

Chapter 16

THE PETITION

In the fall of 1971, soon after the Federal Communications Commission announced its composite week on which the renewal of Alabama broadcasters licenses would be based the next year, we at WACT intensified our efforts to compile all of the required paperwork. The licenses of WACT and WACT-FM both would expire on April 1, 1972, but renewal applications must be delivered to the FCC in Washington no later than December 31, 1971. As I told you in the chapter on regulations, the purpose of the three months between filing and when the renewal application would even be considered by the Commission was ostensibly to give members of the public an opportunity to file comments about a station's performance, whether the comments were favorable or not, it made no difference. All comments from the public, were supposed to be filed and at the Commission on or before March 31 in order to be considered.

With the help of my secretary, Beth Berry, I undertook to fill out all forms and analyze program logs as to percentages of news, weather, music, sports, public affairs, political, and religious programming. On the seven logs representing the past three years, all spot announcements, including commercial, political and public service for each individual hour had to be counted, recorded and compared to our promises of three years before. All files pertaining to the ascertainment of community needs had to be checked for accuracy and completeness. All technical information had to be covered in statements from Dave Peacock, the engineer, regarding performance of the equipment, and field strength measurements had to be included.

For a renewal application there was so much more work

required, I will not bore the reader with any more details here, but you do need to know a large part of our time between October and the end of December was involved with license renewal. In the third week of December we packed all of the paper in two cardboard boxes and shipped them, certified, with return receipt requested, to the FCC, in plenty of time to arrive there before the 31st.

I was in my office on the afternoon of March 30th about 4:00 when Beth came in to tell me that there were three men out front requesting to see our public file. That was the first time since the public file rule had been in effect that anyone had ever actually asked to see it. Naturally she was nervous and apprehensive about it. I told her to bring everything in to my office, while I was clearing my desk, making room to display the material. I, too, was suspicious but thought maybe it was just some folks wanting to see our files out of curiosity or three university students with a class assignment.

However, when they entered my office, and I saw them for the first time, I knew in my gut they were up to no good and really not concerned about my welfare. One was a very small, thin, well dressed man with a squeaky, high pitched voice, appearing to be in his thirties. Another was a young black man, dressed like a typical University student, having very little to say and appearing uneasy, as if he had no idea why he was there. The third, about forty, was dressed in blue jeans, with a denim shirt and wearing over it what we used to call, back in Cullman County, an overall jumper. He wore sandals, with no socks, and a ponytail.

I was immediately suspicious of him when he, instead of hanging his denim jacket on the rack in the corner of my office, took it off and threw it on the floor. I told them that on the desk was the complete public file and that they were welcome to look at it, but reminded them that we were only required to make it available during business hours, and our business office would close in about thirty minutes, at five p.m.

They were not allowed by the FCC to remove any files from the office but were allowed to make copies, at their expense, if they desired. I asked if they would identify themselves. The skinny one said, "We are not required to tell you who we are or who we represent." I said, "Yes, Sir, you are absolutely right, you are not required to tell me who you are, but I thought we might understand each other better if I at least knew who I'm talking to, especially since, I'm sure, you know who I am, or you would not be here." They did not identify themselves, but when they left at 5 p.m. we put everything back in the cabinet, hoping that was the end of it. As it turned out, that afternoon was only the beginning.

The three returned just before noon the next day, March 31. Squeaky did the talking, saying, "Mr. Price, we are going to file a petition with the FCC to deny renewal of the license of WACT." Having read and heard of other broadcasters in every part of the country spending thousands and even millions of dollars to protect their properties from these petitions, I really could not think of much to say, except, "You know today is the last day to file, so if you are planning to do it you had better hurry. And, how could you possibly prepare a petition to deny this license after having spent less than thirty minutes yesterday looking over our files?"

Again I said, "I know you were not required yesterday to tell me who you are, but at this point I believe common courtesy would demand that you at least identify yourselves." Whereupon Squeaky said, "This gentleman," pointing to ponytail and sandals, "is Ronald Kramer, head of the "Citizen's Communication Center in Washington." I am Steve Suitts, from the office of Drake and Knowles, attorneys here in Tuscaloosa, I am the Tuscaloosa director of the ACLU, the American Civil Liberties Union." He identified the young black man as John Bivins, a law student at the University of Alabama. Suitts went on to say, "We know that today is the deadline for filing, but we have taken the liberty of writing a document we would like you to sign requesting the FCC to grant us an extension of the time for filing."

I replied, "I can't believe that you folks in your wildest dreams could think I would ever sign something like that. When

I file with the Commission, whether it be license renewal, EEOC reports, engineering data, or whatever, that has a definite filing date, a late filing would result in a stiff penalty, and a possibility it would not be accepted at all. Seems to me that you people have a lot of nerve to come in my office for a few minutes yesterday, then come back today, asking me to request an extension of time for you to file a petition to put me out of business, the best radio station in town off the air, and all the while my not even knowing what your complaint, assuming you have one, is all about. That kind of foolishness would be like coming in with an unloaded gun, asking me to furnish you a bullet so that you could execute me. I will absolutely not sign your paper, and I would appreciate your telling me what the beef is with our radio station, and if it is a legitimate problem that I can remedy, I will certainly try to do so."

Again, Suitts replied, "The rules do not require that we tell you anything about why we are filing the petition, you will learn that when you receive a copy after its filed."

Immediately after the three musketeers, Suitts, Kramer and Bivins left my office, I was on the phone with my Washington attorney, Leonard Joyce, of Daly, Joyce, Bosari, and George. I explained to Leonard all of the events of the past two days and that I expected they would file the petition as soon as the petition mill, the so-called Citizens Communications Center in Washington, could crank it out. He didn't seem to take the matter very seriously because, as he said, the Commission would most likely not accept a late filing. He told me not to worry, he would follow the Commissions proceedings daily and if anything were filed he would inform me.

On the fourth day after the filing deadline they indeed did file a petition to deny the license renewal of WACT. The petitioners, apparently knowing so little about our station's operations, in their haste to file forgot the WACT-FM station which was under the same ownership and management, even simulcasting for the most part identical programming. That oversight would work in our favor later.

The petition itself was almost a carbon copy of hundreds of

others that were filed by the same group that year and in previous years. In 1972 they filed petitions to deny against WACT, twelve other radio stations in Alabama and three TV stations including WAPI, Channel 13 in Birmingham. All petitions were basically the same, except for changes in names of principles, dates, times and places. The next year they even filed against WSM in Nashville, which in my opinion, was and is still one of the all time great radio and TV stations.

Their petition charged that we had not hired our quota of minorities, that we had over commercialized. That is, in some hours we had run more than the 18 minutes of commercials per hour, that the "Ask the Authority" program was a program length commercial, because John Robert Spiller, sponsor of the program, owned the store, and at the same time was on the air as the authority.

Also we were charged with not devoting enough program time aimed especially toward the black audience, their concerns and needs. Remember our station's music was exclusively "Country" which we as any other station, had a perfect right to program. We were charged with not programming enough "black news," and when we did it was primarily in the morning police report.

We had always been very careful never to identify a person who had been incarcerated as black or white. The kicker was that we did not program enough "black weather,"

I had an answer for all of their charges except that one. I had always believed that when I gave the weather report it was for everyone in the area, but apparently the Citizens Communications Center did not see it that way, and were suggesting I divide the weather between black and white, while at the same time saying that all programming should be aimed at all segments of the population regardless of race. I still don't understand the logic of that, if there was any logic.

They even went so far as to quote an employee, Jack Dimmerling, as saying that I, Syrup Sopper, had said on the air, "We don't play any "nigger" music on WACT," which, of course, he denied telling them, and I know that I never made that statement.

By the time we received our copy of the more that one hundred page petition, and had tried to read and fully understand what we were up against, it was time for the annual NAB convention in Washington. Carol and I had already made plans to attend the convention, go on to New York for a couple of days, see two Broadway shows, for which ASCAP had given us tickets, and then go on to Vienna to visit the Djordjevics, a trip I wrote about earlier. The filing of that petition had thrown such a cloud over our lives, we thought seriously about canceling the whole trip, but decided to proceed as we had planned. Instead of attending the convention we spent most of the time we were in Washington in the office of attorneys Leonard Joyce and George Bosari going over even the most minute details of the petition and deciding how we would answer the charges.

We prepared a preliminary answer, explaining to the Commission that we would file more as time permitted, but insisting because the petition was filed late, our position was that it should not be accepted. I wanted to cancel the trip, but the attorneys insisted that we go ahead as planned, saying, "There's absolutely nothing you could do here and besides this thing will probably drag on for years before it's settled." That was a truly prophetic statement, the filings and refilings of briefs by both sides would drag on for six years.

Answers to their charges about programming and employment discrimination were easy. The one thing that I had already admitted and explained to the Commission even in my original application was the charge of over commercialization, that is, more than 18 minutes per hour. We had, on occasion during political campaigns, when we were required to provide time for candidates and during the Christmas shopping season, exceeded the maximum of 18 minutes by running as much as five minutes more on the Syrup Sopper show, the most commercial show on the air, It was the program that really paid the bills for the station. There were many more hours of the day that we did not run any commercials.

The other charge, that the Spiller program was a program length commercial, we maintained that even though a listener would sometimes ask John if he had a certain product at the store, his answering yes or no did not constitute a commercial, and that during the course of the program we made a distinct break for a commercials, keeping those messages separate and apart from the program content.

I realize a whole book could be written about the period of my life from 1972 to 1978 when this thing was finally brought to an end, but don't worry, I'll not dwell on it much longer. There was one time about 1976 that I paid Leonard Joyce $1000 a day plus expenses to come to Tuscaloosa for a meeting in my office with Suitts, Kramer and a woman ACLU lawyer. I was hoping to reach some kind of settlement with them. I told them, "There's nobody who wants to settle this thing more that I do. I'm spending money that I don't have sending a check to the attorneys every month, hundreds of hours on the telephone, and overtime for my staff, not to mention the time I spend working on this instead of working for the station." That female lawyer spoke up and said, "What you need is some lawyers paid by tax-free foundations like we are." I have never had such a desire to slap a woman's Liberal ACLU teeth down her throat. I didn't, but sometimes wish I had. I would probably still be in jail, but I'm sure I would have felt better.

Absolutely nothing was accomplished by that meeting, although I was convinced then and still believe if I had offered a sizable bribe, maybe ten thousand dollars, they would have gladly withdrawn the petition. But I was determined to beat that blood sucking bunch if it took me years and everything I owned. Mind you, I'm not accusing them or even suggesting they asked for money from me, except the subject was brought up, something about if we drop it, would you be willing to pay our attorney fees? That, to me, sounded like a request for a bribe, considering they had just told me they were being paid by the tax-free foundations. I refused to agree to pay them, so the question was pointless.

It would be impossible to list all of the hours, telephone

calls, and trips to Washington that I spent trying to settle the matter and to prevent it progressing to a formal hearing, which would be so terribly expensive. I could never afford it. In the meantime, when all was said and done, it seemed that the two major points of contention were the commercials and "Ask the Authority." At the suggestion of Leonard Joyce my attorney, we took every daily program log, not only for the composite week, but for the entire previous year and analyzed 365 logs, hour by hour for commercial, public service announcement and types of programming. I could not even begin to estimate the number of hours Beth Berry, my secretary, and I spent counting and recording on charts I had prepared, the number of 30 and 60 second commercial and free public service spot announcements we had broadcast and the percentages of time devoted to each in the past 365 days.

Through the years I had taped many of the Spiller programs, Beth and I listened to the tapes and recorded the number of seconds of commercial time in each, with some having no actual commercials except that the program was being sponsored by Spiller Field and Garden Shop. In addition I began recording every program and sending them to Washington for review by the attorneys.

I don't have the words to describe the anger, frustration, disgust and even hatred for the parties involved, nor the disillusionment and disappointment I developed toward the liberal bureaucracy in our nation's Capitol, during those six years.

The most frustrating thing was that my friends and, sometimes my own family could not fully understand what I was going through. To my business associates and customers, it was beyond comprehension that a pip squeak attorney, who was not really an attorney after all, having dropped out of law school at the University, a hippie lawyer from Washington and a black college student, in conjunction with the all mighty ACLU, could arbitrarily file a petition to deny the license of a legitimate business without even attempting to prove just cause.

I appealed to my Congressman Walter Flowers for, if

nothing else, sympathy, but he cited a "hands off" rule that prevented a Congressman even expressing an opinion on a pending case before the FCC. The FCC was all powerful in deciding the life or death of a broadcaster, and the sad thing was, the broadcaster was considered to be guilty until he could prove his innocence, regardless of how ridiculous the allegations might be, exactly like the Internal Revenue Service.

It was in the summer of 1978, after the April renewal period, and our FM had been renewed twice, in 1975 and 1978, that I had taken just about all I could bear having spent well over $100,000, in attorney's fees, thousands more on the telephone, at least twelve trips to Washington, and countless man hours of over-time. I was about ready to give up, fire the attorneys and say to the FCC or anyone else to take that AM radio station and as Johnny Paycheck said in a song, "Shove It."

I was even becoming upset with my own attorneys accusing them of not wanting to settle the case because they were enjoying the big check I was sending to them every month. The way I saw it, I was a good customer for them and why should they really, sincerely want to settle the question and lose the income. Not only Joyce and Bosari, but hundreds of Washington lawyers were making millions in the seventies off radio and TV stations all over the country as a results of petitions like mine.

One afternoon I was in my office trying to make some sense out of the whole situation, when I had an idea. I got Leonard Joyce on the phone and told him how I felt, that I had just about gone as far as I could go, and that I wanted this thing settled right away, or let's get on with a hearing, but something has got to be done before I completely lose my mind.

He again said, "You don't want to go into a hearing." I said, "Well what do you suggest?" He said, "We should do nothing that we haven't already done, just let it run it's course and sooner or later the Commission will rule, either to dismiss or set it for a hearing." I said, "I can't wait any longer, I want you to get me an appointment with someone at the FCC, I'm coming to Washington to talk to somebody as soon as possible." He said,

"You can't do that, no one over there would even speak to you about it."

I said, "I have met Mr. Richard Wiley Chairman of the FCC, and he is a reasonable man. I know that it would be improper for me to even approach him, but somewhere down the line among the 700 lawyers at the FCC there has got to be someone I can tell my troubles to." He said that in his opinion my coming to Washington, with the crazy idea of talking directly with the Commission's attorneys would be unprecedented, and totally useless, maybe even making matters worse.

I told him that as for as I was concerned they couldn't get any worse. I was going directly to the Commission even if I had to camp out on M street in front of the building until somebody spoke to me, and that he could go with me if he wanted to, or I would go alone.

Leonard called the very next day, saying that he had contacted a couple of his attorney friends at the FCC, telling them about me, and my plan, and that to his surprise, they had agreed to see me at a date to be set within the next two weeks. He went on to say it is imperative that you and I are completely on the same page as to what you are going to say to them and that I should come on up there, and be sure to bring a witness with me who would be able to substantiate everything I would tell them.

The only eyewitness to everything that had actually happened during the period was my former secretary, Beth Berry. She agreed to go with me to meet with our attorneys. We met with both Leonard Joyce and George Bosari for a full day at their office on Jefferson street. They, as good lawyers do, worked diligently, coaching us on everything and every possible question they felt the Commission lawyers might ask.

I was not really a whole lot interested in the legalities, just wanting to talk to someone over there who might understand what a little old broadcaster down in Alabama had been going through for the past six years.

The big day for our appearance at the FCC was the next week, so Beth and I went back to Washington We met again, briefly, the morning of the session with my attorneys, then all four of us walked the block to the FCC building. All cases before the Commission were assigned to an Administrative Law Judge, who was responsible for the case from beginning to end. Without our knowledge, the FCC attorneys had cleared what they were doing with Judge Alexander before agreeing to meet with us, gaining his approval. To our surprise when the four FCC attorneys, the ACLU attorney, Leonard Joyce, George Bosari and I gathered around a long conference table, with me at one end, there was an older gentleman, facing me from the other end of the table, that I had never met.

After appropriate introductions he spoke first saying, "I am administrative law Judge Alexander, and I have decided to sit in on this unusual session strictly as an observer. I am not allowed to participate in any way in these proceedings . You folks just go ahead as if I were not in the room. Something like this has never been done before, and I want to see it." We set about discussing the WACT case and the charges, mostly frivolous, that had been filed six years ago, in a meeting that would eventually last for more than three hours.

In my opening statement, I assumed my best "pore" mouth voice and country boy, Syrup Sopperish delivery, and attempted to tell them about how it is to own and operate a little old radio station down in Tuscaloosa, Alabama. I explained that our station programmed country music, with news and weather for everyone, regardless of race.

I explained the former "Breakfast at the Stafford" program we had aired for ten years, but in 1970 had switched it back to the studios, creating the first telephone talk show in Alabama and most of the country, giving all listeners the opportunity to call in and express opinions on any subject.

I told them about the John Robert Spiller program and that our listeners, especially the old folks, faithfully listened to it in the morning, for all kinds of information about planting, cultivating and harvesting their crops and gardens. I told them how on the program John would give advice about ridding their places of pests, rats, snakes, or whatever was bothering them and, at the same time, Syrup Sopper and John would usually provide a good laugh early in the morning for folks who, probably due to health or other situations, did not find anything to laugh about the rest of the day.

I explained that because we played country music exclusively, we could not program very many "black" artists and their music. I pointed out that in the whole country-music industry there was only one black person making records, and that was Charlie Pride, even though most listeners thought he was white, until he would walk out on stage. But, as much as the radio audience loved him, we could not play him all day. I mentioned that it was extremely hard to find black deejays, they just did not like the music; however, I did have one. Howard, "Lip" Lanier, known all over the city and the University as the Tuscaloosa Lip. That he was our all night deejay on the FM station, with a large following by the high school and college crowd.

I told about the time I had hired a black lady bookkeeper. She was to report for work on a Monday, but on Friday she had called to say she would not be coming to work at WACT, she had changed her mind. When I asked what the problem was, she said, "I don't like the music ya'll play." I told her I was not hiring her to listen to the music, but to keep the station's books. She did not come to work for us.

I told them about a very qualified black lady named Florence who had formally been a program director for a station in Los Angeles, but had decided to return to school at the University for her masters degree. I said she was in charge of our programming until she resigned telling me she would be awarded a government grant for school expenses and have enough money left over to buy herself a new car, if she were not working.

I talked about the few occasions on which we had run more that the recommended 18 minutes per hour of commercials, telling them that the way I saw the rule, and as much as we had tried to abide by it, sometimes in peak periods it was impossible,

It would be wonderful if we could run 18 minutes every hour, but we had many hours with no commercials at all.

I also pointed out another problem with that the rule which applied to WACT in Tuscaloosa, Alabama and WNEW, New York, WLS, Chicago, KPAN, Los Angeles, WBAP, Fort Worth, or WSB Atlanta. These stations charge advertisers as much as $1000 or more for a spot announcement, whereas our average rate was about $5.00. However, when I bought a piece of equipment, a transmitter, turntable or microphone, Harris Radio Equipment sales people didn't say, "Now lets see, your spot rate is $5.00, so we will sell you that $25,000 transmitter for only $1250." No, I pay the same price for equipment, I pay people, rent, and utilities just the way the big boys do."

I concluded my statement with the fact that our WACT-FM license had been renewed twice, in 1975 and 1978, since the petition was filed in 1972 and that both AM and FM had identical programming, staff and management. I had a lot more to say, but had the feeling after my opening statement I was ahead because the lawyers, and especially the judge, had been listening very intently. After I finished, they started firing questions at me, and surprisingly the old judge, who had said in the beginning he was just there as an observer, started to ask me questions too. He was especially interested in the Spiller program, saying it sounded like something he would like to listen to himself.

After more than three hours, the session with me ended. I was excused from the room, they sent for my witness, Beth, who had been patiently waiting in an adjoining room. She went into the meeting and was back out in no more that thirty minutes. I was concerned they had not taken more time with her. As I learned later, they reviewed some of my statements, asking her if she would verify that I had told the truth. She, of course said that she agreed with everything I had said. I was asked to return to the conference room, as the judge was speaking, telling the FCC attorneys that in his opinion this license should have been renewed a long time ago, And, unless they could come up with a good reason not to, within ten days it would be renewed.

As we left the building it occurred to me that neither of my lawyers had said anything during the whole proceeding. In less than two weeks, I received the brief the FCC attorneys filed, a pleading that was much more in my favor than any my own attorneys had ever filed along with the judges final ruling, about two hundred pages, in essence saying. "This petition should have never been filed, should never have been accepted because it was filed late, the license should have been renewed a long time ago and certainly should be renewed now. Fortunately the Judge agreed with the government attorneys and issued a final ruling in our favor. I could have kissed me a judge.

I apologize, Reader for taking so much time and space with this story, but of all the hundreds of petitions to deny licenses of radio and television stations that were filed, by so many groups and individuals in the late sixties and throughout the seventies, I have never read anything about the trials and tribulations they caused the broadcasters of this country. So, in my way, I wanted to record some of the events, if for no one else other than my grand children, so that they might know what an overgrown, bureaucratic government can do if we become too complacent and allow it to happen.

True, very few actually lost their license, but the industry spent millions trying to protect itself from the self appointed leaches, including some lawyers, with nothing better to do.

With the election of Ronald Reagan in 1980, things began to change. When I heard that our new President was changing the make up of the Commission, and was going to recommend deregulation, abolishing assertainment, commercial restrictions, allowing program-length commercials, restrictions on ownership, program logs, quotas, and a seven-year license instead of three, and, best of all, disallow frivolous petitions to deny, I could not believe it. I said to many of my friends, "That will never happen." But it did happen, all except the equal opportunity employment policies, which actually became tougher.

You remember I said that in 1972, when we filed for license renewal, it took two boxes to hold all the paperwork? In 1985, the renewal application consisted of answering three questions on a post card. I suppose we are never satisfied, but like everything else in which the government becomes involved, I actually believe in some ways they have carried deregulation too far. One thing's for sure, it's better now than it was then.

After all was said and done my own attorneys admitted to me they believed that due to the attitude of the Commission and it's staff toward broadcasters, at that time, we would have lost our case if it had gone to a formal hearing.

Chapter 17

ME, THE FCC AND THE NAZI

During the period of the sixties and seventies, the FCC instituted what was known as the equal time rule, which in effect forbade the discussion of controversial subjects on the air, unless everyone with an opposing view, regardless of how far out from the mainstream their reasoning might be, were sought out by the station and given "equal time" to express their opinions. This rule resulted in most stations not even attempting to present discussions of a controversial nature, for instance, taxes, zoning, war, or politics, and hundreds more, because of the trouble seeking out all views and the liability that might occur if challenged by someone who had been overlooked. It certainly discouraged stations from editorializing. Ironically, at the same time the Commission was encouraging stations to do so.

With the deregulation of broadcasting that President Reagan began, the so called equal time rule was eliminated and a more workable method was instituted, that is, editorialize, broadcast controversial matter, but make a diligent effort to present legitimate arguments from all sides. However, even after the Reagan deregulation era we were still required to provide equal and like time to political candidates, local, state, and national. Rules were so strict that we had to place in the public file "requests for political time" regarding rates and scheduling, even if the candidate never purchased time at all. And, we were extremely careful to invite each candidate to appear on our talk shows, sometimes alone and sometimes with all candidates for a particular office, depending upon the number of candidates and the office for which they were running.

Two cases stand out as I think about this equal time rule, one was during a wet-dry liquor referendum for Tuscaloosa County. The "dry" forces staged a rally from 2-4 p.m. on a Sunday afternoon at the First Baptist Church of Tuscaloosa. They wanted to pay for the two hours to be broadcast on WACT. We agreed, and the rally went off as planned.

The next morning I received a call from the head of the "wet" forces who had listened to the broadcast, demanding equal time to express their views. I said "Sure, what Sunday do you want the two hours?" His reply was, "We don't want it on Sunday, we're not going to talk about the advantages of drinking beer on Sunday, and we don't want two hours at one time." "What we want", he said, "is 120 sixty second spots to run as we see fit." I said, "Now, Grover, you know that would not even be close to equal time, in fact it would be much more favorable to you. One hundred and twenty spot announcements would be much more expensive than two hours on a Sunday afternoon."

They, of course, declined my offer of two "equal" hours on a Sunday of their choosing. The city and county went wet, however. I was offered no beer advertising, which was all right with me, because as long as I was in control of the stations, we never advertised beer or wine anyway.

Another case was when I received a letter from the infamous Madeline O'Hare, the atheist who brought the original suit before the Supreme Court in which the court ruled that prayer in schools was unconstitutional.

In her letter, Ms. O'Hare stated she had been informed that WACT broadcasts some religious programs and that her group was demanding equal time to express their atheistic views. You know, it just occurred to me as I wrote that, these people like her and the dozens of others, never asked for equal time, they demanded it. It seemed to me there is a vast difference.

My reply to her was, "Yes, we do broadcast religious programs, but in my opinion and that of a previous decision by the Supreme Court, the existence of God is not a controversial issue. It is an opinion held by an overwhelming majority of people throughout the world. Therefore, you will not be granted equal time on our stations." I never heard from her again. A while after that, she disappeared from the face of the earth and reportedly has not been seen or heard from again. Madeline, wherever you are may God have mercy on your soul and on all of your kind.

Most cities, large and small, have one thing in common, and that is, they all have a town idiot, a town drunk, a town genius, and a town political boss. Sometimes it is hard to tell the difference between the individuals. In our town, we had more than our share of mentally disturbed people out on the streets, especially after federal judge Johnson released most of them from Brice and Partlow hospitals, and sometimes it seemed as though everyone of them had a direct line to me.

For the most part they were all harmless, and never caused any problems. A lot of those people listened to WACT and would show up at our remote broadcasts or at our studios carrying their transistor radios, requesting songs, registering for prizes or for free soft drinks.

However, Tuscaloosa's number one idiot was not fresh out of the mental institution, but from the University of Alabama. Morris Gardner was his name. He had indeed attended the University, never graduating, but according to him, he had graduated with honors, even had played football for the Tide. Morris lived in the West End section, on Herman Avenue, in a primarily black neighborhood. He could be seen almost any day riding his bicycle all over town, wearing a military type khaki uniform and cap. He was everywhere, but apparently went nowhere.

In 1970, we ended the Stafford program and began a telephone talk show we called the WACT Action Hot Line. usually featuring prearranged guests. Listeners could call in and ask them questions about the topic for the day. If there were no guests, we would have what we called an "Open line" program. In 1974, our host for the "Hot Line" was a young Jewish fellow who was also our program director, Don Parden. I never knew how Morris Gardner happened to begin listening to the program, but suddenly I began getting calls at home and at the office complaining about the "nut," or even worse names than that, who was calling in to the Hot Line every day. I was usually busy at the 9:00 a.m. hour and had not paid much attention to the program. After hearing so many complaints, I began to listen and what I heard was unbelievable.

Without fail, every day there was a call from a very distinguished network-quality, very educated sounding male voice trying to express the most radical, downright crazy views I had ever encountered. It was Morris Gardner. He had learned that our host on the program was Jewish and that just tore him apart. Morris, being a hater of all Jews, would call every day espousing the same filth and insisting on discussing with Parden his three favorite subjects.

No matter what the day's topic happened be, apple pie, motherhood, church, school, United Way, or whatever, Morris would call wanting to talk about one or all three of his favorite subjects, which were, The Jewish conspiracy to take over the world, Martin Luther King was a Communist and that Hitler was right. You can imagine how such trash could really upset a radio audience, therefore the calls to me complaining and asking why I allowed such crazy talk on WACT.

We had a young lady in the office whose job it was to screen callers before allowing them on the air, but she had no real authority under the rules at that time, to deny any member of the "public" equal access to the program.

Unlike now, on the talk shows such as Rush Limbaugh, Larry King, and many others, both on radio and TV, where calls are screened as to what the caller wants to talk about and if they don't suit the host, they don't get on the air. Now, the host sometimes spends more time expressing his own opinion than taking calls from listeners Programs like that would not have been allowed in the 1970s. Finally, after several weeks of this foolishness on my radio station I had had enough. I told Judy, the phone operator to just tell Gardner when he called that I had said not to put him on the air if he wanted to continue talking about the Jews, Martin Luther King or Hitler. He promised not to do it again, but before long he was back up to his old trick of telling her he wanted to talk about a subject under discussion. But, as soon as he got on the air he would take off on one of his favorites, and I would get more phone calls.

At last I said to her, "Under no circumstance will we put this idiot on the air and let him expound on things that are totally untrue and disturbing to our listeners." So from then on we never put him on the air again. He came to see me, stayed an hour or more complaining that he had a right to get on my radio station and say anything because the First Amendment and the FCC, the government, said he could. I tried to explain why I could not permit him the say those things, but I could not reason with a crazy person.

After awhile I asked Morris, "Who is your hero, who do you admire most, living or dead? He replied, "Adolph Hitler, the greatest man that ever lived." He went on to say, "He never killed all those Jews before and during World War II, that was all British and American propaganda." That was when I realized for sure that I had made the right decision, not putting him on the radio.

Gardner was not through. He went to my old friends from the previous chapter, Jack Drake and Ralph Knowles, the attorneys who had supplied Steve Suitts office space and had held his coat while he, only two years before, had filed the petition to deny our license. That case was still pending. I have no idea who furnished Gardner the money, some said his parents had left him an endowment, but of one thing I'm sure Drake and Knowles did not file that complaint against me and WACT out of the goodness of their hearts, they must have charged Morris plenty. They, in their filing only said that WACT was running an audience participation talk show and that we had discriminated against their client, Morris Gardner, by not letting him on the air to participate in the discussions.

They conveniently forgot to tell the Commission the reason we would not permit him on the air. Basically, that was their complaint, but before the lawyer talk and pure BS was complete, it was many pages long.

I turned the whole thing over to my Washington attorney, Leonard Joyce, who made light of it, saying, "I don't think you have anything to worry about, it's obvious the guy is a nut." I told him about Gardner, and showed him some of the letters he had written to me calling black folks "monkeys, baboons, niggers, jungle bunnies," and more, his writings were full of stuff like that. Vicious ramblings of several pages about Jews and blacks and about how great Hitler was and how he should have defeated the Americans and British, were all part of his letters to me during that time.

After telling Leonard all of that, he was even more convinced the Commission would throw the entire complaint back to Drake and Knowles, chastising them for taking the Commission's time with such a complaint, from a certifiably mentally-deranged person. I became curious as to why Morris never drove a car. Checking with the police department, I found he had not had a drivers license in years and that he had been arrested nine times for shooting his BB gun from his front porch at black children playing in their yards across the street.

The complaint was filed, our answer was filed, their answer followed, we answered again, after many months, no more filings, just waiting to hear what the Commission would do. My lawyer's fees had been paid, and I had just about forgotten all about the Gardner affair, when one morning I got a call from a reporter at "The Tuscaloosa News" inquiring if I had a statement regarding the fine that had been levied against me by the FCC on behalf of Morris Gardner.

I did not lie when I said, "I don't know anything about it, I have not been informed of any fine, how much is it? She said, " $1000, what do you have to say about it?" Again I said, "Absolutely nothing until I see it in writing." They went ahead and published the news about me and WACT under the byline "LOCAL RADIO STATION FINED" on the front page that afternoon, even contributing quotes to me, when actually I had said nothing.

The next day in the mail, I received notice from the FCC that due to the fact that I had refused to put a member of the public on the air while providing others an opportunity to participate in a call-in program, they were assessing a forfeiture against WACT in the amount of $1000 and requiring me to put Gardner on the air any time he so desired.

I am convinced that had my lawyer taken the case more seriously and used the material I had dug up and forwarded to him about Morris, we would have won. As I write this and think about this case and the other one, I am deciding that I didn't have very good representation from my attorneys. Maybe I should sue for some of my money back.

The morning I received notice of the $1000 fine and instructions from the FCC to put Gardner on the air, I determined to fight that order with everything I had. Thinking to myself, "What have I got to lose, the license renewal is still pending, but I am not going to sit around and spend a lot of unnecessary money on an idiot like Gardner."

I called Leonard Joyce and told him I was leaving for Washington that very afternoon and asked him to arrange an appointment for me to meet the next day with Mr. Richard Wiley, chairman of the FCC. Leonard almost had a fit saying, "You can't do that. Nobody goes directly to the chairman with anything, if you are going to appeal the decision, you will have to go through the proper channels."

I said, "No sir, I have met and heard the chairman speak on several occasions, and he always says to broadcasters, "If there's any way the Commission can help you, please let us know." I had always thought him to be a reasonable, a very approachable man, a former Washington Communications Attorney, a Republican, having been appointed to the chairmanship by President Nixon. I told Leonard, "I'm going to find out tomorrow if he really means it." He still protested, saying such a meeting would never happen and the chairman would think we had both lost our minds for suggesting such a thing for a matter as trivial as the Gardner complaint, and a thousand dollars. If anything, we should go through the compliance and complaint division headed by a Mr. Milt Gross.

I told him that it might be a trivial matter to him, but paying the fine and putting Gardner on the air would completely destroy my own confidence in how to manage a radio station.

Before noon that day, I had gathered all of my Gardner file together, tapes of his ranting and raving about the greatness of

Adolph Hitler, his letters and postcards to me and other members of the staff, letters to the editor from the local newspaper, which, by the way, had limited him to one letter per month, and taken the liberty of editing all of his letters before publishing them. I included in my file, which by that time was about three or four inches thick, a briefcase almost full, his police record, a sample of the swastikas he always stuck to his letters, bearing the slogan, "Hitler was Right," I had a copy of a letter on his behalf that J. B. Stoner, head of the Georgia KKK had written. Stoner was the Klansman who was convicted for bombing the 16th Street church in Birmingham on a Sunday morning, killing three little black girls.

With all of the above in one hand, an extra shirt and drawers in the other, I headed for the Birmingham airport, got on a plane bound for Washington, arriving there on a cold, dark blustery afternoon in January, not knowing whether I had an appointment with Mr. Wiley for the next day or not.

After checking in at the Mayflower, I called Leonard and found him almost in a state of shock. He had contacted one of the Chairman's Aids, he and Wiley had agreed to meet with us at 2:00 p.m. the next day. Leonard Joyce could not believe it, saying, "This kind of thing is just not done." I really think he was troubled by the fact that some more big fees would be out the window, if I were successful with the Chairman.

When I looked out the hotel window the next morning there was a snow storm in progress. My heart skipped a beat or two, realizing that my meeting would probably be canceled, having been in such storms there before, knowing that when it snows in the Capitol, it's not very different from Tuscaloosa. Everything closes down, the bureaucracy stays home. I had not even taken an overcoat with me, certainly no overshoes, but I walked in the storm from the Mayflower Hotel about two and a half blocks across Connecticut Avenue and down Jefferson street to Leonard's office.

He expressed his concern that I had come all the way there, but was very sure our meeting at the FCC would not happen that afternoon, because the whole town was shutting down, with people leaving work for home.

To our surprise, we got a call from the Chairman's office saying that he would like to cancel the two o'clock meeting, but would see us at ten o'clock that morning, less than an hour away. Leonard and I, with my briefcase full of Gardner paraphernalia, walked over to the building where we were escorted to the ninth floor and into the palatial offices of the FCC chairman. Leonard seemed to be more nervous than I. We were directed to a large conference room, which I assumed was the room in which regular meetings of the Commission were held.

In just a few minutes Richard Wiley, Milt Gross, and three other fellows I didn't know, (I figured they were probably lawyers,) came in. The chairman knew Leonard, but I think only had a vague memory of seeing me sometime before. He, however greeted us very warmly, introduced the other gentlemen, talked about the snow storm a while and finally said, "Mr. Price what can we do for you today?"

He, of course, had never heard of Morris Gardner, the fine or any of the details of my case. The decision to fine me and order Gardner's return to the WACT airwaves was made at a much lower level, certainly not at the full commission and without the knowledge of Wiley.

When he asked that question, I took that as my cue to explain to him why I was there. I opened my briefcase and simply spread all of the Gardner filth, letters, swastikas proclaiming Hitler was Right, the letters and tapes about the Jewish conspiracy and Dr. Martin Luther King as a Communist theory, the letters with burning crosses as letterheads and Gardner's police record of being arrested for shooting at black children with his BB gun.

As I spread all of this stuff from one end of the long conference table to the other, I was saying, "Mr. Wiley, I know you are a very busy man, with a lot more important things to take up your time than to worry about me and some nut down in Tuscaloosa, and I really appreciate you seeing me today in spite

255

of the storm, but all I ask is for you to take a look at this vile stuff and if you can honestly tell me it's in the public interest for me to put this idiot on the air in Tuscaloosa Alabama, then I believe I have wasted twenty-five years of my life, and haven't learned the first thing about managing a radio station."

He walked around the table, picking up and briefly reading some of the material as he went. Saying it would not be necessary to listen to the tapes, he sat in his chair, thought a minute and said, "I see you really have a problem down at your station." I said, "Sir, I respectfully disagree with you, but the problem is right here in this building. I handled it the way I still think I should have, by just not putting Gardner on the air. Your people have said that I must, and have fined me $1000 for not doing so." Mr. Wiley agreed, thanking me for bringing the matter to his attention, and promised to do something, saying you will hear from us soon.

As Leonard and I left the FCC building, I was walking on top of the deepening snow, feeling great about the way the unusual meeting between a small broadcaster from Alabama and the Chairman of the Federal Communications Commission had gone.

I told Leonard goodbye, hailed a cab and headed for National Airport and back home where it was not so cold.

I have seen a lot of wonderful sights in my lifetime, but I believe the most beautiful was the view from an airplane as it took off from National Airport, out over the Potomac river, banked left and exposed the passengers on the right side to a sight like no other, the US Capitol building, the Washington Monument, the Lincoln and Jefferson Memorials, the Smithsonian and the White House all covered in a deep blanket of snow as a winter sun was setting. I wish I had an actual picture of the view, but I can still remember it and how good I was feeling after my meeting with the FCC chairman.

Within a week I received notice that the Gardner decision had been reversed and the forfeiture had been canceled. When it was all over, I had spent about $10,000 in travel, phone and attorney fees, but I had won and it was well worth it.

When Gardner, Drake and Knowles heard of the reversal they filed an appeal at the Washington District Court of Appeals, not against me, but against the FCC for reversing its decision. About six years after that the Appeals Court upheld the Commission's decision, and that was the end of my troubles with the Tuscaloosa Nazi.

During all of those proceeding I never even formally met Drake or Knowles, only seeing them at a restaurant or a public gathering. Richard Wiley has long since retired from the commission and is now a partner in one of the most prominent law firms in Washington. I see him every year at the annual BMI dinner during the NAB convention. He never fails to mention and tell his associates about the snowy day we met in Washington. He is still grinning about Morris Gardner and me.

I think it was my success at the meeting with the chairman in 1974 that caused me to persist in my effort to meet with the Commission's attorneys in 1978, even though a petition to deny a license was a much more serious matter than a complaint filed by an unbalanced person and his greedy lawyers. In any event, my efforts worked in both cases.

A footnote: During the time the case against the Commission was on appeal, Gardner would call and threaten to file again, if I didn't put him on the air. I explained to him that the matter was completely out of my hands because the FCC had ruled that I could not put him on, even if I wanted to. I gave him the name and address of Mr. Milt Gross, head of the complaint and compliance division at the Commission. Morris started writing letters to him about me and the station, always including his 2 by 5-inch "sticker" with the swastika, and "Hitler was Right" slogan on the bottom of each letter.

If the thing had not been so serious, it would have been funny. You see, Milt Gross was a Jew and you understand now that the letters from Morris did not win any favors from Gross. He called me one day and said, "I wish you would get that Gardner SOB off my back." I said, "I'd rather he were on your back than mine."

Reader, if you have stayed with me for the past two

chapters, I really appreciate your patience. I promise now, not to mention the FCC, petitions, complaints, shyster lawyers, ACLU, or town idiots anymore and will try to move on with things more pleasant and interesting.

I will add though, that Jack Drake is now an attorney in Birmingham and has been working very hard for several years, trying to receive an appointment to a federal judgeship. God help us all if he ever succeeds. Ralph Knowles practices law in Atlanta and is one of the lead attorneys in the Dow Chemical breast implant case. And by the way, the "Tuscaloosa News" forgot to print a front page story proclaiming, LOCAL RADIO STATION DECLARED INNOCENT OF DISCRIMINATION AGAINST LISTENER.

Chapter 18

OTHER BUSINESS VENTURES

When my father-in-law, W. H. Bailey, became very ill in 1958 and had to leave his job with Blue Plate Foods Company, he wanted so desperately to contribute to the financial well being of himself and Carol's mother, he and I decided to open a coin operated laundry on 9th street in Alberta City, near our home. We planned that with the help of the Norge Company, and the supervision of Mr. Tom Keeler, we would install twenty coin operated washers and eight dryers.

The Baileys would move to Tuscaloosa so that he could operate the laundry, and in case his condition worsened, he would be near us, and Carol could help out with his care. The plan never worked out. By the time we had the laundry up and running, he was not able to work at all, never moving to Tuscaloosa, although we did move the boys grandmother into a house on 26th Avenue East after the death of Mr. Bailey.

It was about that time that I learned I was not cut out to be the "Westinghouse Repair Man." We could not afford a full-time attendant at the laundry, so we trusted our customers not to abuse the machines. Most did not, but some would overload the machines with rugs, bedspreads, even oily rags, causing breakdowns and flooding of the place. I found there is no madder woman on earth than one who has washed her linens in a machine that had just been used to wash a load of grease rags from a service station.

One of the major problems was clogged water pumps, usually caused by mamas washing the kids overalls with BBs in the pockets, clogging a water pump, causing the water to back up and me to have to drain the tub and tear down the machine to fix the problem. I learned very quickly to hate the laundry business. Working all day at the radio station and half the night at the laundry, sweeping water and repairing washing machine, was not the reason I had worked so long and hard for a college degree.

I was almost relieved the night someone broke into the building, and stole all of my tools. I had an excuse for not working for a while. The last straw happened the night they robbed our change maker using home made slugs for quarters. A washer of clothes was $.20, a dryer was $.25, so we had a change maker that would give two quarters for $.50 or two dimes and a nickel for a quarter. Some genius devised a slug made of copper with a center of lead that would work just like a real quarter every time.

The next day I called on one of my sponsors, Raymond Case at the Royal Crown Bottling Company about his advertising. I mentioned that I had found these fake quarters in my change maker, showed him some I had in my pocket and asked if he had seen any of them in his drink machines. He said, "No, I've never seen one like that, but I'll bet you an RC Cola they will not work in our machines, our machines are slug proof." I said, "Let's try one in your machine in the office." I dropped the fake quarter in the slot, out came an RC with $.15 change. I drank the RC as his payoff of the bet. Not very long after that we closed the laundromat. I still don't like washing machines.

This section deserves its own chapter, but I will try to condense about twelve years into a few pages. I met Max Biggs in the late 1960s. He was manager of a Garden Cemetery located on what is now Skyland Boulevard in Tuscaloosa. About ten years previously a man by the name of John Walton and his wife Evelyn, had come to town to establish a cemetery, as they had already done in Cullman and Jasper, Alabama. Shortly after moving to Tuscaloosa Mr. Walton died suddenly leaving Evelyn and his manager, Max Biggs to take over the cemeteries. The Waltons had two small daughters Elaine and Debbie. A few years later Max and Evelyn were married, and Max moved into the family home in Woodland Hills, one of Tuscaloosa's newest and most beautiful subdivisions.

The first time I met Max was the day he called asking me to come down to the cemetery office and discuss a program he had in mind for the upcoming Easter Sunday. Max was a big man, tall, muscular, athletic, blond, with a big smile and a warm handshake, a former football player for the Purdue University Boilermakers, and as I would find out later, an excellent golfer.

We discussed promoting an Easter Sunrise service at Memory Hill Gardens at daybreak on the following Easter and broadcasting it on WACT. We did, with a very large crowd attending, music furnished by the Alberta Baptist Church Choir and a sermon delivered by Dr. Allen Watson, pastor of Calvary Baptist Church. We repeated the service the next year, with other members and churches in the community participating. A tradition was established that lasted for many years, with Max and Evelyn, Carol and me developing a strong friendship.

About that time the custom of cemeteries building funeral homes on their grounds was just becoming popular due to the traffic and inconvenience of having a funeral at a church and then driving a "procession" from there, sometimes all the way across town to the cemetery.

Max and Evelyn, Clem Duckworth, J.C. Faulkner, and Lloyd Wood built a funeral home at the cemetery naming it Memory Chapel. The one and only "white" funeral home had been owned and operated for generations by the Speigner family, but at the time had been purchased by one of the late George Speigner's employees, Rufus Strickland, who kept the best known funeral director in town on his payroll, Mr. Clayton Hayes. Rufus had just built a new building on 17th street calling it Hayes Chapel.

Because of the competition from Strickland and Hayes, and the custom of most families using the same funeral home from generation to generation, it was rough going for the new upstart funeral home, Memory Chapel. Before long Wood, Duckworth and Faulkner became discouraged because they were not receiving a return on their investment, they wanted to sell their interests. Max wanted me to have some ownership, not only because we were friends, but because of my name and promotional abilities.

He and I bought out the other three, Max with 75% and me with 25%. I was in it strictly as a long term investment, not really expecting an immediate return on my money. Neither

Max nor I had any ownership in the cemetery. His wife, Evelyn, and her children were owners and Max was the manager of both the cemetery and the funeral home. Over a couple of years we gradually built the funeral home into a respectable position in the minds of the community and were beginning to service more and more families, but we just never could break into the older, established families in town, because they just could not break away from the funeral home that had buried mama and papa, even though it was under different ownership and management and in a new location.

There was only one thing to do. We needed to buy Hayes Chapel. Our attorney Sam Phelps began negotiations with Rufus Strickland, and before long Max and I were the proud owners of our primary competition, assuming a 4% loan from Liberty National Insurance Company.

We later built our own vault plant, hiring James Rogers who had been making septic tanks to run it for us. We made two or three trips to Bald Knob, Arkansas trying to buy a small foundry that made the bronze markers for garden-type cemeteries such as Memory Hill Gardens. That never worked out. We could build the vaults and sell them much cheaper than we could buy them from Cement Products Company in Birmingham.

In the meantime, some folks in Northport had built a small funeral home on the Highway 82 bypass. Not being at all successful, they offered to sell it to us. We bought it, operated it for awhile and then sold it to Harold Wilcutt and others who turned the building into what is now Open Door Baptist Church.

Before the 1980s it was customary for funeral homes to be in the ambulance business too, so we were providing the only ambulance service for the County, and losing money. Somehow community leaders looked upon the situation as an obligation of funeral homes to operate emergency ambulances at no cost to the local governments. It didn't matter to them that we could only collect about 35% of our fees, but somehow fate had dictated that we furnish the service.

We told the city fathers that within three months we were closing down the ambulance service because we could not afford to lose the three to four thousand dollars a month we were losing. The Council got busy and passed an ordinance making not paying an ambulance fee a misdemeanor, provided a monthly cash supplement, and awarded a contract to a Birmingham firm, which suited us just fine.

Except for the cost, the switch to professional service was the best things that ever happened to emergency situations. Our people had only brief training for emergencies, but the pros charged enough to pay for more modern equipment and trained paramedics, which resulted in saving many lives.

The city bought very modern vehicles and operated them out of the fire department by paramedics, but the cost has been greatly increased to the people being served. Our average fee for transporting a patient from a wreck or home to the hospital was $30-$40, with transportation to and from a nursing home being free. Now, a simple transport can cost as mush as $500.

Max and I had a very good relationship, and although I never actually worked as a mortician I did stay in close touch with him and was out front in public relations.

In 1979, I sold my interest in the funeral chapels back to Max, because that was the year I was building a permanent home for the radio stations. We were planning for a new building with studios, tower and transmitter on the south side of town, just off the new I-359 spur, which was on the drawing board at the highway engineer's office. I needed the money to help with the almost half a million dollar expansion.

Max and I spent many happy hours on the golf course, traveling and just being together. In 1985 he retired, turning the business over to Evelyn's daughter Elaine, and her husband Jimmy Moore. The Biggs bought a beautiful home next to the PGA National golf courses at West Palm Beach, Florida. We enjoyed visiting them several times. In 1987 Max died suddenly from a heart attack and about a year later Evelyn followed him, the cause of her death was cancer. Carol and I lost two good friends, we still miss them.

In 1970 another investment opportunity came along that, at the time, I just could not let pass. You remember architect,

Howard White, whose office was next door to the radio station. Somehow, Howard became friends with a Mr. Kelly, owner of several businesses, including a concrete company, a seafood restaurant, several charter fishing boats and many acres of land at or near Destin, Florida. Mr. Kelly agreed to lease 400 acres of prime land bordering the airport to the west and the bay to the north with about a mile of waterfront. Highway 98, the coast road, was only a few yards to the south of the property. It was a perfect spot for a golf community, but would need a lot of developing, being completely covered in scrub pines and palmettos.

Howard put a group of investors together, real estate broker, Charlie Sealy, banker, John Owens Sr. the owner of a chicken processing plant, Edgerton Harris, owner of a hatchery Herman Hickman, himself and me. After several meetings with Mr. Kelly, we agreed to a 99 year lease at $10,800 a month, with no rent to be paid for the first year. We named the future development Indian Bayou, because a nearby bayou already was known by that name. Our corporation was Indian Bayou Inc. We elected Mr. John Owens president Soon after signing the lease, Howard got busy designing condominiums, with one different twist. Because our land was adjacent to the airport, we would offer "fly-in" housing. A person could land his private plane at the airport and taxi right up to his house or condo, park in the driveway and be ready to take off again. That was a great idea, too bad we never got it off the ground.

With temporary financing, we hired surveyors to lay out streets and utilities, hired Stone golf course architectural company, and made plans to clear the land that would be needed for the first phase of our development. I could not believe how fast that first year, the "rent free" one, went by. At the end of the year we had plans drawn for condos, streets and utilities and were almost through designing the golf course, but had not begun any construction.

Suddenly we were paying rent and were nowhere near selling anything or playing golf. The early 1970s was when interest rates shot up to 15%-16%-even as high as 20%, and sales of condominiums on the coast dropped to unprecedented lows. A buyer with $25,000 could buy just about any condo on the beach. Several high rise buildings had gone bankrupt. A development much like ours, Sandestin, was padlocked by creditors. The best offer we could find for the 7 to 10 million dollars we needed to get our development underway was at interest rates of 16% or more. In the meantime Mr. Owens had died, Mr. Hickman had dropped out and I had been elected president of the corporation. With interest so high and prices so low, I could not see how we could possibly proceed with our plans at that time.

I told Howard to look around to see if he could find someone to buy us out and take over the balance of the 99 year lease on the property. By some miracle we had an offer from a group to buy our lease for enough that we could pay off all of our debts and each clear more than $25,000.

I remember at the meeting I convened to discuss the offer, Charlie Sealy, a real estate man for whom I have the highest regard, said, "My daddy always said, "Son, you will never go broke taking a profit."

The company we sold the lease to went bankrupt. After another bankruptcy, the golf course, and club house were built. The land was subdivided into residential lots, and Indian Bayou is now one of the most beautiful and enjoyable places on the North Florida coast. Our timing was just not right for the economic conditions at the time. I would still like to have that big beautiful lot on Apalachicola Bay, that I had selected for myself and the family as the perfect spot for our own house.

One other business venture I will tell you about is my banking experience. In the sixties a group of local investors, including Mr. Lewis Harper, Chairman of the Board, started a new bank with a new building at Greensboro Avenue and 11th Street.

As most independent banks do, First State Bank began with a very small capitalization. The bank had some very good people on the board, Dr. Cletus Hand, Grover Burchfield, Albert Pitts, Red Reynolds and others good, solid, well respected citizens, but it's management left a lot to be desired. I will not mention any names, but the President of the little bank helped himself to some of the money, then another individual bought enough stock to gain control, lining his pockets, and finally the biggest crook of all wound up with what was left.

An entire book could be written about those days, but no one would believe the bank could go through what it did and still survive.

After pledging the stock as collateral for a large loan to Union Planters National Bank in Memphis the owner of the majority of the stock at the time declared bankruptcy and finally went to prison. As a result Union Planters was the new owner of the bank. Interstate banking had not been approved, regulations prevented them from owning an out of state bank for more than two years.

The people at Union Planters appointed their attorney here in Tuscaloosa, John Owens Jr., to find some more board members and try to straighten out the mess that had been made by the previous owners. John asked me to join the board, which I considered to be an honor, not really knowing anything about the history of the bank. I had never had an account there. I had a surprise at my first board meeting when we began at 2:00 p.m. with the first item of business being a report from the FDIC examiners, covering their last inspection. We were in session for four hours, and to sum it all up, they were saying that if we did not get the bank turned around soon and on a good footing very soon, they would close it down. I was thinking, "What have I gotten myself into?"

As a result of bond claims we filed with our bonding company, USF&G, we collected approximately $4,000,000 of the missing money. I should say that not one of our depositors were ever in danger of losing any of their money.

Union Planters sent an employee of the bank in Memphis, Homer Lee, to be President of the bank, with Rudy Holmes their trouble shooter riding herd on all of us. We were gradually picking up some new business, cutting expenses, and things were beginning to look a little better, when Mr. Harper, our

Chairman resigned because of poor health. I was elected Chairman of the board.

One of my first goals was to increase the size of the board with a few more good people. I added Bill Strickland, owner of Drake Printers, John Dill, from Dill plumbing company, Tom Tarleton, a well known educator and high school basketball coach

Dr. Cordell Wynn had just been appointed President of Stillman College, a predominantly black, Presbyterian, four year institution here in Tuscaloosa. Throughout the years Dr. Wynn and I have become close friends. When he moved here to take over as President of the College, he opened his checking account with us at First State Bank. I was curious as to why he chose to bank with us when I was sure he must have been contacted by all of the bigger banks in town, soliciting his business. I called him one morning and invited him to lunch. He readily accepted. We went to the Landing Restaurant, had a good lunch, after which he said, "I appreciate the lunch, but I know you must want something. What is it?" I said, "Dr. Wynn, I want to invite you to consider joining our board of directors at First State Bank." He said, "What do you think I could add to the board?" That caught me by surprise as I replied, " I hardly know you, and you may not add anything, but I've heard so many good things about you, that I'm certain you will be a valuable asset to our bank, and besides you are black and there is not one black person on any bank board in Tuscaloosa, and I believe there should be."

Cordell said, "I appreciate your honesty, I think I will accept." "Now." I said, " I want to ask you a personal question. Why, when you first came to town did you open your checking account with us?" Dr. Wynn said, "You know that preacher at the church behind the bank, he is on our staff at the college and he told me ya'll have a good looking black teller, that's the reason."

I knew then that I had made a friend in Dr. Cordell Wynn. He retired from the board this year after reaching the mandatory retirement age of 70. I really miss him sitting next to me at the meetings. He also retired last year from the Presidency of Stillman College.

At one of his many retirement dinners that different groups in our community sponsored, Dr. Wynn told the crowd a story about how he came to be hired as President of Stillman College. He said that Dr. Frank Rose, President of the University of Alabama was on the search committee and during an interview asked him a question. The question being, "Dr. Wynn, you are a Baptist preacher. Stillman is a Presbyterian school. How do you propose to reconcile the differences between the two?" Wynn replied, "I don't think that will be a problem, we all worship the same God." Dr. Rose said, "That's not what I mean, I want to know how you feel about SCOTCH. Dr. Wynn came back with, "I love it." President Rose said, "You're a Presbyterian already and don't know it." He got the position and joined the Presbyterian church.

Dr. Wynn and I have enjoyed many discussions about how hard we had to work and how poor we were as children and young men, my growing up in poverty at Nebo, and his raising near Macon, Georgia, in really bad circumstances. We like to see who can "pore mouth" the best and tell the most tales about hard times.

One day he came in and sat by me at the bank board meeting and said, "You know, Clyde, I've been thinking about what you have said about your growing up and how rough you had it at Nebo in Cullman County, and I've decided that you are right. You did have a much harder time than I did." I said, "Well, I'm glad you have seen the light. What made you change your mind?" "You had it much worse than we did, because in Cullman County ya'll didn't have any of us to do the work." When he was young someone must have recognized some real potential in Cordell. He was awarded a Pepsi scholarship to Boston College and the opportunity to live with a very prominent family in Boston while he was in school.

Meanwhile, back at the bank, the next year Union Planters sold their stock to James Cox, a flamboyant, rich, robust, attorney, from the Georgetown suburb of Memphis, who just loved to represent plaintiffs in the court room in big cases like plane crashes, train wrecks and class action suits with big fees. I used to call him the "poor man's Perry Mason."

Cox would charter a plane to Tuscaloosa for our board meetings when one was available, if not he would fly commercial to Birmingham, rent a car and drive here. I think the maddest I ever saw him was the day he arrived at the bank in a Birmingham taxi. He had flown in, tried to rent a car, as usual, but not having a credit card with him the rental agency refused to rent the car for cash.

I will say one thing for Jim Cox, he traveled at his own expense, and never charged anything to the bank, including Christmas parties and luncheons for himself and others.

Union Planters had sent one of their bank auditors, Bill Barnes, to Tuscaloosa to try to get the books in shape. Jim Cox did not like some of the methods of Homer Lee, so he let him go and named Bill President. The first thing I did was resign as chairman, but Jim refused my resignation, saying, he could not live in Memphis and serve as Chairman himself. So, I remained chairman until Jim sold the bank to Lloyd Wood.

It seems that my path and that of Lloyd were always crossing, the trouble being he was the wealthy one. When he bought the bank we had just about doubled the assets from $10,000,000 to roughly $20,000,000. Besides his construction company, Lloyd had experience in banking, having been chairman and a major stockholder of First Alabama Bank, one of the largest in town.

With his infusion of cash and that of some of his friends the bank began to grow steadily. Soon after Lloyd bought the bank it became obvious that Bill Barnes was too conservative for him, and they could not work together. I recommended Bill to my buddy Leroy McAbee, telling him, "If you want the most honest, trustworthy, conscientious, person you have ever met to help with your financial affairs, you need to hire Bill Barnes." Leroy hired Bill and he is still at McAbee and Company.

When Lloyd Wood took over I again resigned the Chairmanship, which was the thing to do. He accepted my resignation, but he asked me to stay on as a member of the board of directors. The fortunate thing for the bank was the retirement of Tommy Hester from AmSouth, formerly First National Bank of Tuskaloosa. Tommy had been with the largest bank in town for over thirty years.

Lloyd hired him to be our President. Tommy with all of his contacts in the community, his vast knowledge of every phase of banking, his outgoing personality, and ability to work with people, was the perfect answer to our leadership situation. For several years the bank continued to grow and prosper, until Lloyd sold the stock for about four times what he had paid for it to the National Bank Of Commerce, with headquarters in Starkville, Mississippi.

NBC holding company owned banks in several Mississippi cities, 'but ours was their first acquisition outside the state. Our relationship with the folks at NBC has been nothing but pleasant. Lewis Mallory, CEO, and Mark Abernathy, President and all of the employees with whom I have come in contact are the very finest, and it is a pleasure for me to continue to work with them on the board. With the purchase this year of the First National Bank of the South, our little First State Bank, now a National Bank, NBC, has assets of roughly $140,000,000 and is part of a massive $1,000,000,000 banking and insurance corporation.

I am happy to have had an opportunity to experience other business ventures besides broadcasting. They have helped to broaden my perspective and my entire outlook on the business world. I was able to do these things because of a hard working staff and family. However, whatever I have done or will do, radio is still my favorite and I thank the Lord and some wonderful people like Carroll Eddins, Lon Waters, Tom Todd, Ruth Harris, Joe Carson and Eddy Holiday for giving me the chance.

Chapter 19

WORKIN' ON A BUILDING

In spite of the aggravation and expense of the previously described events, the petition to deny our license to operate the radio station and the Gardner fiasco, the 1970s were good. I was busy managing the station and doing a large portion of the advertising selling, still doing the Syrup Sopper show, a lot of civic and community work. and keeping up with the other ventures that I described in the previous chapter.

Wally graduated from the university and went to work at the station full time. The death of "Buckshot" in 1970 had left a large hole in our "on the air" staff. I could not possibly remember all of the staff for that period but we were fortunate to have people like Bob Inman, Bob Tanner, James Ellington, Don Parden, Jerry Kalenz, Jack Hamm, "Lip" Lanier, Jim Vance, Dan Berry, Jack Dimmerling, Mike Dale, Wally, and Ron, on the air, Mike Travis Sales Manager. David Peacock, engineer, and Florence Howard in programming, Kaye Stallworth, Pat White, Beth Berry, Tilly Woods, Marilyn Norris, Judy Trantor and Betty Vance in the office

One of my favorite hobbies has always been my love and appreciation for music. I have enjoyed country music, naturally, that's how I got into broadcasting in the first place. I am proud to have had a small part in the music's fantastic growth during the sixties and seventies.

When I was stationed in New Jersey in 1956, I could only find one radio station in the whole New York, New Jersey area that programmed any country music. In the sixties that all changed with the advent of national TV and radio coverage of awards shows, The Grand Ole' Opry, weekly shows by Tennessee Earnie Ford, The Mandrel Sisters, Roger Miller, Jimmy Dean, Porter Waggoner and "Hee Haw." In a few short years our music advanced from "hillbilly" to "country", America's favorite music.

I was proud to be a country music broadcaster, but I

especially enjoyed and liked participating in religious music, choir, quartet and solo performances. Even as a boy, I was fascinated by the southern gospel quartets. My first recollection of a quartet on the radio was a group from Birmingham called the "Yellow Label Happy Hitters" on WAPI each Sunday morning at 8:00. Their sponsor was Yellow Label Syrup, therefore the name.

Then later, I liked listening to the groups such as the Blackwood Brothers, Statesmen, Oakridge Boys, John Daniel and so many more, not only their records, which I played so many times on the radio, but going to their concerts when they came to town, especially the Wally Fowler All night singings. I believe every modern gospel singer owes a debt of gratitude to men like John Daniel, Wally Fowler, James Blackwood, Hovie Lister, Jake Hess, J.D. Sumner and the Stamps Baxter publishing company for the rise in popularity of gospel music, not the least of which was the winning of the Arthur Godfry Talent Scouts TV program on CBS by both the Blackwood Brothers and the Statesmen on separate occasions.

The nationwide recognition converted gospel music from a southern regional form of entertainment to nationwide acceptance almost overnight. I really enjoy singing the old familiar hymns and convention type songs and learning the newer songs.

I remember RCA Record Company sending a new Blackwood Brothers album to the station, on which was a new song I had never heard before. The song was "How Great Thou Art." When I first listened to it I loved it, so I painstakingly listened to the record and wrote down the words. I called Mary Ruth Finney, pianist at the Alberta Baptist Church, telling her that I had a new song I wanted us to learn, but did not have the music, only the words. We got together and she played along as I sang the best I could, until we learned it. Then we performed the song at the worship service the next Sunday.

Since then I have sung it many times on the radio, at church and especially at funerals. Now "How Great Thou Art" is in the

Hymn book, one of the most loved and most performed songs in religious music.

I was privileged to help form a local quartet, we called The "Goldentones," with four of my good friends. We began with no name at all, promoted a quartet naming contest on the radio station, inviting listeners to win a prize by submitting the best name for the group. "Wint" Patterson a barber at the VA Hospital sang lead, his brother Royce Patterson, assistant city schools superintendent, baritone, Charlie Smith, a district engineer for the state highway department, tenor, and I sang the bass.

At the piano we had a young man, Steve Hoyle, who could play with the very best. Steve is a great musician, plays in any key, any song he has ever heard, and he would always say "If I don't know the song, just hum a little of it, and I'll play it." Royce, Charlie, Steve and I all sang in the choir at Alberta Baptist Church, and Steve was the church pianist, having been playing for church services since before he was ten years old. We drafted "Wint" from the Circlewood church., where he is now the fulltime music director.

We formed the group primarily to sing at church, and for our own pleasure, but because we would practice in the studios of WACT, we decided one night to put some songs on tape. With the acoustics of the studio and quality recording equipment we sounded really good. I started playing some of our tapes on the gospel segment of the Syrup Sopper show. The radio audience response was terrific, with people calling for more, so each week we would try to record at least three more songs and pretty soon we had enough recorded for me to begin a regular Sunday morning program of the Goldentones songs. We were sponsored by Acker Appliance Center, and enjoyed a long run on the station.

The quartet sang at many churches, concerts, fairs, remote broadcast promotions and nursing homes. We had a great time, because we all liked what we were doing. My all time favorite gospel quartet is the Cathedrals form Stowe, Ohio. George Younts, bass and Glen Payne, lead, have been singing for over fifty years, now, with them, they have two young fellows, Earnie Haaus, tenor and Scott Fowler, baritone, with Roger Bennett at the keyboards. It has been my pleasure to introduce the group on several occasions at their concerts.

I dare not leave the subject of gospel music without mentioning one of my favorite people and musicians. Jack Marshal, from Holt, Alabama, just outside of Tuscaloosa. Jack began playing piano for the famous Blackwood Brothers when he was only 19 years old. The first time I met him was when I was working at WFMH in Cullman. The group came to town for a concert and stopped by the radio station, as they often did, sang for thirty minutes to promote that nights concert. Little did I know that day that the skinny kid playing the piano like no one I had ever heard before would some day be one of my very best friends.

Soon after we moved to Tuscaloosa, Jack Marshal opened the first Kentucky Fried Chicken store in our town. He and I became better acquainted and have remained good friends since. Jack introduced me to Colonel Harland Sanders, the originator of KFC, and I had the privilege of interviewing him on WACT. Jack named his first born son Harland, which was the colonel's name. He now owns more than thirty KFC stores through out the South. I like his chicken, but I still I enjoy his music much more.

Locally, a man named W. G. Snider was a great promoter of gospel music. He headed the "Rainbow Quartet", traveling within our region every Sunday to sing at all day singings in churches and usually at a different church on the same Sunday evening. They sang live every Sunday morning for two hours on WACT. Although personnel in the quartet varied from time to time, some of the more prominent ones were Paul Barnett, James Adams, "Hoot" Windom, Jack Hannah, Circuit Judge Fred Nichol and of course W. G. Snider.

Of my three major past times bowling, golf, and music, my favorite would have to be music. I really admire these people who are so professional and dedicated to the music we love most. Bill and Gloria Gaither from Alexandria, Indiana are the most prolific song writers and promoters of the music now, having recorded and released more than two dozen video and audio tapes featuring what they call "Homecoming Friends", as many as two hundred voices singing primarily the older gospel songs. They are great. I own and enjoy just about all of their tapes.

Other than the problems which I have already covered, the seventies were fairly uneventful. I did make a change in my on the air schedule. After Don Parden left, I decided that I would start anchoring the WACT "Hot Line " program from 9:00 to 10:00 A.M. Monday through Friday in addition to continuing the Syrup Sopper Show from 6:00 till 9:00. I had a lot of fun with the Hot Line, with listeners calling in and expressing opinions about every subject imaginable. I would normally schedule a guest or two, but sometimes I just had an "open line" for the folks to talk about whatever they desired.

Politicians loved to be on the program, especially just before election time. We were always very careful, because of the equal time rule, to see that every candidate for a particular office was invited to appear, and what I liked to do was have all candidates for the same office on at the same time. That resulted in some pretty heated debates.

During the fifteen years that I did the Hot Line program, I had so many interesting guests that I could not even begin to name them, but a few stand out. Coach Paul "Bear" Bryant had been interviewed hundreds of time on radio and television, both nationally and locally. Some of his best friends were sports announcers, like Keith Jackson, Curt Gowdy, and of course, John Forney, who did the play by play of all Alabama's football games, but he had never been on a show that invited listeners to call in and ask him questions. He finally agreed to come on. After our promoting that Coach Bryant would be on the hot line on a certain day, I'm sure we must have had the largest audience we ever had.

The great coach came in that morning, and before we went on the air he said to me "We're probably going to get a lot of crank calls". I said "Coach don't worry about that, I don't think we will, but if we do, I've got a switch here to cut them off." He was extremely nervous at first, but after about ten minutes he was relaxed, sitting there with a Chesterfield, for you young folks, that was a cigarette, between his fingers and chatting with the friends and neighbors in radio land about his favorite sport, football, and even answering personal questions. One little old lady called and said, "Coach I'm worried about your quarterback, I'm afraid them big old boys are going to kill him." Bryant replied, "If he doesn't get rid of the ball in three and a half seconds, he ought to get killed".

The Tuscaloosa Quarterback Club met at the Tuscaloosa Country Club each Monday evening after a Saturday football game. The Quarterback club was a group of men and a few women who liked to get together, enjoy a steak supper and hear talk about football from one of the Alabama coaches, or Charlie Thornton the sports information director at the University, Delbert Reed from the Tuscaloosa News, and a special paid speaker such as retired head coaches, TV and radio sports people, comedians like Jerry Clower, or Leonard Post Toasties, and former NCAA and NFL players. Coach Bryant would always speak to the club the week preceding the Auburn game. That was a vacant week in the schedule in order to give the team a week off to rest and heal minor injuries before the most important game of the year.

I served as program chairman for one year and president of the club the following year. The fifth week of the season, I had booked coach Bobby Dodd the retired, famous Georgia Tech head coach, a long time friend, and an old adversary of coach Bryant. Late that afternoon I called Rebecca, Bryant's secretary, asking her if she would tell coach that Bobby Dodd was speaking to the Quarterback Club that evening, and if he could come and eat with us, I would like for him to introduce coach Dodd.

She said, "He's at practice now, but when he gets back in the office, I'll tell him what you said, but I doubt he will be there, he's so busy." To my surprise, just before we started, the old coach came in. I had reserved a place by coach Dodd at the head table just in case he did find the time to come to the meeting. Everyone in the room was shocked to see him there, because he just did not ever attend a meeting except on "his" night. My having no idea that he would really come, I had not told anyone that I had invited him.

After the meal, I introduced coach Bryant as the introducer of coach Dodd. He got up and started telling old stories about Dodd and talking about some of his most memorable games with Georgia Tech, and about thirty minutes later got around to introducing Dodd, who, when taking the podium, took about another thirty minutes for rebuttal of all the things Bryant had said about him and his great program at Tech.

That was the best Quarterback Club program I ever attended, and I doubt very much that ever before had one club meeting been entertained by two of the most famous and respected coaches in the entire football world. After the meeting I told coach Bryant that I knew it was a sacrifice and problem for him to be there, and how much I appreciated him attending. He said, "I'm glad you asked me. I wouldn't have missed it. I'm the only one who knows the old SOB well enough to introduce him."

When I tried to give coach Dodd his honorarium, he refused the check saying, "I'm not charging you anything, I haven't had so much fun in a long time." It was at another quarterback club meeting, in 1974 coach Bryant's regular speaking occasion, that he showed up late. The meal had already been served when he arrived and took his place beside me at the head table. Instead of a steak he told Bessie the waitress to bring him a double Scotch on the rocks. Sensing something was wrong, I said, "Coach what's wrong, are you not feeling well?" He said, "I've got the worst toothache I've ever had." Alabama had played Kentucky the previous Saturday and while in Lexington the coach had gone to a dentist, without getting any relief from the pain.

After our meeting was over he asked me if I knew of anything that would help his toothache. I said, "How about holding a little brandy on it, that might dull the pain, I don't really know. I have never tried it."

He said, I'm willing to try anything, I believe he liked the idea of the brandy whether it did any good or not. The two of us went into the lounge of the Tuscaloosa Country Club, we were the only patrons that evening, he started holding brandy in his jaw, and I got him started talking football. I asked him about some of his former players, his favorites, like quarterback Babe Parilli at Kentucky, John David Crowe at Texas A and M, his only Heisman trophy winner, and Joe Namath. His only comment about Namath was that, "If he could have gotten in school at Maryland, he would never been at Alabama." He readily admitted that his all time favorite player was an average player, talent wise, but an outstanding leader and a great person, a quarterback from Scottsboro, Alabama, named Pat Trammel.

He liked Trammel not only because he was a winner, but because he was a very good person, with character that placed him above many of his peers. Pat Trammel received his degree in medicine and before he really had a decent chance to begin his practice and make a name for himself as a physician he was stricken by cancer and died shortly there after.

Other coaches and critics of the coach had always accused him of personally arranging the year-end bowl schedule in his favor, which I'm sure was at least partly true. That night being in late November, the bowl pairings had not yet been announced, but I asked coach Bryant what bowl the team would be playing in at the new year. His answer was, "You know I can't tell you that, you'll put it on the radio."

I assured him that I would not tell anyone, much less announce it ahead of time. I don't know if it was the brandy or that he simply trusted me, but he gave me the scoop, saying, "We will be playing Southern California in the Liberty Bowl. The regular season game between USC and UCLA will decide who we will play. The winner of that game goes to the Rose Bowl and the loser plays us in the Liberty Bowl. The looser will be USC, because UCLA will beat the hell out of them." As it turned out the coach was wrong, USC beat UCLA and then in the 1975 Liberty Bowl Alabama won over UCLA.

Back to the hotline program, there were so many interesting guests, we had preachers, teachers, lawyers, doctors, judges, law enforcement officers, business people, nurses, civic leaders, county and city commissioners, youth groups, and politicians both local, state and national. During his first term Governor Fob James became a regular. About once a month he would be my guest in person, or from his office in Montgomery. My only problem with the governor, was I could never get him off on time. He would be so wrapped up in answering questions, and there were so many calls, that I would usually give him an extra thirty minutes.

There was one person that I could never persuade to come on the air with me, and that was Mary Harmon Bryant, the wife of the coach. I called her and she called me so much that we became good off the air "telephone" friends, talking for several minutes at a time, about all sorts of things. She was a very interesting person, could have been a celebrity in her own right, but she preferred taking a back seat in the publicity department to "Papa", her famous husband.

During the seventies all radio stations were required to "seek out" and make time available for minorities, especially if one programmed a "talk" show like our Hot Line. Regular guests on the Hot Line were representatives of the NAACP, SCLC, Stillman College, predominantly black churches and ordinary black citizens.

Therefore, I was not hesitant in granting a request that was presented to me by telephone from Detroit, Michigan. The lady caller said to me "I understand that you have a talk show on your radio station". After I answered in the affirmative, she went on saying, "The prophet Jeremiah A. Lewis will be in your area in two weeks and would like to appear on your program."

I was thinking the prophet was just a title for an evangelist who would be conducting revival services, the sort of which we had on many times before, said, "Sure we would like very much to have Prophet Lewis on our station", knowing, of course, that I dare not refuse the time. A refusal of that type of request would no doubt result in severe punishment from the FCC, if the prophet's church filed a complaint, and I did not know at the time whether it was a legitimate request or a test of our compliance with the rules.

The morning came for the prophet's appearance on the Hot Line. Just about five minutes before air time, from the control room where I was finishing the Syrup Sopper Show, I could see two of the biggest, meanest looking black men I had ever seen enter the building. With them was another large black man clothed in a multi-colored robe, sandals and a little round cap that matched his robe. I figured the one with the robe matching cap had to be the prophet. One of the others looked like Mr. "T", big, muscular, gold chains around his neck, rings on his fingers and in his ears. The other one looked like his twin.

I immediately went to the front to greet them, but when I offered the prophet my hand he refused to shake hands simply bowing and not saying a word. I don't remember if I bowed back or not, but seeing that they all looked so serious I probably did. I explained that we needed to get back to the control room, because it was almost time to go on the air.

I assumed the twins would sit in my office or the coffee lounge while the prophet and I were on the air. I was wrong. They both followed us into the small control room where the interview would take place. By the time I had chairs brought in for them and had the prophet settled in behind the guest microphone, we were on the air. Up until that time the guest had not said a word, not even good morning. I'm thinking to myself, "I'm gonna have some fun today".

I opened the program with the usual good morning and chit chat about the weather, an announcement or two and in a couple of minutes said, "Today we are privileged and very fortunate to have as our guest, for the entire hour, The Prophet Jeremiah A. Lewis, from Detroit, Michigan, good morning Prophet Lewis." He bowed again, which is not real good for radio. So. I continued, "Prophet Lewis, I have never had a prophet on my radio station before, what is it that you prophesy?"

At that, the prophet sorta leaned back and in a loud, rumbling, windows rattling bass voice said, "I HATES NIGGERS". When he said that the twin towers in unison said a hearty "AMEN". I broke out in a sweat, trying to recover from the shock. I said, 'Whoa, wait a minute I wish you hadn't said that, we don't use that word around here." By that time all four of my telephone lines were lit up, and I was saying to the prophet, "Why do you talk like that, you are obviously black yourself?" "I'M NOT A NIGGER, I'M A JEW." All I could think of to say was, "You mean like Sammy Davis Jr." He said "NO, SAMMY IS NOT A JEW, HE'S STILL A NIGGER.' "AMEN", went the echo from the two bruisers. I thought then that it might relieve some of the tension if I took a phone call. The first caller a black lady said, "Syrup Sopper, where you get that fool"? I told her again who he was and where he came from. After a couple of more calls like that I knew we were getting nowhere, so I went back to the prophet with another question.

"What is it that you hate about black folks?" He said, "NIGGERS IS FOOLS, THEY'S ALL NO GOOD, THE WORST THING THAT EVER HAPPEN TO DE NIGGER WAS INTEGRATION. WHAT DE NIGGER NEED IS FOR DE SHERIFF TO WHOP HIM UPSIDE DE HAID WIF A STICK AND SEND HIM ON BACK TO DE BACK A DE BUS WHERE HE BELONG." "AMEN!!", from the two behemoths. By that time I'm trying to decide whether my radio station would be bombed, set on fire or stuck by lightning. I was catching it from both sides, when I would answer the phone, from listeners fussing about me putting him on the air and from my guests. I asked another question which I really wanted to know the answer to, "Prophet how do you go around all over the country talking like that about your own people without someone killing you"? I had assumed that he must travel a lot and had not randomly selected WACT on which to appear out of the thousands of stations in the entire country. He came back with, "DE LAWD PROTECK ME." "AMEN". That gave me an opportunity to say, "I'll bet these two big guys you have with you are not doing too bad either." and to explain to the listeners that it was not me yelling "AMEN" every time the prophet said something.

Finally, I took a call from a man who said, "Now look here, I've heard all that mess I want to hear, if there's any fools around here it's that so called prophet, and not the black people. I want him to know that the best friend I ever had while I was in the army was a black soldier. We went to Vietnam together, fought side by side, and just before we were to come home that black man, my best friend, stepped in front of me and gave his life for mine by taking a bullet that was meant for me." Prophet Lewis answered "SEE, I TOLD YOU NIGGERS IS FOOLS." "AMEN"!!!

I don't know how I managed to get through the whole hour, but somehow, by running a lot of commercials and talking to the prophet as little as possible, I made it. I have not discovered yet what he prophesied, but I did learn later that he was from Eclectic, a small town just outside of Montgomery, and had gone to Detroit to start some kind of cult. I never heard from him again.

The next day I was still getting calls from listeners about the prophet, and I tried as best I could to explain how and why I had put him on the program. Luckily I had taped the whole program, because I had calls from just about every black group in the area wanting copies of it, which I gladly provided.

By the mid seventies, our offices at #3 Office Park had become totally inadequate for the staff and both the AM and FM stations studios. Another problem was, our AM tower and transmitter were located west of town on highway 11, and our FM was on the east of the city on 15th street. I started making plans to move all three to a single location if I could find enough land available that would meet the FCC engineering specifications, and was not too far from town.

My friend William Campbell owned approximately nine acres on the south side, just off Greensboro Avenue to the east and bordered on the west by the proposed I-359 spur from I-59 into downtown Tuscaloosa. I took an option on the property until I could have consulting engineer, Claude Grey, from

Birmingham do enough studies to see if the location would accommodate our facilities and provide enough space for one tower holding both the AM and FM antennas and a building. The sight was perfect except we had to obtain a waver from the FAA for the 400 ft. tower, because they claimed it was in the flight path of the Tuscaloosa airport about 10 miles away.

In 1977, I bought the land for $59,000 and soon was working with architect Howard White on a building plan. At his suggestion, and with my approval, we came up with a most unusual design for the building.

It would have 16 sides, with a detached, concrete portico at the front, rock columns at each of the 16 corners, and the outside walls would be West Coast cedar, board and batten. The outer space would house our reception area, and to the right, my office, two sales offices, the employees lounge, transmitter room, engineers office and technical supply room, storage room, music room, computer room, program directors office and finally the bookkeeping office.

All of the separate offices would occupy one sixteenth of the outer space except my office was doubled, as was that of the lounge and transmitter room. Across the circular hall from the offices, were the main studio, FM control room, production room, news room, and AM control room. Each room would have a large round double glass window, four feet in diameter in keeping appearance of the building, four feet in diameter, providing an excellent view through out the entire broadcasting facility.

The inner core would have a glass dome at the top to provide light and access to the wiring from one control room to the other. Access to the wiring would be provided by simply removing panels at floor level in the center core. The natural pine ceiling would be open with large beams supporting it and the roof. The interior walls were all unfinished West Coast cedar. It was truly a unique building, and very serviceable.

It was so unusual that Broadcasting Magazine ran a feature story and picture of it. When our plans were finally finished, there was only one contractor that I wanted to build it and that was my friend "Red" Reynolds owner of Reynolds construction Company.

He agreed to build it for $189,000, so in early 1979 construction began. My plan was to buy all new broadcast equipment, replace most of our furniture and in effect create a whole new beginning for WACT and WACT-FM. For all of that including $40,000 for a new 400 ft. tower, I spent well over $250,000, which I had saved and for which I was able to pay cash. I financed the building at First State bank and paid the note off in five years. On New Years eve, December 31, 1979 we moved into our new home at number 3900 11th Avenue.

Chapter 20

THE EIGHTIES

The 1980s began with the WACT staff getting settled in our all new surroundings, and becoming accustomed to our new broadcast equipment at our new location. For the first time we had the room and facilities to completely separate our AM and FM programming. At that time it seemed that the future of AM radio would lie in the conversion to AM stereo by all stations, so as I bought the new equipment for the AM station I was particular to go ahead and buy a stereo transmitter, control boards, turntables, recorders and playback units, and spent many extra dollars on wiring for AM stereo.

The problem with AM stereo was that the manufacturers actually marketed very few AM stereo radios, and the automobile manufacturers refused to make AM stereo radios standard equipment in their new cars and trucks. AM receivers were strictly optional, unlike when television added UHF channels to their existing twelve VHF channels and the government required set manufacturers to add the reception capability of the new channels to their new sets. AM stereo radio never got off the ground, causing a lot of broadcasters to lose a considerable amount of money on it.

Our new building was beautiful and very serviceable. Carol decorated my office the way she thought it should be from the grass cloth on the walls to the plush carpet on the floor, with a large mahogany desk and credenza, a triple row of mahogany book shelves over cabinets, two wing chairs, a sofa and a coffee table, with suitable pictures and plaques on the walls.

For the first time we had a "break" room with cabinets, table and chairs, a microwave oven and a refrigerator for the enjoyment of the employees and guests.

After working hours were over on late summer afternoons I enjoyed cutting the nine+/- acres of grass around the building and tower with my new John Deere tractor and Bushhog mower, which I stored in the adjacent storage building that was constructed of the same expensive West Coast cedar as the main building. Although I had grown up on the farm, I had never driven a tractor. It was fun for a while, then got to be sort of like work.

When we moved, I continued to work the 6-9 a.m. Syrup Sopper Show and the 9-10 WACT Action Hotline, having a good time with both. Business was good and the staff was working very hard. I installed our first computer, an IBM 5120. Compared to today's super fast and efficient machines the 5120 was a Model-T. However, it was much better than the old methods of bookkeeping, payroll, accounts receivable and payable and producing daily program logs. I paid Jerry Jackson in Opelika, Alabama $8000 for the program and $14,000 for the hardware in the early eighties. The machine I'm typing this on was less that $1500 and will do thousands of times more in a fraction of the time it took the 5120.

I was elected to the board of directors of the Associated Press Broadcasters in 1979 and while attending my first meeting of the board at the New York Hilton, received a call from The National Association of Broadcasters in Washington asking if I would accept a one-year appointment to fill out the unexpired term of Bill Stakelin our Southeastern representative, due to a shakeup in the NAB brass. I agreed, and because of my two consecutive elections for the maximum of two terms, I was on both boards for the next five years, from 1980 till 1985 and continued on the AP board for another three years until 1988 for a total of eight years.

Serving on the AP and NAB boards was very rewarding and a lot of fun, offering both Carol and me a wonderful chance to experience new people, places and things that would not ordinarily have been ours. Each of the boards met twice a year, either in Washington or preferably in some really nice exotic places, especially the winter meetings.

The AP board met in Palm Springs several times, in Sarasota, Florida, Seattle, Vancouver during the Worlds Fair, Disney World; San Francisco; San Diego; New York; Boston; Carmel, where I got to play Pebble Beach golf course; and after one meeting in Seattle, we took the inland water-way cruise of Alaska from Vancouver, B.C. to Anchorage, Alaska.

From there I went with some of the other board members, at the invitation of Shell, BP and Exxon Oil Companies on up above the Arctic Circle to Prudhoe Bay, where the Alaska Pipe Line begins. That's 800 miles from it's Southern end at Valdez. The purpose of the trip was to show us the undeveloped oil plateau, about a two hour helicopter ride from Prudhoe Bay called the Answar section, an area of Northern Alaska about the size of Indiana, which reportedly contains more oil in the ground than Saudi Arabia. That is the area that congress has consistently refused the oil companies permission to explore and develop because of environmentalists' objections. . Returning to Prudhoe the helicopter landed at an Alaskan Eskimo village called Ketchtovic, where we ate our box lunches. We rode in the only motorized vehicle in the town, an old school bus, from the small World War II air strip to a rundown shack that reminded me of our chicken house at Nebo with the sign over the door reading "Hotel."

The little village was one of the most desolate areas in which one could imagine any human being actually living. The only way in or out was by air or boat during two months of the summer. I could not help but notice in the small dining room there was a 17-inch television set mounted on the wall with CNN news broadcasting. An old man was in the kitchen, I assumed he was the cook, so I went in to talk to him, asking him if anyone else had ever brought their own lunch to his restaurant? He said, "Yes, but I don't blame them."

Kechtovic is a small village where the temperature often drops to 75 degrees below zero in the winter, with its only support being the Federal government and the permission to kill up to three whales a year for food.

Back at Prudhoe, we were assigned rooms for the night in the dormitory shared by the pipeline workers. The rooms were simple but nice and clean, the food was excellent, a wide variety of vegetables, meats and deserts. The dining room never closed due to the shifts of the workers, they could eat any meal at any time. I stayed awake most of the night to see if it really never got dark, as I had always heard. It was the first part of August, there was a twilight all night, even though it snowed enough to cover the ground, but quickly melted the next morning

They served a fabulous buffet breakfast, my first chance to eat reindeer sausage. I couldn't help but think about Rudolph. Then they gave us an extensive tour of the facilities covering an area of approximately 50 square miles. Of particular interest to me was the actual pipeline that begins at the main pumping station and runs over land for 800 miles. Another fact I had not heard was that in Northern Alaska, they don't have to pump the oil from the ground, they just bore a well and the pressure forces the oil to the surface at a temperature of 140 degrees.

The pipeline is so well insulated that by the time the oil reaches its destination at Valdez, 800 miles to the South, the temperature of the oil is just a few degrees cooler. Another thing I didn't know was that they don't turn off their truck engines all winter. They run all the time, because it's so cold they would not start again if they were stopped. A highlight of our flight back to Anchorage was the sight of snow-covered Mount McKinley, the tallest peak in North America. The weather was clear and we had an excellent view of the mountain.

I had left Carol back in Anchorage at our hotel, where she had the time of her life. The public relations director of BP Oil Company picked her up in a helicopter and showed her the entire area, even landing on a glacier. The night after I returned to Anchorage, Carol had contacted our good friend from Tuscaloosa, Norm Hibbard who was pastoring a small Presbyterian church in Palmer, Alaska, about forty miles from Anchorage. He picked us up and took us back to Palmer to show us the small town where they grow the giant carrots, cabbages, other vegetables and flowers, and the only musk ox farm in Alaska. Then after a great supper, he drove us back to our hotel. Our trip to Alaska, including the eight day cruise from Vancouver to Anchorage was a wonderful experience that we will never forget.

We were having such a good time we decided not to come

directly home, flew from Anchorage to Salt Lake City, Utah Neither of us had ever been there. After a day or two we rented a car and drove North, up through parts of Utah and Idaho to Jackson Hole, Wyoming. Then we continued north to a lodge just a few miles outside the entrance to Yellowstone National Park. I know of no more beautiful place even though much of the Park was still charred by the terrible fire that had burned much of it the previous year.

After touring the Park we drove down through Wyoming back to Salt Lake City. Having driven about two thousand miles we were ready to board a plane for home the next day.

A favorite meeting place in January for the AP Board was Palm Springs, California. The weather was always nice and the facilities were great for meeting, dining and playing. We usually met the week of the Bob Hope Desert Classic pro golf tournament. I was thrilled to be invited by one of the members to play the PGA West course at LaQuinta. I didn't play it very well, and I have no desire to play it again, if I had an opportunity. It was the toughest golf course I had ever seen.

Palm Springs is a beautiful city, with all underground utilities, no visible power lines and no ugly signs and billboards. There are no buildings taller than the tallest palm trees, about three stories. In January we played golf in shorts, while the mountains surrounding the area were snow covered.

At our meeting in 1987, former President Gerald Ford came by, ate lunch with us and visited for about two hours, before heading for the golf course. His visit was very informal, just chatting about anything we wanted to ask him. He impressed me as being a real gentleman, a nice person to be with.

I asked the former president, "If you had it to do over again would you pardon President Nixon as soon as you took office, and do you think the pardon caused your defeat in 1976?" His answer was, "Yes and yes. I would pardon Nixon again because I thought at the time it was good for the country, and I do think the pardon was one reasons for my defeat by Jimmy Carter in 1976."

I decided that day that Gerald Ford has the best job in

America. He served just long enough to garner the world-wide recognition and acclaim we afford past Presidents, the extremely high honoraria for speaking engagements, the pension, the security and honor, but not long enough for the job to sap his strength and his mental and physical abilities.

Carol and I enjoyed our eight years on the Associated Press board, not only the travel, but the many friends we made and those with whom we still share cards and calls regularly. At the time I went on the board, the President of the AP was Roy Steinfort. Roy idolized Coach Bryant. He had worked as Bryant's sports information director when the coach was at the University of Kentucky. Later as the owner and publisher of a newspaper in Greenville, Mississippi, Roy followed closely Alabama football, so he and I became instant buddies.

Carol and I invited Roy and his young wife, Patty, to visit us the weekend of the Penn State football game, which Alabama lost, but we had a great time. Patty, originally from New York City also worked for the AP covering the Long Island beat as a reporter. She was so "citified" I don't think she had never seen dirt, especially the kind we have in Alabama. She had never been further south than Washington D.C. and at first was very nervous about our unfamiliar surroundings.

The night before the game, we had made reservations to eat at the North River Yacht Club. With Roy and Patty in the backseat, we stopped by the McAbee house to pick up Ruth and LeRoy. As I drove the long fence lined lane to the house, Carol said, "We had better go to the front door, because they have the front porch light on, and not to the back as we usually do." I said, "That's right, the guineas have probably crapped all over the back patio." Their guinea hens roosted every night in the two tall pine trees near the house and droppings were not particular about where they fell on the yard and rear patio.

When I said what I did about the guineas, I immediately heard a commotion and whispering in the back seat. Roy tapped me on the shoulder and said, "Patty thinks you're talking about Italians." Roy told that story to everyone who would listen when he returned to Washington.

After the ballgame on Saturday we took Roy and Patty to the Kentuck arts and crafts show and sale at Kentuck Park in Northport on Sunday. It had rained all night the night before leaving the unpaved parking lot and the trails through the park almost too muddy to negotiate. Somehow we managed. After sloshing through the puddles and the mud viewing every type of "country" art imaginable, on the way back to the car, I said, "Patty I'll bet you have never had so much culture in one weekend." She replied, "I'm just about to O D on it." We all had a good laugh, especially Roy, having been originally from the South.

In 1985 Roy retired and at the next board meeting at The Parker Meridian Hotel in New York we had a special retirement party for him. As a retirement present Carol and I took the front page of the "Tuscaloosa News" that ran the day after coach Bryant became the winningest football coach in America, with 315 victories, and the page announcing his death in 1983, to Jack Andrews having him to encase them in Plexiglas frames and we presented them both to Roy after the dinner. That night I saw a grown man cry.

Roy was replaced as President of the AP by another good friend of ours, Jim Williams, from Sylacauga, Alabama. Jim was a graduate of the University of Alabama, a friend of Wally and Ron, and a former employee of Bert Bank at WTBC. Jim is still the President of the broadcast division of the AP in Washington. We still correspond by letter and phone with him and Rosie, his beautiful wife.

Like the AP board, the National Association of Broadcasters board met each January or February at some warm place, resorts like St. Maartens Island in the West Indies, Key Biscayne and Orlando, Florida, Puerto Vilarta, Mexico; Palm Springs and Laguna Niguel, California; or Maui, Hawaii, and each June at our headquarters building on the corner of Connecticut Avenue and N street in Washington. In addition to all of these biannual meetings, Carol and I always attended the annual NAB convention in April.

The board meetings lasted for five days allowing plenty of

time for our meetings, socializing, golf, and or sight seeing. We always invited several members of Congress to attend our meetings, especially those on the Commerce Committees of the House and Senate. That gave the board members and the Congressmen a chance to become better acquainted, was a free vacation for the members and gave us a good chance to do some effective lobbying on behalf of Broadcasting.

Talking about sight seeing, on our last visit to St. Maartens Island, Carol and I rented a car and were driving around the small island which is half French and half Dutch. As we drove from one side of the island to the other, I spotted a small sign by the road which read "Au Naturale Beach." I told Carol that if I remembered my French language, the sign meant there were naked folks out there. She said "Let's go see."

I turned down a small road for about a quarter of a mile until we could see the ocean. I parked the car then we walked down to the beach. I was right, everyone on the beach was naked except us. I asked if she wanted to join them. She said, "No, I'm just looking." As we strolled along the beach stepping over, around and very near the many nude folks, no one seemed to mind us looking. It was easy to identify those that had just arrived from the states that morning. They were the ones sunburned in places that were normally covered by their bikinis. They were staring at us, two freaks wearing clothes.

Soon we met Mike and Ann Harwood, they were clothed too. Mike was the long time Secretary/Treasurer of NAB. Finally we came upon a small lean-to, a shack where an old native was cooking and selling hotdogs. Mike and I each bought one, sat down on the ends of a well worn bench to eat. Mike anchored one end and I the other, to balance it. As we were eating, a true blond young lady, slim, trim, beautiful and buxom, about 23 years old, came and sat right between Mike and me on the middle of the bench.

She was not only naked, but she was as we said at Nebo, "Nekked as a jaybird." Mike and I both had a very difficult time trying to concentrate on eating our dogs and looking straight ahead. We ate with one eye and stared with the other. The last time I saw Mike Harwood, about fifteen years after that incident, he said, "You know, I still dream about that girl at St. Maartens."

The annual NAB conventions were very special occasions for board members, associating with old friends and fellow broadcasters, being entertained by some of the world's great entertainers, and numerous political celebrities as well as some of the greatest names in broadcasting.

One year we flew the entire Mormon Tabernacle Choir to Las Vegas for the opening of the convention. Other opening acts were Glen Campbell, The Oak Ridge Boys, and Bill Cosby. Besides congressional leaders, the President of the United States was always invited to speak at one of the major joint luncheons. They all accepted our invitation, usually bringing with them members of their staff and cabinet. We were privileged to meet Presidents, Nixon, Carter, Ford, and Reagan, Henry Kissinger, all members of the FCC and numerous members of congress.

The NAB sponsors the Broadcast Hall of Fame in Washington with new members being inducted at the annual convention. With that, and my membership in the Broadcast Pioneers organization I met a lot of the all time greats in our industry, Pat Buttram, Gene Autry, Carol Burnette, Mel Allen, Paul Harvey, Walter Cronkite, Barbara Walters, and Larry King. Jack Clements, president of the Mutual Network and I became good friends and he always invited me to play golf at the famous Congressional Country Club in Washington. Leonard Joyce, my Washington attorney was a member of Columbia Country Club, and Vince Wasilewski belonged to Burning Tree, the only exclusively male country club in Washington. When I was there, I always had an invitation to play, if I had the time.

The highlight of the annual NAB convention was and still remains the BMI dinner. Broadcast Music Incorporated (BMI) is a corporation formed and owned by broadcasters for the licensing of music. It was formed in the 1950s due to the high performance rates being charged by ASCAP the major service and SESAC the European licensing company. For a while the broadcasters refused to play any ASCAP music and only that which was in the public domain, until BMI could begin operation.

For many years most of the "country" music was licensed by BMI, however with the increase in popularity of our music ASCAP decided to become more involved. Do you remember Charlie Monk, the employee of WACT that sold me his old golf clubs and moved to Mobile? After a few years in Mobile, Charlie moved to Nashville to work for ASCAP signing country song writers.

Meanwhile, back to the BMI dinner, the affair paid for by BMI is the most fancy, elaborate, multi-course meal imaginable especially for an old boy from Nebo, Alabama. Invitations are sent to all current and some past NAB board members and past and present members of the FCC.

It is customary for some old, retired former broadcasters like me to make the trip to the Las Vegas convention not only for the food, but to visit with old friends. The dinner is always held at The Desert Inn or Caesar's Palace hotels. Dress for the occasion is strictly formal. For years all attendees wore over their tuxedos a long white apron with the name of the individual and the number of dinners he had attended embroidered on the bib.

My first one was in 1973. I never knew how that tradition got started, but it helped to set the occasion apart from an ordinary event, besides it was sorta fun for me to be dressed exactly like some of the real giants in the broadcasting industry, network executives, group executives, large station owners and managers and of course many small station owners. There were the former FCC members, many of whom had moved on to other high positions in government and industry, and the current members of the Commission. I still see Richard Wiley when I attend, even though he has been off the Commission for more than twenty years. I'm sorry to say that the apron tradition has run its course and now instead, we wear a large gold medal with our name and year of our first dinner inscribed on it. The medal is on a large ribbon worn around the neck

The dinner itself is truly extravagant, beginning at 7:00 p.m..

with a cocktail party and very heavy hors d'oeuvres, including my favorite, Alaskan king crab claws, followed by the seated dinner, usually French, from 8:00 to 10:30 or eleven p.m. with no speeches just good conversation and good food.

Before I leave the BMI dinner, I must tell you about one that I still remember, not because of the food, but a funny thing that happened. The closest I have ever been to a professional championship fight was at Caesar's Palace Hotel. I don't remember the year, but that doesn't matter. My friend Bob Hilker and I had ridden with the President of NAB, Eddie Fritz in his limousine from the Hilton over to Caesar's. When our driver pulled up in front, there were hundreds of people pushing and shoving, crowding around asking for autographs and yelling at us.

We didn't know for a few minutes, but soon figured the mob was a part of the crowd that was there to see the fight between Hearns and Hagler, which was also at the hotel that evening. The mob, mostly black, decked out in more gold chains, rings and bracelets than Fort Knox could afford and their very finest, to me, odd looking attire, thought we were celebrities there to attend the fight because we had arrived in a limousine.

After making our way through the throng and the crowded casino, we made it to our BMI dinner and donned our long white aprons with our names embroidered on the front. Everything was going well, the food was great, the company at our round table was good, we could hear the boisterous fight crowd cheering. Even though the actual fight was in the outdoor arena, the large ballroom across the hall had been set up with closed circuit television for the overflow crowd, and it too was packed. Sometime between the pheasant, the ox tail soup and the salad, (I have never figured out why the French serve the salad last,) I tried to remember if I had already eaten and forgot it by the time the salad was served. Speaking of salad, at one of the dinners the salad was a single leaf. One leaf covering most of the plate with a little dab of dressing on it, looked like pore folks eating to me. My good buddy Bill Hanson from Cicero, Illinois said, "What is this?" I said, "I don't know what ya'll up north in

Illinois call it but in Alabama, we call it kudzu, and our cows won't even eat it." We didn't either.

As I was saying, sometime between the main course and the salad I needed to go to the men's room. I walked down the wide hallway to the room, where to my surprise, I was the only one in the largest, fanciest toilet I had ever seen, except for the old gentleman that handed me a towel as I went in. I thought to myself, he must think I'm gonna take a bath, when all I've got to do is pee. Just as I entered the bathroom, I heard a loud commotion in the hallway outside. Hagler had knocked out Hearns in the third round and all the "brothers" in the ballroom were running to see who could be first in the men's room, apparently having held it all evening and as long as they could. By the time the first ones arrived in there I was standing at a urinal with my white apron pulled way up to my cummerbund, my pants unzipped and relieving myself. The men's room that just a few seconds ago was empty was now bedlam, with men pushing, shoving and yelling. I thought they were going to continue the fight that had ended so abruptly in the ring. About that time I saw I was completely surrounded. I'm six feet tall, but as I stood there with my apron in one hand and my little tallywhacker in the other, I was suddenly between two of the biggest, meanest looking, black men I had seen since I interviewed the prophet.

There was no doubt they were men, while I was holding mine between my thumb and forefinger, they rolled theirs out and held them with both big hands. "Why did I look?" you say, "I had to, I was eye level with them." All I wanted to do was finish and get out of there, but the one on my right looked at me and said, "Hey Man, you wid de Klan?" I replied, "Naw suh I works in de kitchen." About that time big Willy Davis, the former Green Bay Packer lineman, walked in with his apron on and saw that I was being hassled. He asked me if everything was all right, but before I could answer the one who had mentioned the Klan looked up to Willy and said, "Everythings's cool, Man everything's cool." I had always liked Willy Davis, but I could have kissed the big guy that night for coming into the men's room when he did.

All of the NAB conventions were special for their display of all the very latest equipment in broadcasting, their programs, hobnobbing with celebrities, lunches and dinners and the opportunity once a year to visit with old friends from across the nation.

However, there was one, 1984, that was a disaster for our circle of friends. Len Hensel, was a friendly, outgoing, tall dark and handsome man, always with a joke and a big smile who became a very good friend of ours. Len, originally from Florence, Alabama, had worked his way up through the ranks of radio to one of the best jobs in the country, and that was manager of WSM in Nashville. Carol and I both enjoyed the company of Len and his wife Pat every time we could be together. Pat was a lovely lady, with a great sense of humor, much like her husband's.

It was a Friday night in Las Vegas before the convention was to begin on Sunday, that six of us earlybirds went out to dinner. There were Charlie and Carol Jones from Columbia, South Carolina, Len and Pat Hensel from Nashville and Carol and me. We had a great time catching up on all the things that had happened to us and our families during the past year. I was seated beside Pat Hensel, and as we talked about our favorite places to vacation, she said that she and Len had gone to Maui, Hawaii the previous winter and that she just loved the place, saying, "I just can't wait go get back there."

The NAB sponsored an annual golf tournament on Saturday, presided over by Gert Schmitt from Jacksonville, Florida, that being one reason for Len, Charlie and me being in Las Vegas early. That night Len and I agreed to share a cab to the golf course the next morning, which we did. When we arrived, we found that we were not scheduled to play in the same foursome, so we agreed to meet after the game at the Desert Inn club house and return to the Hilton together.

When it was over, I couldn't find Len anywhere, but was told that someone had come out to the golf course during play to pick him up, telling him that his wife was ill.

That morning after Len had left their room very early to meet me, Pat got up, dressed, and did the usual things that women do to get all " prettied up" in the morning. She went down to the Hilton dining room where she met Carol Jones for breakfast. She ordered, and before it was served she died. She, without saying a word, simply fell over.

The night before she had been perfectly healthy, even bragging to me about how good she was feeling. The autopsy confirmed that she died of a cerebral hemorrhage. Len never saw his dear wife alive again. She was an organ donor, and while he was making arrangements for the transfer of her body to Los Angeles and the removal of her vital organs to be used for transplants, he asked my Carol to go up to their room and pack all of their clothes and prepare them for shipping back to Nashville.

I found that Las Vegas is not a good place to die. A person falls over in the big coffee shop, the paramedics come, a doctor pronounces her dead, she is taken out among the diners, and through the casino to the front of the hotel for a waiting ambulance, and very few people even pause in respect from their eating, drinking and gambling. What shook me most, was when I asked the grief-stricken Len, about funeral arrangements, assuming she would be buried in Nashville, he said, " As soon as our two daughters can get here we are going to have Pat cremated and take her ashes to Maui and scatter them at sea." My first thought was the statement she had made to me the night before, "I just can't wait to get back to Maui." Neither of us thought that it might be so soon.

Len retired from WSM, took a job traveling from state to state for BMI and a few years later married a gracious lady who owned a television station in Phoenix, Arizona. Later he developed circulatory problems and died. He was a good man and a good friend.

The 1980s brought a lot of change, not only in the business

lives but the personal lives of the Price family. After graduating from the University of Alabama, Wally came to work full time in sales and on the air at WACT. On March 23, 1980 he married Judy Kline, a registered nurse, and they bought a small house on Camellia Drive.

On February 28, 1983 our first grandchild was born, Walter Bailey Price II. We have always called him Bailey, his grandmother's maiden name. Bailey is a straight "A" student, planning to go into the field of medicine as a career. I predict he will be a wonderful doctor someday or maybe he will discover a cure for diabetes or cancer.

Exactly two years later, on February 28, 1985 another son Bradley DeFoor Price was born. The DeFoor comes from my mother's maiden name He has always and forevermore will be known as "Brad." He is also a very fine student and athlete. He has played baseball, soccer and football, but plans to concentrate on football this fall at Tuscaloosa Middle School. Brad is a "people" person, possessing an outgoing personality, liking and being liked by almost everyone with whom he comes in contact. He won the "Good Citizenship" award and other special recognition at Tuscaloosa Middle School last year.

On March 24, 1988 our little doll, Mary Leah Price was born. I say little doll, because that's what she was. Being two months premature, and weighing less that two pounds at birth, she seemed not to have a very good chance of survival, but by the grace of God, and Dr. Choy with his fine staff in the neonatal unit at DCH Medical Center, and a strong will to live, she made it. She remained in the hospital for five weeks, but was then able to go home weighing three pounds.

Of course, we were all concerned and praying that she would be perfectly normal, which I'm glad to say she is in every way. She is smart, making good grades as she enters the sixth grade this fall, and, like her brother Brad, she won the "Good Citizen" award at Verner Elementary school last year. I could never say that one grandchild was my favorite, but you can bet that Leah would be close to the top if I could, and she would say the same about me. She loves her "Pop." With the birth of Leah,

Wally and Judy's family was complete. As I write this Bailey is 16, Brad is 14 and Leah is 11.

When Ron graduated from the University, he went to work for the Associated Press as a station representative, along with his friend Jim Williams whom I have already mentioned as current president of the AP Broadcasters. On May 9, 1980 he married Terry Elizabeth Davidson from Northport at St. Luke United Methodist Church in Northport. They lived in Atlanta for a while, Ron working for the National Association of Broadcasters. When the NAB discontinued their station representative program and went to direct mail and phone correspondence with member stations, Ron and Terry moved back to Tuscaloosa into a very nice house in the Covington subdivision. Ron came back to work with us at the radio stations, and Terry went to work for the Red Cross.

Their first child was born on July 12, 1989. They named the new baby boy Ronald Blaine Price II and he is known as Blaine. Less than two years later a daughter, Caroline Sommers Price was born. Caroline was born on January 29, 1991. Just a week or so before she was born, Ron and Terry were granted a divorce.

Ron was remarried in November of 1994 to Deborah Kapan, giving Carol and me three more instant grandchildren, Julie, Haley, and Amy. Julie is married now living with her husband Tom in Seattle, Washington. Julie has recently given birth to a baby girl, Josey, making Ron a "Grandfather" and Carol and me "Great Grandfather" and "Great Grandmother".

Ron, Deborah, Haley and Amy live in Tuscaloosa in the Riverdale section. Blaine and Caroline live with their mother in Guntersville, Alabama. They get to visit us and their daddy every other weekend, a week at Christmas, spring break, and six weeks in the summer. They are both great kids, and we love them dearly, which makes seeing them when we can even more special. Ron is now employed by the Alabama Brick Corporation with headquarters in Birmingham.

After fifteen years of marriage Wally and Judy were divorced in 1993. Their three children, Bailey, Brad and Leah have lived with Wally since that time, with a lot of help from Carol, advising, cooking, shopping, dressing and taking the place of a mother. They live less than two miles from us on a fifty-five acre plot of woodland just off Rice Mine Road, owned by Leroy McAbee. Wally is involved in real estate and other ventures, also doing a morning talk program on WTBC, and has full custody of the children.

As I think about the eighties the one event that changed my life and lifestyle more than any thing else, was the heart attack on August 11, 1984. I have already mentioned that, but I need to tell you that in 1978, during a routine physical examination by Dr. John Todd, he discovered that I was a "borderline" diabetic.

I was able to control it somewhat with oral medication, Diabonese, for a few years, but during a hospitalization for pneumonia and pericarditis in 1983 the doctors decided that I must go on insulin. I did, and have remained on both regular and NPH since that time.

Before the heart attack I thought the radio station could not exist if I were not there by six a.m. and stayed till late in the afternoon, but I found I was wrong. While I was away for a month the boys took over and business wise we had the best month ever. That was when I began thinking about slowing down, decreasing my work schedule and increasing my golf.

Wally took over the early morning Syrup Sopper Show. I continued to do the Hotline program, manage the station, and call on some advertisers. Wally was in sales and promotions, while Ron was selling and doing some on-the-air work. We brought Carol in after a while, to try her hand at collecting from some slow paying accounts. She was the best collector I had ever seen. I used to say, "She's got people trying to pay that don't even owe us anything."

Later, she took over the sales department, outselling everyone, proving that she could sell advertising as well as collect for it.

As the decade of the eighties progressed, my health was not any better, the boys' families were growing and the strain of the radio station's ever increasing need for more revenue for the twenty-five employees, and our families Wally, Ron and I began talking about expanding our business or selling WACT since prices at that time were extremely good. I had been in the business for almost forty years and was ready for Carol and me to retire.

Nothing would have suited me more than for Ron and Wally to take over the station, own and run it, if they could assure us that we would be able to survive on the amount they could pay us. Separately, they each told me that they did not believe they could work together, without me in the middle, so I said it seemed to me the best thing to do would be to sell it.

We hired a brokerage firm from Atlanta and put the station on the market. After almost a year of negotiations in 1989 we sold it to Taylor Broadcasting, headquartered in that city. I don't think it necessary to disclose the exact selling price, but I must admit, it gave me great pleasure and a humble, grateful feeling to think about how from nothing we built a business that sold in the seven figures range.

However, I still become a little sad when I pass the round building on I-359 that I built in 1979. Sometimes it seems as though I have deserted one of my children. During the years before the sale, I had given Wally and Ron each 15% of the stock in New South Radio Inc. and when it was sold I gave them the equivalent amount of cash for their stock.

People still ask me if I miss the radio station and being Syrup Sopper, and I say that sometimes I miss it, but it doesn't take me long to get over it. The thing that's really strange to me, the younger generation has never heard of the Syrup Sopper, but the older folks still talk about Lum 'n Abner, John Robert Spiller, Buckshot, Hank, Granny, the Groundhog Man, occasionally the Prophet and other characters that made the Syrup Sopper show the most popular radio program in the entire area.

Chapter 21

THE NINETIES

We completed the sale of WACT & WACT-FM to Taylor Broadcasting on December 31, 1989. For the first time in my life, when I awoke on the morning of January, 1, 1990, I did not have to get up build a fire in a wood heater, milk a cow, slop a hog, feed a chicken, chop stove wood, plow a mule, chop cotton, plow cotton, pick cotton, "tote" water from the creek, catch a school bus, go to a class, answer reveille, pull KP, play records on the radio, try to be informative and entertaining when I really didn't feel like it, worry about the FCC, worry about meeting a payroll, worry about paying corporate taxes, selling advertising, keeping sponsors and a staff of twenty-five or more people happy. or write the longest sentence in this book.

In other words I felt completely free. I said then, "That was the first time in my life I didn't have to start the day kissing somebody's rear end." Steve Taylor hired Wally to remain with the stations as manager, that being one condition of the sale. Ron and his boyhood friend from across the street, Bill Lavender, purchased his father-in-law, Buddy Davidson's paving business. They soon found out that pouring and spreading hot asphalt on parking lots and driveways in the summertime was not their calling, so they sold that business right away.

Ron went to work for a company called Superock, sounds like a radio station, but it is a concrete block company. He later moved on to Alabama Brick Company. Wally, after managing WACT for a while formed a partnership with Jimmy Shaw and they put a new radio station, WLXY, on the air in Northport. When Wally sold his interest in the station, he went into the real estate business.

As for Carol and me, we retired. At the time of the sale, we received enough cash to pay all sales costs, brokerage fees, lawyers, and accountants' fees, tax, and cash to Wally and Ron for their 30 % interest in WACT, then financed the balance for the Taylor family.

These last chapters, I must admit will be the most difficult for me to write primarily because they concern my health. I know that there is nothing more boring or less interesting than someone telling about his "operation". If you prefer you may feel free to end your reading with chapter twenty but if you read on you may find what I'm saying a little bit interesting. I have often said, "It's a good thing I retired when I did in 1990, if not I wouldn't have had time to be sick."

My problems began as early as 1962 when Dr. Maxwell Moody diagnosed a hiatus hernia in my chest and also discovered I had a slightly elevated blood pressure. I was so sure that I was having a heart attack when the hernia would flare up that he prescribed nitroglycerin pills, telling me to always have them with me and if the pain started, take a pill. The idea being, if the pain stopped it was indeed a heart attack, but if it didn't stop, it was the hernia. I never took a single pill, but I always carried a small bottle of them in my pocket, until they all turned to powder. I was really too busy in those days trying to get the radio station on its feet, with new personnel, and programming. When I had a pain I was afraid that if I took a pill the pain would stop and that would mean I was having a heart attack. The hernia cured itself, however the high blood pressure continued, controlled by medication.

For many years I had annual physical examinations at Dr. John Todd's office, blood tests, x-ray, prostate exams, the works, and everything was fine except for the usual wear and tear. The first treadmill I ever saw was at his office. He said, I've got this new machine, and all you have to do is walk on it and it will tell me all about your heart. He didn't say the nurse would shave spots all over my chest, then take a sand rock and rub the spots till they were raw, hook up enough wires to light a Christmas tree, start the tread moving, while I was supposed to jump on it like a hobo catching a freight, and walk fast enough to stay on and keep up with it.

At the beginning, it was easy, staring straight ahead, holding on to the handrails, and walking, but suddenly the thing was going faster and faster, with the front end of it rising so that I was going up hill becoming more and more difficult for me to stay even with it. Soon I was running up hill and hanging on to the rails. After about fifteen minutes which seemed like an eternity, it began to gradually slow down, finally to a stop. They helped me off and let me rest a while on the table. Since that day I have been on many treadmills, and I have learned one thing about them. That is, if you survive, you pass the test. I told the doctor that instead of having me look at a blank wall while on that thing, the very least he could do would be to hang a picture of a mule's rear end on the wall for me to look at, so it would seem like I was back home on the farm plowing.

John Todd would always fuss at me about smoking, but I never really had the desire to quit. I remember one day in his office, he said, "Clyde, you are a fairly intelligent fellow. You know those cigarettes are killing you, that they cause heart, kidney, and lung disease and a bunch of other health problems, and besides, you're already being a diabetic and cigarettes will compound your risk of having a fatal heart attack.

I would always say, "Yeah, I know all that and I'm going to quit someday," knowing I didn't really mean it. Soon after one of those conversations one of my problems was solved, I changed doctors. John Todd suddenly started having heart problems himself, so he retired, leaving me the opportunity to change medicine men, to a doctor who himself smoked, my neighbor, Dr. Ted Cone.

It made me feel good when I would see Ted and he would bum a cigarette from me. I found out Ted didn't buy them he just smoked them, he had a lot of "smoking" patients. I soon changed doctors again, this time going to Dr. George Miller. The first time I was in his examination room, I was checking out his diploma hanging on the wall when I saw that he had graduated from the Louisville School of DENTISTRY. That made me nervous. I've never liked going to dentists. When he came in I said, "Doctor, I think I'm in the wrong office I'm here for a physical examination, not a toothache. Miller said, "I was a dentist before I was a doctor, I worked my way through med school by practicing dentistry in Louisville." Dr. Miller is still our "family" physician, although I personally have not seen him recently, except socially, because I have had to spend so much time with heart, lung, kidney, urology and orthopedic specialists.

I have suffered much physical pain, but the most excruciating pain I ever had was in the spring of 1983. It was an early Saturday morning when I began developing a hurting, burning sensation on both sides of my rib cage. By noon, it was so bad, I described it like railroad spikes being driven into my sides. Carol drove me to the DCH Medical Center, where they soon determined it was not a heart attack, but after many tests, diagnosed my problem as pneumonia and pericarditis, an inflammation of the "sac" around my heart.

I was admitted to the hospital and treated with several drugs, one called Ativan. Not knowing I was allergic to the drug, they kept giving me big doses of it for several days, even though I was completely unaware of everything that was happening. Carol and others told me later about some of the wild and crazy things I did and said, during that time. From Saturday until the following Friday, when I began to recover, everything is still a complete blank.

I came out of it not remembering anything except checking into the hospital. During the time I was ill, my blood sugar shot up to the 300 range. That was when the doctors put me on insulin, both regular and NPH, and I have not missed a day giving myself two injections a day since then. A quick calculation reveals that I have given myself over 11,000 insulin injections and have stuck one of my fingers drawing a drop of blood for testing at least 5000 times, and I'm the one who used to faint at the sight of blood or a needle. Before 1983, I had sworn that I would never be able to administer a "shot" to myself, but I found that you do what you have to do.

Diabetes is a terrible disease, unlike a massive heart attack or a brain hemorrhage, it is a slow killer. It affects the circulatory system, therefore the heart, kidneys, eyes, lungs, liver, your libido, and especially the extremities, lower legs, feet, toes, and fingers.

All I know about diabetes is from my own experience and what I have read, and been told by the experts, so I will not try to get into the medical aspects, leaving that to specialists like our Dr. Keith DeBell here in Tuscaloosa.

My purpose here is to tell you that if you are experiencing extreme thirst, weight loss, itching, unusual tiredness, or frequent urination, all or any of which could be symptoms of the disease, for goodness sake see a doctor, and have a check-up right away. Most early stages of diabetes can be treated with oral medication. If you are diagnosed a diabetic, remember it's not the end of the world. Be sure to follow your doctor's advice regarding exercise, diet, regular blood sugar testing and you can live an almost normal life for a long time. The condition will never be cured, unless medical science discovers a miracle.

Looking back, at this state of my life, I wish I had taken more of the advice I'm giving you. I went through a long period of rejecting the idea that I was a diabetic, not wanting to follow the advice of the dieticians and doctors, counting calories, avoiding sweets, which I dearly love, and exercise. Remember, when you are a diabetic, you are gradually dying, but you may slow the process by taking good care of yourself. This is for every reader, but especially for my five grand children, any one or more of whom are subject to inheriting my condition. I certainly hope not.

In an earlier chapter I wrote about August 11, 1984. That was the day I suffered a heart attack on the golf course, smoked my last cigarette and Dr. Bill Hill performed an angioplasty by running a tube from, my groin to my heart. After that I took a few days off from the radio station and found they really didn't need me anyway. That's when I determined to change my working and playing habits. I began exercising more and eating less of good things, and put myself under the care of Cardiologist, Dr. John Mantle. He reminded me, that if it tastes good, spit it out.

After the heart attack in 1984, Carol and I both continued to work at the radio station, while enjoying more time off. The boys were taking on more responsibility. We purchased a three-bedroom condominium in the new Regatta building on the beach at Gulf Shores, Alabama. We spent a lot of time there, in addition to traveling to Associated Press, and NAB board meeting. Healthwise the 1980s were pretty good. I continued to see Dr. Mantle about every three months for check-ups and Dr. Miller for the diabetes.

The year was 1990, shortly after we sold the radio station, that my friend the late Carl Knight introduced me to his friend Gene Brett from Gulf Shores. Gene, his brother, Tillis Brett and Tommy Robinson owned a real estate and construction company with offices in Saraland, just north of Mobile. They had built two high-rise fifteen-story condominiums called Phoenix I and II, at Orange Beach.

Brett/Robinson company was trying to raise money to purchase a lot on the beach adjacent to Phoenix II. They needed $800,000 to buy the lot from the Federal Government, which had taken it over after the bankruptcy of the Baldwin Savings and Loan.

I was one of several individuals who participated in the loan for the property with a guarantee that when the building was finished, Carol and I would have our choice of a condominium. That turned out to be a great investment, because in 1992 when the building was completed we had a lot of fun furnishing our brand new home-away-from-home, on the eleventh floor of the fifteen story Phoenix III. Our final purchase price was less than half the going rate for similar condos.

The first time our four year old grandson, Blaine, visited us he walked out on the balcony and exclaimed to his grandmother, "Woof, you're the only one I know who has an ocean in their backyard." Several of our friends bought units after the completion of the project, the McAbees, Hahns, Knights, Peakes, the Ways, and others.

Shortly after Phoenix III was completed Brett/Robinson acquired the lot next door and constructed Phoenix IV. I bought a condo in that building which we still own as rental property.

The company has been very successful since 1990, having built Phoenix V, VI, VII, VIII, Phoenix East, and Phoenix East II. Phoenix X, the largest of them is under construction now at Orange Beach near the Florida line. All Phoenix buildings are fifteen stories tall.

In the fall of 1990 I began having more heart problems, with some angina during exercise, irregular heart beats, and just not feeling well. When Dr. Mantle checked me with the electro-cardiogram, treadmill and ultra sound, he said that he did not think heart surgery was required at the time, but if my condition worsened that was definitely in my future. In early January of 1991, I developed pneumonia. I was feeling so bad that Carol drove me to the emergency room at DCH. By the time we got there, I was having chest pains and irregular heart beats. Dr. Posey said, "We need an e.k.g. right away to see about your heart." When it was completed, he said, "That's the worst looking one I've ever seen." You need bypass surgery now, but I want to see if we can cure the pneumonia first." So, in consultation with the cardiologists, they all recommenced that I go home, take handfuls of medication for the pneumonia, hopefully improving enough within a week or two to have the heart surgery.

Two nights later I woke Carol and told her that I needed to go back to the hospital, I was really in pain. I spent that night and most of the next day in the emergency room, until I was finally admitted and assigned a private room. The doctors still were hesitant to operate before my pneumonia was cured. They treated it for three or four days, with heavy medication, achieving no success at all.

Dr. John Summerford, one of Dr. Miller's partners came in to see me about the third day I was in the hospital. When I asked him if they were going to operate, he almost shocked me into a fatal attack. He replied, "I don't know, first we've got to decide what we're going to do about your CANCER!" I almost jumped out of bed, saying, "What are you talking about, I don't have cancer. I've got pneumonia and a bad heart. What do you mean cancer?" He asked, "Didn't Dr. Miller tell you?" "Tell me

WHAT?" "The lab tests have revealed that you have some "suspicious" cells in your sputum, which could be cancerous, even though x-rays don't show any sign of it.

We think you may have a cancer in the lower lobe of your left lung, the only place one would not show on x-ray." After that, all the medics got their heads together and came in to tell me what they had decided to do. First we could not wait for the pneumonia to improve, I must have surgery, but they didn't know what kind. The only way to tell if I actually had cancer of the lung was to perform a broncoscopy, a light inserted into the lung, but they figured that might trigger a fatal heart attack. They would prepare for the bypass operation, then after I was anesthetized, perform the cancer test first. If it revealed any sign of cancer they would not perform the heart surgery, however, if there was no cancer, they would go ahead with the heart bypass.

In either case there would be no lung surgery, because they believed my heart could not take it. The decision amounted to this. If there was no cancer, a heart operation, if there was cancer, no operation at all and I go home to die.

The afternoon before the operation was scheduled, a good looking young man came in my room and said, Mr. Price, I am Dr. Ford Simpson, and I am going to perform your surgery in the morning." Another shock, I said, "No, you're not either Young Feller, I remember you in high school just a few years ago, you are Wally's age, and I sure wouldn't want him taking my heart out and messing with it. I want your daddy." Ford said, "Daddy's retired and besides he doesn't know the first thing about performing a heart operation." That same afternoon my golfing buddy and retired surgeon, Dr. Floyd Fitts came to see me to cheer me up and ease my mind about the things that would be happening the next day. Floyd said, "Clyde, you are in one of the finest hospitals with some of the most competent surgeons and heart teams in the country. If I had to have what you will have, I don't know any place I would rather be." When he left he said, "I'll see you early in the morning before you go into surgery." Dr. Fitts, my good friend and adviser never showed up the next morning. I learned later that he had gone home the day he had given me the pep talk he had accidentally sawed off the ends of three of his fingers working in his wood working shop. Did he go to DCH, to the wonderful facility and great surgeons to treat his fingers? NO! He went to Northport General Hospital. I think maybe it was because they would let him perform the operation on himself and save money.

I had a lot of company that afternoon, including Bill David Smith, my accountant. That gave me a chance to refresh his memory about my personal business affairs, my insurance, living will, and last will and testament, just in case I didn't make it. My pastor, Dr. Rick Lance from The First Baptist Church, came and stayed a good part of the afternoon. I felt much better about the whole situation after he prayed asking God to be with me and the doctors during the ordeal.

That night about 8 o'clock one of the nurses asked if there was anything special I would like to eat. Since I had been eating hospital food for about four days, I said, "Do you mean I can have ANYTHING I WANT?" She said, "Sure, anything you want now, but you get nothing after midnight." Louis went to the Waffle House on McFarland Boulevard, my favorite restaurant, for one of their best meals, scrambled eggs with cheese, bacon, grits, raisin toast and apple butter. He brought back enough servings for himself, his mother, Ron, Wally, me and the nurse. We went in the waiting room and ate the "whole thing" like it was my last meal, thinking maybe it really was.

They wheeled me into the operating room shortly before 7:00 a.m. on January 18, 1991. The operation was performed by Drs. Simpson and Newsom assisted by Dr. Olivet, the head of the department. My next recollection was waking up in the recovery room with all kinds of tubes, and wires protruding from every part of my body. There are seven places in the body that will accommodate a tube. I had one in each of them, and they had even made holes where none had existed before. I could not speak because I had a tube in my mouth that seemed as big as a stove pipe, the most uncomfortable thing I had ever experienced.

I was so nauseated that I began throwing up, every few minutes everything would come up, out my mouth, around that tube and all over me and the bed. I don't know what kept me from choking to death. The nurses would change me and the bed and soon the whole process would be repeated. I remember one nurse saying, "What did you eat last night? I see bacon and eggs, wait a minute, it's even got raisins in it." All I could do was nod that, indeed, that was what I had for supper. They finally realized I could not tell them, that I was allergic to the Morphine they were giving me for pain, but they finally switched me to Demerol. About the only two other things I remember in the recovery room other than visits from the family for five minutes every few hours, are when I was awake enough, I motioned for a pad and pencil. Since I couldn't talk, and had no other way of communicating, I took the pencil and scribbled, "lung?" on the pad. The nurse informed me that my lung was O.K. and that I had a three-way heart by-pass operation and that there was no cancer. I felt better already.

That night they removed the big exhaust pipe from my mouth with the inflatable football bladder attached to it that had been inserted in my chest. After another day in intensive care, I was moved to a private room, where I remained for another week. Still with the pneumonia, it seemed as if I was coughing every breath, and would surely tear all of the staples out of my chest. The pain was almost unbearable when I coughed, but they would not give me anything for it because they wanted me to "cough It up".

After heart surgery the next big event is when the patient has his first bowel movement. During the surgery ones entire body is shut down, and at the end, they have to get everything cranked up again, so the best indication that the patient is returning to normal is that first movement.

Six days after the operation, I still had not been to the bathroom. That afternoon one of the nurses came in saying, "Mr. Price, I'm going to give you a suppository, you must have a bowel movement." I said, as I was pulling the sheet up around my neck, "No, you are not either, just hand it to me and I'll do it." She said, "No, I'm supposed to do it. It's against the rules for me to let you." I said, "This is one time you and me are going to break the rules." She said, "Well alright but don't you tell anyone I let you do it or I'll get fired." She handed me the two inch long, paraffin looking suppository and left the room. I placed it in the proper place.

In a few minutes Ron came in to visit me, and as we were talking, the nurse came back in, as I was casually telling Ron, "That big old suppository didn't do me a bit of good, I might as well have stuck it up my ass." The nurse almost fainted, and went wild, saying, "Did you swallow that thing?' I said, "Why sure wasn't that what I was supposed to do with it?" Ron and I almost had a dead nurse on our hands . Even after I told her I was only kidding, she still didn't think what I had done was very funny, but she did admit that I must be getting better.

I went home from the hospital after the seventh day, still coughing and hugging a pillow to my chest for about another two weeks. As part of my recovery program I started attending Dr. Mantle, the cardiologist's, exercise sessions three days a week continuing for the next three months. Then I began a daily exercise program of walking at least two miles a day. When the weather was bad Carol and I would join with the early morning walking club at University Mall.

With quarterly check-ups, my heart seemed to be doing O.K. but my blood sugar continued to rise in spite of increased dosages of insulin. In the summer of 1995 Dr. Mantle became suspicious of an increased level of creatnine showing up in my blood tests. I decided to go to Kirklin Clinic, in Birmingham, to see Dr. Hunt, a diabetes specialist. Because he was leaving Kirklin shortly and going into private practice, he referred me to Dr. Curtis. He, after reviewing my medical history and reading my blood tests made a startling statement that still rings in my ears. He said, "A normal creatnine count is one. Your creatnine is at 2 points, meaning you only have one half normal kidney function. If the number goes to four, you only have one fourth and your kidneys are shutting down. If the number rises to seven or as high as eight, you will have practically no kidney function at all. You will have to go on dialysis, but if I were you, I wouldn't worry about my kidneys, your heart will most likely kill you before your kidneys will." I said, "Man thanks a lot, I'm glad I saw you today, you are just what I needed, someone to give me some good news and cheer me up." Needless to say I did not go back to Dr. Curtis, instead I started going to my friend and neighbor, Urologist, Dr. J.D. Askew here in Tuscaloosa.

Kidneys are nothing more than complicated filters. Their sole purpose is to filter impurities from the blood as it passes through them. I had always thought that kidney failure was a condition in which urination was not normal, but in my case the problem was that my kidneys, with their millions of little filters, were simply clogged from the diabetes. Then, as the disease progressed, the condition worsened.

Several times, Carol had said, "Why don't we see if we can get you a kidney transplant?" My reply was, "They don't give kidney transplants to 64-year-old heart patients with diabetes, resigning myself to a short future of dialysis if it should become necessary. Dr. Askew's partner Dr. Dirk Berry, another neighbor of ours, was in charge of the dialysis clinic. I talked to him about the possibility of having to go on it, and he even took me to the clinic to explain the procedure, which I will not go into here, because it never became necessary.

In November of 1995, during a regular visit to Dr. Askew, my blood creatnine level was at six. We knew something had to be done soon. Carol asked the doctor about the possibility of a transplant. He said, "Because of your previous history, age and general health, I doubt very much that you would even be accepted for an evaluation in the transplant unit at University of Alabama Hospital (UAB) in Birmingham. However Dr. Deithelm, the head of the transplant unit, is a friend of mine. I will call and tell him about you and your condition, just to see if by chance they will take you for an evaluation."

To our surprise, they did accept me, so, in December I checked into the kidney transplant unit, where I stayed for a week. Until that time I thought I had endured complete physical examinations, but I had never been poked, gouged, squeezed, x-rayed, ekg'ed, eeg'ed, scanned, scoped, mri'ed, treadmilled, and tested in every way possible as the transplant team did. I must have answered several hundred questions about my history, even about my mama and papa, and about my mental attitude.

They even had classes to attend for those of us who were being considered for the transplant waiting list. At the end of the week the social worker paid me a visit, talking about the expense, in addition to insurance and Medicare, how that if accepted, I would have to stay in Birmingham for at least four weeks in order to go to the lab for blood work every morning, those first weeks being the most critical time for a rejection.

In the final analysis I was told that it would be very unlikely for me to get a matching kidney within three years, even if I were added to the list of 7,000 people already on the waiting list in Birmingham, and 45,000 more nationwide. The doctors, with Dr. Diethelm would make the final decision, would let me hear from them.

I left the hospital somewhat discouraged, but not too surprised. I had not really expected to be put on the list when I checked in for the evaluation. I more or less simply put the idea of a transplant out of my mind, thinking that even if I were placed on the list, I would probably die before a match was found for me. I must add here that during the waiting period, Wally and Ron each volunteered to donate one of their kidneys to me. I said, "Positively NO, you both have your families, jobs, and futures ahead of you, and I probably won't be here much longer anyway." At this point I'm going to break a trust. I promised at the time that I would never tell this story, but I feel that now almost four years after the fact that I must.

On a Sunday afternoon in January, my friend and Good Samaritan Sunday School Classmate, "Sonny" Boothe, called, saying that he wanted to come over to talk to me and Carol. He came in, we visited awhile and finally he said, "The reason I'm here is that I want to donate you one of my kidneys. Betty and I have already talked it over, prayed about it and decided that I am going to Birmingham for an evaluation to see if one of my kidneys will match yours, and if so we are going to do it right away."

315

I said, "Sonny, I will not let you do that. You a very special friend, and I love you for offering to make a sacrifice like that for me, but I just can't let you go through that very serious operation, besides, What is your blood type?' He said "Type 0". "That settles it, mine is A+, if I can't get a cadaver kidney, then I just won't get one." I will always love, admire and be grateful to Sonny for offering to give a part of himself that I might live. To paraphrase our Lord, "Man hath no greater love for his fellow man than to lay down his kidney and his life for him." That was what Sonny wanted to do. In a day or two I received a letter from UAB saying that I had indeed been put on the waiting list for a transplant.

In January of 1996, my creatnine was up to seven and a half. Dr. Askew said, "Clyde, it's time we started making plans for your dialysis treatments. You have a choice to make and that is, which of the two types do you prefer. There is hemodialysis, a process that pumps the blood through a machine which acts as an artificial kidney, requiring you to go to the clinic, about a four hour process three or four times a week. Then there's is peritoneal dialysis, a process that allows your abdomen wall to act as a filter, that you administer to yourself at home, and you will remain ambulatory. That type requires a twenty-four hour, seven days a week schedule.

I had opted for the peritoneal and had gone to Dr. Charles Gross, surgeon, made an appointment for the next Wednesday for him to perform the operation that would place the tubes in my abdomen for the dialysis. On Friday before the fateful Wednesday surgery, I went for my regular visit to Dr. Mantle. I told him what was about to happen the next week. He checked the numbers, and said, "I don't think you should do that right now, your creatnine is down just a little, and I would hate to see you go on dialysis until you absolutely have to, because it will put a strain on your heart."

We postponed the operation. The very next Sunday morning on February 16, 1996, at 6:30 while Carol and I were drinking our coffee at the kitchen table and preparing to go to the 8:30 Sunday School, our phone rang. I answered. A voice on the other end said, "Mr. Clyde Price, 7609 River Ridge Road Northeast, Tuscaloosa?" I replied, "Yes, this is he." "I'm calling on behalf of the kidney transplant unit to tell you that we have a kidney for you. You will need to be checked into the hospital by 2 pm today." I was so shocked at the sudden news, I don't believe I even said, " Thank you."

Both Carol and I were running around like crazy, laughing and crying at the same time. I did remember to call Dr. Hayes Boyd, our Sunday School teacher to tell him the good news and that we would not be there that day. He could tell the class that our many prayers had been answered. I always had mixed emotions about praying for a cadaver kidney, knowing that for me to receive one, someone else had to die. I don't believe in selfishly praying for something bad to happen to another person for my benefit. As Dr. Charles Carter, our minister put it though, "Don't pray for any one individual to die, just someone in general, and pray that their kidney will match yours. After calling the boys, Carol and I threw some things in the car and headed to Birmingham to begin a whole new life for a while.

I was so excited that I never even thought about the fact that at the hospital I was being prepped for a very serious operation, and that I might not even survive. I had never been paid so much attention in a hospital before. They checked and rechecked my blood pressure, pulse, temperature, scrubbed me with something that smelled like mama's lye soap. A young nurse shaved me all over from my chin to my toes. I told her if she didn't hurry up and finish, she would have to marry me, A surgical assistant inserted a shunt in my left shoulder. Nurses and aids were in and out of the room constantly. One nurse came in and said, "Mr. Price, I understand you are here for a "renal transplant". I thought she said "penal", replying, "No I'm in here for a kidney but if they have an extra one of those I'll take it."

The operation was scheduled for Sunday night. Carol, Wally and Ron were all in the room anxiously anticipating my going to the operating room. We waited and waited, finally they told us that the operation had been delayed until 7:00 the next morning. I don't think any of us slept that night. I know I didn't. Shortly before seven on February 17, 1996, I was taken into an operating room, lifted off the bed onto a table, noticed how very cold the room was, and a bunch of folks all wrapped up in white and blue masks and robes gathered around.

That was all I remember until I woke in intensive care. Thankfully, I had not eaten a big meal from the Waffle House before that operation. The first familiar face I saw was Carol bending over me, saying it was over, and I had done fine. I must have been really hungry, I asked for some watermelon.

Soon a young doctor, about Ron's age came by and introduced himself, "Mr. Price, I am Dr. Keith Rhynes, your surgeon. Everything went really smooth and great, no complications," I said, "Dr. which one did you take out?" He replied, "We didn't take one out, you still have your two old ones, we put the new one right here, pointing to the right side of my abdomen" I was so drowsy at that time, I really didn't care where they put it, but I was surprised to learn that the new kidney was in the front instead of my back. Later, Doctor Rhynes explained that unless a person's kidney is badly damaged from cancer or some other disease, they leave them as is and insert the new one. The operation to remove a kidney is much more dangerous and serious than that to install one. I asked how he got it in, with everything else that was in that area. He said, "Oh, I just moved some stuff around and took out some of the fat that you didn't need anyway, to make room for it ." I have been amazed at the number of people, even medical personnel, who don't know that the procedure is not really a transplant, but more like an implant. I have had many professional people ask me "Which one did they take out?"

After two days in the intensive care unit I was transferred to a large, very nice room in the transplant unit, where I remained under constant monitoring for the next seven days by nurses, doctors and interns. The care could not have been better. Dr. Rhynes spent a lot of his free time with me . We became good friends. He was from Baton Rouge, Louisiana, a graduate of LSU, a Tiger Fan. That winter I invited him to come to

318

Tuscaloosa to attend the Alabama vs. LSU basketball game. Another time, on his day off, we played golf here at North River. About two years ago he moved back to Louisiana. I still visit with him on the phone occasionally.

During the time I was at UAB Carol lived at a hotel just about two blocks from the hospital. When I was released, we had to stay in Birmingham so that I could be there each morning for lab work, and in case my body began rejecting the new kidney. The hospital transplant division owns an apartment building across the street called the Towne House. All units except the top floor of the seven story building are small "efficiency" type apartments. We were lucky. The day I was released, a very big, nice, two bedroom, two bath, kitchen, living, dining, and laundry room unit became available, which we rented for $700 a month.

The next week after moving into the Towne House, I went to the lab at Kirklin Clinic as usual on Sunday morning. About 9:00 a.m. they called and told me to report to the hospital as soon as possible, my blood test that morning was showing signs of rejection.

Within ten minutes I was back in my old room, and soon Dr. Gaston was supervising the treatment. I was immediately given an IV of the drug Solumedrol. After only two treatments the rejection was reversed, but I remained in the hospital for another week.

At the end of six weeks we came home, but I still had to return to the lab twice a week, then weekly, then every two weeks, then monthly, quarterly and now biannually.

There are two really good things about a kidney transplant. First, it prevented me from a short lifetime of constant dialysis, and unlike a heart by-pass operation, not very many people have had one. After my heart operation, every time I tried to tell someone about it, chances are they would say, "Oh yeah, I know all about that, I had five by-passes, or in the case of my buddy Bill Strickland, who had six, How many did you have?" I would mumble something about three, change the subject, and slink away. I have yet to tell anyone about my transplant and have him or her say, "Yeah, I know all about transplants, I've had five."

I never learned the identity of my donor, but Doctor Rhynes told me it came from the Washington D.C. area. I said, "I hope it was a Democrat, so there would be one less of them up there." He explained that there are six major characteristics that ideally should match between the donor and the recipient for a successful match. Four will usually work, but the kidney I received, matched perfectly.

How did the people in Washington even know I needed a kidney? I asked the same thing. Here's the way it is. UAB sent all the information about me to a huge computer in McLean, Virginia. When a kidney became available in Washington, they sent the information about it to the same computer. The machine started churning out numbers, data, information, and like magic it came up with a match for an old man named Syrup Sopper, down in Tuscaloosa, Alabama.

Seriously, I am very grateful to the person who signed an organ donor card, not knowing that someday they would save my life with one of their kidneys being a perfect match for mine. Whoever you were, God Bless You and Keep You. Thank you so much!

This would be a good spot for me to urge anyone reading this, if you have not already done so, please sign an organ donor card or have it stamped on your drivers license, that you are a donor. Organs are desperately needed, hearts, lungs, kidneys, eyes, livers, are all in short supply. I understand that now there are 1300 people on the waiting list in Birmingham alone and at least 60,000 nationwide. YOU COULD SAVE A LIFE, if you happen to lose yours.

The last procedure a kidney transplant patient has to endure is performed at the urology department. During the surgery a stint is placed in the urethra, therefore a visit to the urologist is a must for the removal of the stint before the patient is allowed to go home. I went to see Dr. Bueschin, having no idea what it was all about or what he would do. His assistant told me to strip down to my socks, put on a gown, that looked more like an apron than a gown, and climb up on a table, place my feet up higher than my head, in stirrups and relax.

I said, "Why don't you try that." The doctor came in and said, "Now, Mr. Price, what I'm going to do is run this light and camera, up through your penis, flood your bladder with water, and try to find that stint." I said, "You're gonna WHAT!!" He explained again, then asked, "Are you ready?" I said, "I'm as ready as I'll ever be." As he began he said, "Just relax, this won't hurt much." It was obvious he had never had it done to him. Just as I was about to let out a scream from the pain, he said "Do you mean to tell me I'm hurting you?" "You sure are," I said. "If you don't believe me, let me do it to you" He came back with, "If I had to have this done, I think I would rather have someone more experienced than you." I told the old doctor that I believed that was the first one he had ever done.

As he was searching for the stint, he paused a moment, saying, "Hey, wait a minute, I see something in your bladder that shouldn't be in there." I said, "Sure you do, it's your two fists, the northern lights, the CNN network and the Tennessee river, and I wish you would quit watching Opera Winfrey on that television you are looking at, and hurry up, I'm dying."

He said, "You have a small tumor next to where the urethra enters the bladder, and you need an operation to remove it as soon as possible." I said "Are you telling me that I have CANCER?" "We can't be sure until it's removed." In a state of shock, after he found and removed the stint, I got dressed and went to his office to discuss his finding, with him and Carol. He called my type of tumor a "smoker's tumor." I said, "Man, I haven't smoked a cigarette in fifteen years." "That doesn't make any difference. Any man who has ever smoked, will sooner or later have these tumors if they live long enough, and most of the time they are malignant." He went on to say "You are extremely lucky that we found it this early, most people who have them don't know about them until it's too late for simple operation to remove them."

We consulted with Dr. Rhynes about another operation so soon after my kidney transplant. The procedure was set for two weeks hence.

Those were some really dark days for Carol and me, recovering from the kidney transplant and facing the possibility of bladder cancer. The tumor was removed, tested and indeed was cancerous. It was so small that no radiation or special treatment was required, but at the end of six months, I had to return for another search of my bladder. The Doctor had said that type of tumor has a habit of "coming back." Sure enough it, or one just like it was back, requiring another bladder operation. That time the tumor was not cancerous Since then, I have continued to go back every six months for an examination with, so far, negative results, but that doesn't ease my concern that one day it will return.

Chapter 22

THE FINAL CHAPTER

Each first Sunday in August the McAbee family tradition is a family reunion at the farm of Leroy's uncle, Al McAbee, about ten miles east of Rome, Georgia. Ruth and Leroy, for several years, had invited Carol and Me to go with them. He liked to brag about the good home cooking the ladies bring, and the great country and gospel music that members of the family sing. After meeting some of the singers and singing with them on the occasion of Harold's funeral, we decided to go with them, for the reunion on August 3, 1997.

On Saturday we drove to Dalton, Georgia, so that Ruth and Carol could shop for furniture and carpet, which neither of them needed, went to Chattanooga that evening for supper at Uncle Bob's catfish restaurant, and back to the Dalton Holiday Inn, where we spent the night.

The next morning we drove to Rome, then on out to Uncle Al's place, arriving there shortly before the big dinner was served under a permanent shed next to the giant size stainless steel barbecue grill that Leroy had constructed in his shop and taken over there several years before. The setting was beautiful, on the bank of a creek across the paved road from the house.

When all the people had gathered, there must have been at least 100. The fun began. I never knew there were so many McAbees. The only ones I had ever really known were Leroy, Harold and their immediate families.

They came from Georgia, Florida, Alabama, Tennessee, with all the little babies, all the way to the older ones, some as old as eighty and ninety. Some of them brought their musical instruments, guitars, banjos, fiddles, piano keyboards, drums, with a public address system and several microphones. The McAbee band warmed up before dinner, but the music really got under way after we had our fill of meats, fresh vegetables, and wonderful deserts, a spread like I had not seen since we used to have all day singings and dinners on the grounds at Mount Zion in Cullman County.

While the old folks were clearing the tables or napping, the children wading in the creek, the "pickers and singers" gathered under another shelter and began playing and singing. I listened for a while, but just could not resist joining in. The band played, and we sang every song we knew, and when we couldn't think of another one, we would repeat the last one. We were having a wonderful time.

About 2:00 p.m. I needed to go to the bathroom. To reach it I had to climb up a steep graveled bank, cross the road, then up to the concrete block outhouse that Uncle Al had built. As I climbed the bank, I was thinking, "This is dangerous, some of those old folks might slip and hurt themselves on the gravel. I was on the way back down the steep bank when suddenly both of my feet slipped out from under me and I fell flat on my rear end, and elbows. Only one or two people saw me fall. Embarrassed, I stood up then fell again, thinking something was drastically wrong. I looked down and what I saw was frightening. My left foot had gone straight out, but my right one was still under me and turned completely around backward.

One of the witnesses was an orthopedic nurse. She ran to me, looked at the twisted ankle, and said it was surely broken, which I already knew. The odd thing was, I had absolutely no pain in my foot or ankle. As I lay on the ground, Leroy brought his big Ford Expedition around, several men picked me up, placed me gingerly in the back sear and right away Leroy, Ruth, Carol and I hurried to the Floyd Medical Center in Rome.

Arriving at the Emergency Room we were met by an orderly who helped take me out of the car and into a wheel chair. He rolled me into a room where I was examined by an orthopedic surgeon, who happened to be on duty that Sunday afternoon. After reviewing x-rays, he said my ankle was severely crushed, and that I would need immediate surgery to put it back together. I explained that I was from Tuscaloosa and would much prefer to go back home for the surgery, if at all possible. He said, "I'll put it together as best I can, in a temporary cast, but don't go home when you get to Tuscaloosa go directly to the hospital and check in. Who is your orthopedic surgeon?" I didn't have one, but the first name that came to mind was Dr. Les Fowler. I had never seen him as a patient, but had played golf with him in one of Coach Bryant's tournaments.

The nurse at the Medical Center called DCH in Tuscaloosa, Fowler happened to be on duty, alerting them that I would be checking in about three hours later. Those people were so kind and considerate, making me a comfortable "bed" in the back seat of Leroy's vehicle. Propping my injured ankle in Carol's lap, we started out for Tuscaloosa. We arrived at DCH about 9:00 p.m.

The next morning Dr. Fowler performed the operation, a large incision on each side, putting my ankle back together with a plate, pins and several screws, then placing my entire foot and leg, to up above my knee, in a hard cast. I remained in the hospital for five more days, taking daily therapy, trying to learn how to walk and get around on one leg with a walker. Before leaving the hospital they removed the heavy cast and replaced it with one that was much lighter.

At home it was very difficult trying to move around even with a wheelchair. We hired John Wedgeworth, a longtime orderly at the hospital, to come every morning help me get in and out of the shower stall (taping the bad leg in a garbage bag to keep it dry) and get dressed.

Two weeks after the operation I went to Dr. Fowler's office so he could see how my ankle was healing. When Mike, his surgical assistant, removed the cast, the incision on the right side had almost healed, but the one on the inside, right over the ankle bone hadn't begun to heal. It looked really bad. The doctor said that he shouldn't put another cast on it, instead he sent me downstairs to therapy, where they did a pulsavac treatment on it. I will try to describe "pulsavac." They have a small electric pump to which is attached a clear plastic hose, the other end goes to an IV bag of saline solution. Another hose with a gadget that looks and acts like a child's water pistol, only bigger and stronger, is used to spray the water directly into the wound, with an adjustable force, depending upon the operator and the nature of the wound. Dr. Fowler then prescribed daily pulsavac treatments by the DCH Home Health Service, which they did every day for several weeks.

In spite of the treatments, my ankle's condition worsened, until Dr. Fowler sent me to see Dr. Bunch, a plastic surgeon. He said, "It appears to me that the ankle is badly infected. Before I do anything we need to cure that, and besides, your being a diabetic, even if I took a flap of skin from another part of your body and put it on the wound, then we would have two places that might not heal properly.

One statement he made that day still rings in my ears, and has for over a year now. He said as he looked at the bone, "If that bone becomes infected, you could lose your foot." I didn't pay that much attention. Who had ever heard of anyone losing a foot from a broken ankle?

Dr. Bunch decided to do nothing, but sent me to Dr. McDermott. He was in charge of the "Hyperbarac" unit at DCH. Not knowing what to expect when I arrived there on the fifth floor, I found the hyperbaric machine was a large, round glass tube, with all sorts of wires, dials, knobs, on the outside, and a narrow foam pad inside. For the next fifty consecutive days Sylvia or Ginny, which ever nurse was on duty, would slide the pad out the front end of the tube onto a gurney. I would strip down to my all cotton tee shirt and shorts, lie down on the pad and then they would slide me in feet first, close and seal the metal door, then slowly begin pumping pure oxygen into the glass tank.

As the pressure built my ears felt like I was experiencing a swift landing on a jet airliner, about to burst. My ears couldn't stand the pressure, so before I had anymore treatments, I had to let Dr. Bill Walburn put tubes in both ears.

My next visit to the hyperbaric torture chamber was much more pleasant, no more pain in my ears, but being enclosed in that thing for two hours was an ordeal that I hope I never experience again. I could talk to the nurses, and they could talk to me by way of the built in sound system. I could see out because it was made of glass. I would take a movie with me to watch on the television mounted on the wall, which helped to pass the time. The reason for the all cotton clothing, there was less danger of an electrical spark, 100% oxygen under heavy pressure could have been disastrous. I guessed that a small spark of static electricity in the that thing would have blown me and the machine all the way to the courthouse.

The idea for using the hyperbaric machine was, the pure oxygen under pressure should aid in heeling my ankle. It worked, after fifty days in a row of going to the hospital for treatment and seventy-five days of pulasavac treatments there and at home, my wound healed over, but the pain and swelling was gradually worsening. We had healed the outside, but not the inside of my ankle.

I should pause here and give credit to some folks that assisted me during the ordeal of daily visits to the hospital. My neighbors, Jim Leydon, Harry Sherritt, Norman Bobb, Jack Crisler, Tom Davenport, Max Gathings, Dick Dickerson but especially to the members of our couples Good Samaritan Sunday School Class, at First Baptist Church. The men took turns picking me up at home, delivering me to the hospital and then two hours later bringing me back home. Fellows, I appreciate every one of you, Sonny Boothe, Charlie Johnson, Maxie Kizzire, Lanny Gamble, Bobby Kemp, and anyone else I may have forgotten, but most of all I appreciate the prayers, cards, calls and visits of the entire Good Samaritan Class, and our great, devoted teacher Dr. Hayes Boyd.

During the time Carol and I could not attend, which was many weeks, he tape recorded the lesson and would bring the tape to me every Sunday afternoon. Of course, I could never forget how Carol and the boys stood by me in all situations, doing the driving and wheelchair pushing when necessary.

After all of those treatments, it was obvious that even though the wound had healed the ankle was still infected. I wore "ace" bandages to try to prevent swelling, but it became worse and more discolored. We could never find out from the doctors or the DCH lab what type of infection it was. In January, when the pain and swelling had become so severe, Dr. Fowler said he thought the best thing to do would be to operate on it again, take out some of the "hardware", clean it and maybe, given a second chance, it would heal. He operated, put it back in another soft cast, and by that time having called in Dr. White, a communicable disease specialist, they sent biopsies to the lab again. That time they came back with a finding of bacteria they called chorini. Doctor White seemed surprised, saying that type of bacteria usually grow on the outside of the skin and not on the inside.

Before I left the hospital they sent me down to radiology for the insertion of a "pic" line into my left upper arm. That provided a permanent opening for a constant flow of antibiotics from a pump which I wore twenty-four hours a day, seven days a week for the next twelve weeks. They gave me mega-doses of Vancomyacin and Zosyn, trying to kill the bacteria.

I know now that what I had must have been a "Staph" infection, because, from everything I've read, that is about the only medication that is sometimes effective for treating Staph. There are certain strains of the staph bacteria that no antibiotic will kill. The DCH home health nurses started coming back to our house daily to change the IV That continued for 12 weeks and with weekly visits to Dr. Fowler's office there was no sign of improvement.

Finally I decided to take my problem to Dr. Sanders at Kirklin Clinic in Birmingham. He said, after looking at my ankle, it might be possible to save some of my foot with four or five operations, but there was not much he could do other than what had already been done. I asked if he was familiar with a specialist in Atlanta, named Cierney. I had heard about him through Bill Smith, my accountant. Dr. Sanders said that Dr. George Cierney was the very best in the country at performing bone infusions, treating bone infections, and that was obviously what I had.

After a couple of tries Dr. Fowler arranged an appointment for me with Dr. Cierney, at his office next door to St. Joseph's hospital in Atlanta. Carol and I, along with our bone scans,

MRI, and x-rays, drove to Atlanta on a Sunday afternoon, for a 9:00 a.m. Monday meeting with him. He gave us very little encouragement. Saying, after looking at all the things we had taken with us, that he might be able to save a piece of a foot, but if it healed at all, I could look forward to at least eight months of recovery time lying flat in one of those bird cage looking braces, not putting any pressure on it at all, and that instead he thought the best for me would be an AMPUTATION.

I told him I would have to think about that, there's no way I could make up my mind to have my leg taken off, that day. We came home, still continuing the Vancomycin and Zosyn antibiotics, with the pain and swelling becoming worse.

One morning about two weeks after my visit to Dr. Cierney, my ankle was so painful that I told Carol, "I believe I could cut it off myself, if I had a good sharp ax." I called Dr. Cierney that day and told him, "I'm ready for the amputation. When do you want to do it?" He said, "Oh, it won't be necessary for you to come back to Atlanta, I don't do that type of operation, you can get that done at your local hospital." I said, "Thanks a lot", and hung up.

On the next visit to Fowler, I reported what the Atlanta doctor said, and that I was ready for the amputation. We set the date for the following Monday. At 7:00 a.m. on Monday May 3, 1998 my right leg was amputated about half way between the ankle and the knee. By coincidence my sisters Lela, Aria, and brother-in-law Curtis from Indiana were in Alabama that weekend. They came on to Tuscaloosa to be here for the operation, along with Carol, Louis, Maggie, Wally and Ron, which I appreciated very much.

My little grand daughter, Caroline, told her first grade classmates that her "Pop" had his leg cut off and was waiting for someone to die, so he could get another one. After the surgery I had another series of ups and downs, good news and bad, progress and regression, and a total feeling of helplessness and depression. I don't know what I would have done without the assistance of friends, Carol, Wally, Ron, and especially big John Wedgeworth who came every day to help me, and tell me everything will be all right. "Mr. Price you are going to be walking soon," he would say. I had my doubts.

My cast was removed after about ten days, the stump was healing normally. I was feeling pretty good, getting around the house on my walker and in the wheelchair. The next morning the walker overturned, causing me to fall in the bathroom, landing squarely, with my full weight on the end of the stump, opening the incision. I saw "stars" for several minutes.

Dr. Fowler wanted to start the pulsavac treatments, but I said "No, I had seventy-five of them on my ankle without any success, and I'm not going do it again."

Instead, I made an appointment with Dr. Roger Snow at the Carraway Methodist Hospital Wound Care Unit in Birmingham. I saw him every week for several weeks, in addition to the home health nurses coming every day to clean and dress the wound.

I am convinced that if I had been under the care of Dr. Snow from the beginning, I would probably still have a right foot, but there's no way to change the past. During all of that, my eyes were beginning to fail because I had developed cataracts. Dr. Van Johnson operated on the right one first and in two weeks the left one. I see things now that I haven't seen in years without glasses.

After five months of daily treatment for the yeast infection in my leg, it was finally healed enough to begin thinking about a prosthesis. Since December of 1998, I have had four different ones. As of now, I have one that fits fairly well. It's now possible to walk with the aid of a cane, just about anywhere. I bought a new Jeep Grand Cherokee and had Custom Adaptive Vans Company in Birmingham install a left accelerator on it. enabling me to drive wherever I need to go. I also bought, from them, a "Scout" mobile scooter for distances too far to walk. With a lift for the scooter mounted on the back of the Jeep. I am now ready to go to Disneyland.

Well, that brings us up to date, I am about to finish this before something else happens to me. I realize I have already told you more about my health than you really wanted to know, for that, I apologize. This is the only way available to me for telling you about my "operation." you would never stand still long enough for me to tell you in person. Maybe I should take up a new career, writing for The New England Journal of Medicine.

I had hoped to end on a positive, cheerful note, but as of now we are worried about Carol's health. She has been diagnosed as having Chronic Lymphocitic Leukemia. For the past two months she has been taking chemotherapy twice monthly and daily doses of Prednizone, which will supposedly cause the chemo to be more effective. After three months of treatment the medication seems to be working. Her white blood cell count has dropped drastically. Let's all hope and pray that the condition will be completely arrested.

Since I started writing this about six months ago, I have been very concerned about how I would end MY STORY. I wanted it to be light and a little amusing, giving the reader a chuckle or two. I think maybe I did for a while, before I got into all the discussion about my health. I want to be clear about one thing. I definitely am not complaining, feeling sorry for myself, or asking for pity or sympathy for all that has happened to me. I am thankful to God and modern medicine every day that I am still here and able to see my grandchildren grow up.

Had it not been for the discovery of insulin, the development of heart surgery, kidney transplants, bladder cameras, and medications such as Cellcept, Neoral, Prednizone, all anti-rejection drugs, I would have been gone a long time ago. GOD HAS BEEN GOOD TO ME!! My favorite Gospel Singer is Jake Hess. Jake has suffered just about everything I have except an amputation, but in addition, he is bald, having worn a toupee, for years. After all that's happened to me maybe if my hair would just all fall out, I could sing like Jake! That would make it all worthwhile.

I think the best way to end is to give you, the reader a simple multiple choice exam. What I want you to do is choose, from the following, the way you would like for MY STORY--THEY CALLED ME "SYRUP SOPPER" to end.

Please check one of the following....

1. Heart_____   6. Eyes_____
2. Lung_____   7. Old age_____
3. Kidney_____   8. Shot by a jealous husband _____
4. Leg_____   9. Run over by a beer truck_____
5. Cancer_____   10. Live happily ever after_____

THE END

Clyde "Syrup Sopper" Price "on the air" at WACT, 1975.

ABOUT THE AUTHOR

Clyde W. Price was born March 26, 1932, the seventh child of Walter and Gertie Price, on a small farm in rural Cullman County Alabama. The house in which he was born had no electricity or indoor plumbing but his was a family that was close knit and bound together by loving parents who did the very best they could to raise their children to appreciate their God and Country.

He was educated in the public schools of Cullman County, Auburn University, Saint Bernard College and the University of Alabama.

He began his broadcasting career at 16 years of age as a part-time announcer on WFMH in Cullman. While attending the

University of Alabama, he worked as a Country Music Disc Jockey. That is when his listeners first began calling him SYRUP SOPPER. After graduation he served in the army Signal Corps for two years. He returned home to resume a career that would offer him an opportunity to become a radio station owner and manager.

He was very active in the Alabama Broadcasters Assocation and the National Association of Broadcasters. A charter member of the Country Music Disc Jockeys Association, which is now known as the Country Music Association (CMA). He sold his radio stations in 1989, retired and with his wife Carol still lives in Tuscaloosa, Alabama.